Embrace this destined-to-become classic as soon as you can. Doug is a seasoned pastor and skilled guide into the greatest opportunity of your lifetime: to be shaped into the likeness of Jesus through intentional practice.

—Will Mancini
Author of *Future Church*; founder, the Future Church Company

Our intentionality lies at the heart of Doug Rumford's vital, personal, transformative vision for our spiritual lives. Drawing both from Scripture and the deep spiritual traditions and practices, Rumford offers very practical steps and tools for our intentional pursuit of a dynamic life in and with God and others.

—Mark Labberton
President, Fuller Theological Seminary

Wisdom comes from age, but deep wisdom comes from personal experience. Doug Rumford has been a pastor for decades. He knows the human soul. But Doug also knows his own soul: how to care for it and what happens when we don't. This book is a tour of the deep places of human life and an application of Christian spirituality to troubled, weary or broken souls. I applaud the wisdom contained in the second edition of *SoulShaping*!

—Todd Hunter
Bishop in the Anglican Church of North America; author of *Deep Peace: Finding Calm in a World of Conflict and Anxiety*

Life is a journey. From time to time, we can get lost on the way. Doug provides a very useful structure for reflection to help us name our struggles and discern the next steps. *SoulShaping* will equip us to live out the life God intended us to live.

—Igors Rautmanis
Secretary of Staff and Team Development, IFES (International Fellowship of Evangelical Students/InterVarsity, USA)

SoulShaping is a pastoral guide to spiritual disciplines. I used the first edition of Doug Rumford's *SoulShaping* when I taught spiritual formation classes at Wheaton College. I am so glad it is being reissued in a second edition. I look forward to seeing how the Lord will use it.

—Adele Ahlberg Calhoun
Author of *The Spiritual Disciplines Handbook*

All my life I've been taught that being a Christian is not simply about holding a set of beliefs but is about having a "relationship" with Jesus. Yet for years I received little if any vision for what such a relationship might look like. It was difficult to find adequate guidance for how to go deeper and sustain this relationship. I struggled to have much hope that I could experience God's power transforming me—to actually make me more like Jesus. I've found much of what I've longed for in Doug Rumford's book *SoulShaping*. I've found inspiration and practical, creative resources for participating in the process of transformation. This resource will be invaluable for both individuals and small groups alike. Pastors and leaders, take note!

—Patti Pierce
Founder, WellSpring/SoulCARE: A Resource for Christian Spiritual Formation

Oliver Wendell Holmes, Sr. wrote, "Some people are so heavenly minded that they are no earthly good." Dr. Doug Rumford, in *SoulShaping*, masterfully pens the steps that articulate the practical pathway to transform a heavenly mind into authentic earthly good. Rumford, like a spiritual mentor, guides us out of our constant motion and into the peace of God's presence, where he details how we can daily renew our personal power and purposeto truly actualize Christ's abundant life.

—John Van Epp
Founder/president, Love Thinks, LLC

It is very easy for pastors and lay leaders to get so caught up in tending the souls of others that their own spiritual vitality is neglected. At the same time, Christian spirituality can often seem confusing or only for the spiritually elite. *SoulShaping* makes deeply tending to one's own soul attainable for any person. Through his engaging and easy-to-follow writing style, Rumford helps people in all stages of their Christian life evaluate the condition of their own hearts and uses simple exercises to shape and strengthen their souls. Engage deeply with this book and you will be richly blessed.

—Dana Allin
Synod executive, ECO: A Covenant Order of Evangelical Presbyterians

SoulShaping is the perfect instruction manual for the weary traveler. While teaching us how to care for our souls, Doug also offers practical wisdom to answer life's most complicated questions. Most important, it meets us where we are and offers us a blessed assurance that our life has both purpose and meaning.

—Van Partible
Animation producer, Creator of Johnny Bravo

Endorsements for the first edition of *SoulShaping*

Many of us sense something missing in our busy, active programs, and our overcommitted and often draining "Christianity." That something is depth—the need to go down into our very souls, to rediscover there the deep, deep love of God. Doug Rumford has given us a remarkable guide for our spiritual journeying. *SoulShaping* is full of carefully crafted truths, insights from a wide range of wise travelers, stories of fellow pilgrims, coaching for our necessary spiritual exercises, and godly hope. Don't miss the journey. And take this book along.

—Leighton Ford
Founder, Leighton Ford Ministries; author of *Transforming Leadership*

Advice on developing the spiritual life runs the risk of being either too prescriptive or too theoretical. Doug Rumford has now given us a clear, gracious, motivating manual to help all of us in our journey toward more maturity. Through careful biblical counsel and numerous real-life illustrations, Doug has provided a book useful for both those eager to take their first steps and those well along the spiritual pilgrimage. I will be recommending this book for years to come.

—Stephen A. Hayner
President, InterVarsity Christian Fellowship

There is a sweetness about this book.... The stories are universal. The questions gently and effectively Socratic. Rumford's guidance toward the answers is clearly Scripture-based. This is a searching and satisfying book.

—Max De Pree
Author of *Dear Zoe* and *Leadership Is an Art* and *Leadership Jazz*

Underneath all the glitter and veneer, our society is experiencing a tidal wave of hopelessness. As Doug states so well, this is happening because of the widespread neglect of our souls.

Numerous authors have recognized this, but Doug Rumford has approached the issue with a freshness, vividness, and precision that I have not seen for some time. He re-introduces us to a God who is Personal, Passionate, and Present—a God whose love will always find a way to be practical. I think this is what stunned me the most. *SoulShaping* is profound without being esoteric, and Doug makes this wild hope practical without it ever being shallow. He takes us from the "Oh Wow!" of holy awe to a holy boldness, giving us mature tools so that we can take on the challenge of spiritual restoration and growth.

If, like myself, you are deeply concerned about the escalating problems all around us; if you care about your world, your friends, your family, or your "self," this book is a must-read. In the midst of all the pain and confusion, there is a Living Promise—a truth that can and will set us free. Rumford knows that this Truth is not just a principle but a Person—One whom he knows at a level few do and about whom he writes with passion, power, and clarity.

—Tim Hansel
Founder/president, Summit Expedition, and Ignite, Inc.; author of *You Gotta Keep Dancin'*, *When I Relax I Feel Guilty*, and *Holy Sweat*

This book is extremely timely and relevant to the needs of Christians today. Many are searching for practical guidance for shaping their spiritual lives in the context of a crazy-making world. They are hurried and hassled and don't have a lot of time to discover the spiritual disciplines for themselves. Doug's book provides them with guidance, but it does so in a stimulating, scintillating and soul-serving way. New believers as well as veteran disciples will find it tugging at their heart. Hardly a page goes by that doesn't create a hunger within to know the deeper experience of God's presence.

—Archibald D. Hart
Professor, Fuller Theological Seminary; author of *Unlocking the Mystery of Your Emotions*

SoulShaping

SECOND EDITION

DOUGLAS J. RUMFORD

From Soul Neglect to Spiritual Vitality

Lorica
MINISTRIES

Printed and Distributed through Lorica Ministries

The personal stories in this book are true. Many are told with the permission of the people involved. In some cases, names and identifying details have been altered to preserve anonymity.

Scripture quotations marked NIV are taken from The Holy Bible, New International Version. (1984). Grand Rapids: Zondervan Publishing House. All rights reserved.

Scripture quotations marked NLT are taken from Tyndale House Publishers. 2004. Holy Bible: New Living Translation. Wheaton, IL: Tyndale House Publishers. All rights reserved.

Scripture quotations marked RSV are taken from the Holy Bible, Revised Standard Version, copyright © 1946, 1952, 1971 by the Division of Christian Education of the National Council of the Churches of Christ in the United States of America. All rights reserved.

Scripture quotations marked NRSV are taken from the Holy Bible New Revised Standard Version, copyrighted, 1989 by the Division of Christian Education of the National Council of the Churches of Christ in the United States of America. All rights reserved.

Scripture quotations marked KJV are taken from the Holy Bible, King James Version.

Scripture quotations marked NKJV are taken from the Holy Bible, New King James Version. Copyright© 1979, 1980, 1982, Thomas Nelson, Inc., Publishers. All rights reserved.

Scripture quotations marked ESV are taken from Crossway Bibles. 2007. The Bible, English Standard Version. Wheaton, IL: Crossway Bibles.

Second Edition Published in 2022

Published by Douglas J. Rumford. Printed and distributed through Lorica Ministries
Orange, CA 92867

Library of Congress Control Number: 2021925823

ISBN 978-0-578-26009-9 (pbk. : alk. Paper)
ISBN 978-0-578-26010-5 (ebk. : eBook)
ISBN 978-0-578-26011-2 (abk. : Audiobook)

Editor Steve Halliday

Front cover image by Diana Akhmetyanova
Cover design & interior book design by Katie King Rumford | www.katiekingrumford.com

This Second Edition is based on Douglas J. Rumford, SoulShaping: Taking Care of Your Spiritual Life, Wheaton, IL: Tyndale House Publishers, 1996 (first edition).

www.loricaministries.org

First Printing 2022

SoulShaping

DOUGLAS J. RUMFORD

From
Soul Neglect
to Spiritual
Vitality

SECOND EDITION

Table of
Contents

Introduction
God Makes,
We Shape

Life is hard on the soul.

Life's daily stresses drain us mentally, physically, emotionally, and spiritually. We have many resources for dealing with life's issues, but we haven't been trained how to care for our souls, for our inner lives. Attending church, listening to podcasts, reading the Bible, praying, and participating in small groups can help. But these too often miss the soul connection that truly refreshes us.

Even as a pastor, I have experienced times of spiritual drought and emptiness. Outwardly, I looked like I was thriving, but inwardly I was barely surviving. My relationship with God felt stale. I was going through the motions, but not connecting with the Lord. Praying and reading my Bible weren't enough. I needed something more, something fresh.

My spiritual life came alive when I discovered the broad repertoire of spiritual disciplines that have nurtured God's people across the centuries. Though they weren't part of my church tradition, my heart stirred as I read about them and then began to practice them.

Soon I was exploring the many pathways that traverse the geography of the soul. I traveled to the heights of contemplative meditation, and then enjoyed the refreshing valleys of rest. I ventured into the "wilderness" of fasting, silence, and solitude, and discovered the unanticipated power that came from them. I was replenished as I learned how to navigate the terrain of everyday routine with a vibrant sense of God's presence. My relationship with the Lord became a real experience. I began to understand and feel what I think Jesus meant, at least in part, when he said, "I have come that you might have life and have it abundantly" (John 10:10 NRSV).

SoulShaping equips you to connect with Christ's abundant life. The resources in this book provide the tools and coaching for spiritual vitality. These principles and practices will empower you to move from good intentions to rewarding practice.

God makes. We shape.

> Yet you, Lord, are our Father.
> We are the clay, you are the potter;
> we are all the work of your hand (Isaiah 64:8 NIV).

While God makes us and shapes us, God also calls us to join actively in shaping our spiritual lives. Like a wise parent, the Lord cultivates our maturity by not doing all the work for us. We play an essential role in forming our life in Christ. God provides the raw material of personhood. We are given the privilege of forming a healthy life from that raw material.

SoulShaping moves faith from theory to reality. We move beyond intellectual belief to contact with the living Lord. We experience the sense of God's presence that gives us peace of mind, direction, and assurance. The content is formatted in three parts.

"Part One: From Soul Neglect to Spiritual Vitality" overviews the process of spiritual transformation, beginning with an assessment of a person's soul condition. I identify five vital signs of a healthy soul, and then explore the motivation for sustainable spiritual growth by looking first at five inadequate strategies for change. The section concludes with the most energizing strategy.

"Part Two: Pathways to Spiritual Vitality" presents a cluster of three spiritual disciplines to support each of the five vital signs of a healthy soul. The overview of fifteen spiritual disciplines provides a broad frame of reference for spiritual formation.

"Part Three: Walking Toward Spiritual Vitality" pulls together the process described in Part One and the pathways of spiritual disciplines in Part Two so readers can develop their personalized soul plan. Having diagnosed their spiritual condition and learned about the resources for spiritual vitality, readers are introduced to the concepts of seasons of the soul and soul-specific disciplines so they can discern a schedule of spiritual discipline that works best for them.

It's important to remember, amid all this content, that the disciplines serve our souls; our souls do not serve the disciplines. *SoulShaping* provides the tools for a life-long journey of faith. It is a resource for spiritual vitality throughout life's varied seasons. So don't be overwhelmed. You will graze briefly n some chapters and linger longer in others. The priority is discovering the fuel for spiritual vitality.

This book, a major revision of my first edition of *SoulShaping* (published in 1996), has passed through the refining fires of life and ministry. It's not as much about understanding spirituality as it is a book for practicing spirituality.

Spirituality isn't a spectator sport. Spiritual growth and vitality don't just happen. They don't come naturally. To have spiritual vitality we must actively engage in soul care.

The disciplines serve our souls; our souls do not serve the disciplines.

SoulShaping will take you on a journey from soul neglect to spiritual vitality. And it will show you how to invite others to come along with you. You will get the most from this book by focusing on doing, not just learning. I have also developed *The SoulShaping Journal* (a separate resource) that provides additional material to help you translate information into genuine personal transformation.

God wants so much more for us. My prayer is that this will be one of the means God uses to help you experience the life Jesus died to make possible.

Part One
From Soul Neglect to Spiritual Vitality

Chapter 1
From Soul Neglect to Spiritual Vitality

Jesus did not die so we would stay the same.

Jesus did not become flesh, surrender his life on the cross for us, rise from the dead, and send the Holy Spirit to live within us so we could stay stuck in a mediocre experience of faith and life. "I came that you may have life and have it abundantly," Jesus insisted (John 10:10, NRSV).

We commonly think God wants something *from* us, when in reality, God wants something *for* us. Like a loving parent, God wants the best for us.

God offers us in Christ a rich and satisfying life. Although we turned away from God like teenagers demanding emancipation, God didn't hold a grudge. God spared nothing for us to have life and have it to the full.

We commonly think God wants something *from* us, when in reality, God wants something *for* us.

Abundant life means "to have life in excess," "life to the fullest extent," "maximum life." Jesus came to give us a quality of life surpassing our wildest expectations in both meaning and satisfaction.

Abundant Life: What Does That Look Like?

If someone said they would give you the best life ever, what would you picture? Picture a life in which joy carries us through the day and laughter comes as naturally as breathing. We don't feel drawn to the things that take us down, but rather to those that build us up.

Abundant life means trusting ourselves. We have control over our thoughts and words, over our responses and reactions. We have no need to hide in shame and embarrassment.

The distractions and deceptions of the world don't fool us. We learn to live with life's questions.

We live in the moment. We don't make others anxious. We value people for who they are, not for what they might give us.

We are honest with God and others. We admit when we make mistakes. We say, "I'm sorry," and begin again. We confidently accept God's grace, releasing the burdens of lingering shame and regret.

We have courage to do the hard things, even though we dread them. We keep our word and fulfill our responsibilities.

We remain connected to God, who created us in all our uniqueness. By God's grace and power, we are becoming all God created us to be.

We feel at peace in every circumstance. We celebrate God's good gifts when we have them, and trust God when we don't.

We serve others willingly, without seeking recognition. We are free from people-pleasing and live for an audience of One.

I want that kind of life! I confess I experience it far less than I desire. But I know that this, and far more, awaits us in Christ. *That's* why I'm so passionate about spiritual vitality.

How would you describe your life? Would you call it "abundant"? In fact, that's what the Lord wants for you. Abundant life is meant to be yours.[1]

God wants so much more *for* us.

Abundant life is about our quality of life, not a quantity of stuff. It's about becoming a person who lives with confidence, compassion, and an awareness of God's presence. It's an unhurried life. A life of peace amid the storms. A life of generosity, both experienced and shown.

Abundant life is about our quality of life, not a quantity of stuff.

Does it seem just out of reach for you or way beyond your grasp? Why aren't more of us living this kind of life? Why do so very few live this kind of life in Christ?

A Check-Up on the Condition of Your Soul

As you reflect on those questions, complete the following assessment on the current condition of your inner life. Rate yourself in the following ten categories on a scale of 1 (the lowest) to 10 (the highest). A lower number means you identify with this symptom and would like to remove it from your life. A higher number means you do not feel this symptom describes your spiritual life at this time. Total your score once you've completed the assessment.

1 I HAVE A LOW-GRADE "DEPRESSION FEVER"

Need Intensive Spiritual Care   *Need Attention*   *Top Condition*

1   2   3   4   5   6   7   8   9   10

2 I'M BUSY BUT BORED

Need Intensive Spiritual Care   *Need Attention*   *Top Condition*

1   2   3   4   5   6   7   8   9   10

3 I'M LOSING CONTROL OVER LIFE'S ROUTINE

Need Intensive Spiritual Care   *Need Attention*   *Top Condition*

1   2   3   4   5   6   7   8   9   10

4 I'M LOSING RESPONSIVENESS TO OTHERS

Need Intensive Spiritual Care   *Need Attention*   *Top Condition*

1   2   3   4   5   6   7   8   9   10

5 I'M WITHDRAWING FROM RESPONSIBILITY AND LEADERSHIP

Need Intensive Spiritual Care   *Need Attention*   *Top Condition*

1   2   3   4   5   6   7   8   9   10

6 I PAY MORE ATTENTION TO LESS IMPORTANT THINGS

Need Intensive Spiritual Care   *Need Attention*   *Top Condition*

1   2   3   4   5   6   7   8   9   10

7 I FEEL RESTLESS AND DISSATISFIED

Need Intensive Spiritual Care   *Need Attention*   *Top Condition*

1   2   3   4   5   6   7   8   9   10

8 I'M FALLING INTO UNHEALTHY HABITS AND
TEMPTATION

Need Intensive Spiritual Care   *Need Attention*   *Top Condition*

| 1 | 2 | 3 | 4 | 5 | 6 | 7 | 8 | 9 | 10 |

9 I FEEL PREOCCUPIED WITH GUILT AND SHAME

Need Intensive Spiritual Care   *Need Attention*   *Top Condition*

| 1 | 2 | 3 | 4 | 5 | 6 | 7 | 8 | 9 | 10 |

10 I'M BECOMING SPIRITUALLY APATHETIC AND
INDIFFERENT

Need Intensive Spiritual Care   *Need Attention*   *Top Condition*

| 1 | 2 | 3 | 4 | 5 | 6 | 7 | 8 | 9 | 10 |

My total score:

The list above identifies what I call the primary symptoms of soul neglect. I'll define them more fully in the next chapter, but for now, get a sense of your own level of spiritual vitality. How satisfied do you feel?

Your score will help you reflect on your overall spiritual condition as well as some specific areas you may want to give special attention. Please consider seeking professional counsel if your symptoms are severe.

40 points or below: You will find *SoulShaping* an important resource for renewing your faith and your experience of the Lord. Also, you might tend to be a bit hard on yourself. You may have unrealistically high expectations. Discuss your scores with a mature Christian friend who can help confirm or revise your self-assessment.

41–75 points: You are feeling fairly satisfied with your spiritual life, but you will benefit greatly by developing a broader repertoire of spiritual disciplines to keep your journey fresh.

76 points or above: *SoulShaping* will provide a new framework for spiritual growth and for discipling others to experience spiritual growth and vitality.

I've given this assessment at a variety of conferences and used it with both groups and individuals. In my experience, the usual distribution of scores looks like this:

- 10 – 25: About 10% of respondents
- 26 – 50: About 20% of respondents
- 51 – 75: About 55% of respondents
- 76 – 100: About 15% of respondents
- I've never seen anyone score 100!

It fascinates me that we often experience symptoms like these, but rarely stop long enough to check them out. Human beings have an amazing tolerance for misery! How many of us refuse to go to a physician to get the help we know we need? Instead, we tolerate the pain. This hesitancy is also true in spiritual matters.

People feel reluctant to speak with a pastor, counselor, or friend. If we took a chance to reach out, however, perhaps another person could hold up a mirror in which we might better see and understand what's going on inside us.

Start the Journey

The pathway to joy passes through the landscape of soul care. God has given us practical principles and activities to lift us to new heights and open new vistas of life.

Why not engage with a God-ordained process that brings lasting change? This isn't just a matter of information, but transformation. It's not merely about content; it's about change.

Chapter 2

Recognize the Symptoms of Soul Neglect

Even as volcanic activity and shifting continental plates have altered the geography of the earth, so unseen interior forces determine the landscape of our lives. If left unattended, these forces can wreak havoc, not only for us but also for those around us, particularly for the ones we love most.

Beneath the surface of daily experience lies an inner world churning with emotions and motives, hurt and hope, pain and desire, doubt and faith, shame and honor, love and hate—all of which shape our outer, visible life.

But God does not leave us helpless! God's truth, wisdom, and power can harness the energy of our interior world to produce a life that brings joy to others, unspeakable satisfaction to ourselves, and glory to God.

Pay Attention to the Condition of Your Soul

I've already invited you to assess the condition of your soul using ten symptoms of soul neglect. Understanding these symptoms is the first step toward spiritual renewal. Self-understanding begins the process of freeing us from the dark forces that control us. When we exercise faith and courage to take that "inner look," we discover the motives, desires, and fears that drain our spiritual energy.

In his book, *Let Your Life Speak,* Parker J. Palmer writes, "Self-care is never a selfish act—it is simply good stewardship of the only gift I have, the gift I was put on earth to offer to others. Anytime we can listen to true self and give it the care it requires, we do so not only for ourselves but for the many others whose lives we touch."[2]

Paying attention to your heart is the first step toward valuing yourself as God values you.

What's Shaping Your Soul?

You are being shaped every day and every moment. The question is, by what forces? By which people? By what thoughts and ideas? It's not a matter of whether you're being shaped, but of your awareness of those often-unrecognized influences. When we remain unaware of the forces that shape us, we surrender to worldly influences, personality tendencies, wounds, drives, and other factors that harm our spiritual health and impede our growth.

You *can* shift from unintentional to intentional shaping.

The psalmists frequently considered the condition of their soul. "Why are you cast down, O my soul, and why are you disquieted within me?" (Psalm 42:5, RSV). They took time to look within, under the guidance of the Holy Spirit, to discern their soul need and to seek God's solution.

If someone asked you to describe your spiritual condition, what would you say? Consider the following symptoms of soul neglect as tools for diagnosing your heart. They are suggestive, not exhaustive. Feel free to add others that may be troubling you. Understanding your symptoms will help you to understand the spiritual pathways and disciplines that have the power to most readily replenish and sustain you.[3]

Ten Symptoms of Soul Neglect

SYMPTOM #1: A LOW-GRADE "DEPRESSION FEVER"

A melancholy streak often troubles those who care most deeply about faith. I call this a "low-grade depression fever" because low-grade fevers often indicate infections or problems that elude simple diagnostic techniques. I do not have in mind clinical depression, which has psychological and physiological roots. I refer instead to feeling spiritually drained.

A melancholy streak often troubles those who care most deeply about faith.

Indifference and unresponsiveness to spiritual things characterizes this condition. A person may feel guilty for feeling so dull but cannot find relief. The courageous ones continue to live the life of faith, functioning out of commitment but without desire. Activity may continue, but without fire.

> "My tears have been my food day and night," cries out the writer of Psalm 42, "while [people] say to me continually, "Where is your God?'" (Psalm 42:3, RSV).

Charles Spurgeon, often called the Prince of Preachers, pastored a congregation of more than ten thousand in London in the mid- to late 1800s. Yet he knew the darkness of depression. After delivering a great message, Spurgeon sometimes would go home on Sunday evening and curl up in bed, in abject despair. He introduced an insightful lecture to ministerial students, titled "The Minister's Fainting Fits," with wisdom that speaks to all of us:

> As it is recorded that David, in the heat of battle, waxed faint, so may it be written of all the servants of the Lord. Fits of depression come over the most of us. Usually cheerful as we may be, we must at intervals be cast down. The strong are not always vigorous, the wise not always ready, the brave not always courageous, and the joyous not always happy.[4]

God's servants in scripture were no strangers to spiritual depression. Elijah felt overwhelmed by depression following his thunderous victory on Mount Carmel. Consider the complaints of Jeremiah, the struggles of Jonah, and the affliction that nearly crushed Paul so that he "despaired of life itself" (2 Corinthians 1:8, RSV).

Depression stems from a sense of loss.[5] Even before we become able or willing to recognize or admit it, the heart knows something is missing.

If you want to move forward, pay attention to your loss. Examine your life, asking the basic questions: "What have I lost? Is this loss real (such as losing a friend) or imagined (such as not having an opportunity you were never promised in the first place)? What am I telling myself about this loss? Why does it affect me so deeply?"

SYMPTOM #2: BUSY BUT BORED

If you are active but feel weary, you may be facing serious soul trouble.

Initially, we thrive on activity. We love having options, adventures, interesting things to do, people to meet, and places to go. We can feel powerful, needed, important. A full calendar tells us that others value us because we are "in demand."

We have a full calendar but an empty heart.

But such satisfaction may not last. Even good things can lead to burnout. If we assume the way to happiness demands busyness, we may conclude that we can stay happy only by remaining busy, which soon becomes intolerable. We have a full calendar but an empty heart.

Do you feel your soul withering, shrinking, and losing the capacity to care deeply or to experience pleasure fully? Do you want everything to just stop? But then you may find that no activity unsettles you even more than too much.

This was the primary complaint of my friend Jen. She had everything going for her but still felt a gnawing emptiness. She had lost her joy. She felt bored with the very life she had spent all her energy to achieve.

"What was the point of the sacrifice and effort, if this is how I feel now?" Jen asked.

Boredom does not refer to a lack of activity, like children at the end of summer who want to go back to school because they feel all played out. Rather, boredom refers to a lack of meaning we feel despite all our activities. Henri Nouwen writes:

> While busy and worried about many things, we seldom feel truly satisfied, at peace, or at home. A gnawing sense of being unfulfilled underlies our filled lives. Reflecting a little more on this experience of unfulfillment I can discern different sentiments. The most significant are boredom, resentment, and depression. Boredom is a sense of disconnectedness. While we are busy with many things, we wonder if what we do makes any real difference. Life presents itself as a random, unconnected series of activities and events over which we have little or no control... To be bored therefore does not mean that we have nothing to do but that we question the value of the things we're so busy doing.[6]

SYMPTOM #3: LOSING CONTROL OVER LIFE'S ROUTINE

Do you feel overwhelmed by a constant press of demands, unable to keep all the fires fueled that you've started? Unlike the "Busy but Bored" symptom, you may not question the meaning of what you are doing, but you feel overwhelmed by the sheer quantity of your activities. There seems to be no time just to "let down" and catch your spiritual breath. If you stop, you fear disappointing either yourself or others who count on you.

This is one of my struggles. When I began exploring ministry as a church intern, my mentor, Gary, warned me about a problem I've wrestled with my entire life.

"Doug," he said, "you'd better stop building so many fires! You'll wear yourself out carrying all the wood you need to keep them going."

There seems to be no time just to "let down" and catch your spiritual breath.

It's easy to start fires—but can you keep them burning? Or will you burn up or burn out in the process?

When you find yourself always saying, "Next month, things will be under control," only to find next month even worse . . . watch out. While at work, do you feel guilty about your home life? When at home, do you feel preoccupied with your work?

Routine often gets a bad rap, but it is one of life's economies for budgeting our energy. Routine not only saves time, but energy. It reduces the number of decisions we must make so we can conserve our emotional and mental resources for important decisions.

Soul care must anchor your routine.

SYMPTOM #4: LOSING RESPONSIVENESS TO OTHERS

In times of soul neglect, our relationships often reveal the strain. Relationships function like a thermometer, showing the spiritual temperature.

If you see this symptom in your life, you may find it difficult to be with people you used to enjoy. Comments or actions you used to overlook now provoke negative reactions. You feel irritable and judgmental toward others, weary of putting up with or overlooking their flaws and habits. And even if you control your outward expressions, you often find yourself seething on the inside. Spiritual subjects no longer feel like natural, inviting topics of conversation.

Near the end of his journey through the wilderness, Moses lost his composure with his people and so lost the privilege of entering the promised land. Moses' anger had overcome his commitment to obey the Lord (see Numbers 20:2-13).

What happened? Moses ran out of cope! The incessant demands and thirst of the Israelites had finally parched his own soul.

Have you run out of cope?

SYMPTOM #5: WITHDRAWING FROM RESPONSIBILITY AND LEADERSHIP

Have you started backing away from responsibilities, including leadership? When you see another person begin to resist, refuse, or renege on their responsibilities, their soul may be calling out for care.

Men and women sometimes drop the ball when their arms get too full. Compassion, rather than condemnation, will help them manage their burdens.

When we see another person begin to resist, refuse, or renege on their responsibilities, their soul may be calling out for care.

My friend Alan had served in several significant positions of community leadership, when he suddenly resigned from them all. Many of us felt surprised. So, I called Alan.

"I knew it was time to leave," he explained, "when I began to resent those meetings. While I was doing things to make life better for others, my own world was going from bad to worse."

Alan needed soul time and family time. He'd lost his ability to be "response-able."

"Response-ability" is the ability to respond to a need or obligation. When your spiritual reserves get drained, it's all you can do to manage your own life, let alone serve others. If you try to fulfill your responsibilities apart from God's power, they can crush you.

SYMPTOM #6: PAYING MORE ATTENTION TO LESS IMPORTANT THINGS

Have you become preoccupied with projects of lesser importance? You keep doing things, but you switch to less demanding things.

When you find yourself continually clearing your desk instead of writing a report, you may be dealing with a soul problem. Straightening the piles of work instead of eliminating them or making lists instead of completing items on the list can all indicate spiritual malaise. Your lack of energy and motivation may signal that your inner life needs more attention. If you tend it, you'll find the energy to do those other things.

In athletics, coaches spend as much time working on the mental and emotional attitudes of athletes as they do on their physical skills and aptitudes. Our son Matthew and I visited the locker room of a college basketball team before a game. The coach said to his players, "First you've got to win the inner game. Then the outer one will take care of itself."

When you fail to care for your soul, your vision constricts, your hope dims, your energy fades, and you do busywork instead of meaningful work.

Attitude can make or break your performance. When you focus on the important elements of the "inner game," the more trivial, outer elements will feel less distracting. But when you fail to care for your soul, your vision constricts, your hope dims, your energy fades, and you do busywork instead of meaningful work.

SYMPTOM #7: FEELING RESTLESS AND DISSATISFIED

Feeling restless, dissatisfied, and discontent can indicate a spiritual problem. The story is told of King Pyrrhus[7] (319 BCE—272 BCE), ruler of Epirus, who planned to invade Italy. He called for Cineas, his advisor, to inform him of his plan. Cineas asked him why he planned to invade Italy.

"To conquer it," the king replied.

"And what will you do when you have conquered it?"

"Go on to France," the king answered.

"And what will you do when you conquer France?"

"Then I will go on to conquer Germany."

"What then?" asked Cineas.

"Conquer Spain," said the king.

"I perceive you mean to conquer all the world," said Cineas. "What will you do when you have conquered all?"

"'Why then," replied the king, "we will return and enjoy ourselves at quiet in our own land."

"So you may do now," said Cineas, "without all this ado."

Cineas could not relieve the king's discontent nor blunt his desire for conquest. When the king went out in battle, the Romans promptly ruined him.[8]

Restlessness often indicates an unmet need.

Have discontent and envy drained away your joy, leaving you bitter and dissatisfied? Have you lost sight of your own worth and blessings? Do you look in the wrong places for satisfaction? If you answer "yes" to any of these questions, you may be especially vulnerable to the next symptom of spiritual neglect.

SYMPTOM #8: FALLING INTO UNHEALTHY HABITS AND TEMPTATION

You might consider this symptom a combination of symptoms: resurgence of unhealthy habits, diminished impulse control, and diminished resistance to temptation. These often go together to describe spiritual regression or "backsliding."

You binge on sin when you are starved for grace.

This constellation of symptoms acts like a deteriorating immune system. White blood cells are the disease fighters of the body, and when the white cell count plummets, the body cannot defend itself. Similarly, spiritual vitality defends you against the enemies of abundant life. Soul neglect leaves you vulnerable to spiritual attack.

When your soul needs attention, you may try to satisfy the wrong appetite. You may misread the inner discomfort you feel and do exactly the opposite of what you really need to do.

Think of people in a snowstorm. They may become very sleepy and not realize they have begun to suffer from hypothermia. Though they know they need shelter, they may feel an irresistible urge to lie down and sleep. They believe that if they can rest for a while, they'll recover their energy. But what happens if they do lie down and sleep? They die.

Whether the issue is money, food, ambition, pride, envy, lust, laziness, or fear, the warning signs start flashing. Your soul is in critical need. We binge on sin when we are starved for grace. Vulnerability to temptation is the fever of the soul, not the germ of the disease.

Soul neglect leaves you vulnerable to spiritual attack. Spiritual vitality defends you against the enemies of life.

The parched desires of soul drought make you crave the closest "relief," even if it is toxic. While falling into sin is abhorrent, usually a genuine soul need lies beneath the sinful act. If you feel the pull of some sinful act, what heart cry may lie behind your illicit desire?

SYMPTOM #9: PREOCCUPIED WITH GUILT AND SHAME

Guilt is the pain of the soul.

Guilt is an objective state of having violated a law or personal value. Most of us fail to understand that guilt is an indicator, not a cure. Guilt is the God-given, natural response of the human heart to the violation of some objective law, and so has an appropriate role to play in human experience. It functions like pain in the body.

When you feel severe pain, you do not savor the pain. You go to your physician to diagnose the cause of the pain and so find relief. Pain has told you that your body needs attention. Likewise, with guilt.

A woman I'll call Carrie, who worked for an appliance dealer, came for prayer one Sunday. "This is very unusual for me," she said, "but I don't feel God has forgiven me. I know in my mind the Lord forgives me, but I just can't get rid of this burden. It's blocking my fellowship with the Lord."

She described how her manager had asked her to falsify warranty information so the company could get refunds on defective merchandise.

"At first I protested," Carrie continued, "but then gave in under pressure. They called me 'Miss Goody Two-Shoes' and said it was all part of the job. After a while, I did it without even thinking twice. But I finally stopped doing it, and they forced me to resign. But it's still eating at me. I feel so guilty."

Deliberate sin shrinks the soul, wringing vitality from it. Carrie, however, had confessed her sin and repented of it—and yet she still felt guilty. When forgiveness doesn't "take" and we don't feel forgiven, we face a significant soul issue.

Carrie had dealt with her guilt, but not with her shame.

Shame is often guilt's twin. Shame is not guilt, but a sense of lowered self-esteem that can accompany guilt. Think of shame as the lingering echo of a guilty action. Some have described the two like this: "Guilt says, 'I did wrong,' while shame says, 'I am wrong.'" When shame attacks a person's self-worth, it can be very destructive.

Carrie found herself stuck in "worldly sorrow," a biblical expression for shame. Scripture says, "For godly grief produces a repentance that leads to salvation and brings no regret, but worldly grief produces death" (2 Corinthians 7:10, NRSV).

Someone with a healthy soul who has committed sin experiences "godly sorrow," then embraces forgiveness and moves forward.

Guilt is the pain of the soul.

Are you stuck? Does shame keep you from moving forward? Do you feel as though God has not forgiven you for some sin, even though you have confessed it and repented of it? If so, you may need to give Symptom #9 some urgent attention.

SYMPTOM #10: SPIRITUAL APATHY AND INDIFFERENCE

This is the most frightening symptom of soul neglect. We see it when we knowingly refuse to do what is right or refuse to stop doing what we know is wrong. It's as though we stand outside ourselves, spectators in a tragic situation.

I believe this is what the Bible has in mind when it mentions the hardening of a human heart. When Pharaoh continually resisted God's call to liberate the Israelites, he developed spiritual calluses. The author of Hebrews gives a sobering warning: "Therefore we must pay the closer attention to what we have heard, lest we drift away from it" (Hebrews 2:1, RSV). Those who refuse to care for their souls will be less and less able to care unless the Lord intervenes.

When dryness reaches this stage, it becomes like the Sahara Desert. Just a century ago, that area was a lush region of plants and wildlife, but drought extinguished its life. Even so, the coming of rain would awaken new life.

Are you indifferent toward the health of your soul? Are you moving toward apathy regarding your spiritual life? Do you feel blasé about God, the church, Jesus, evangelism, or ministering to others for Christ's sake? Do you feel spiritually drowsy? If so, you may have a serious problem with spiritual apathy and indifference—and it will only grow worse if you don't address it.

The Power of an Honest Look

"Why do I have to bother with all this introspection?" a friend once asked me. "I just want to serve the Lord!"

The man had an imposing presence and impressive ministry. Over the years, he had helped many to become faithful disciples—but he felt soul weary and had already begun the slide toward burnout.

"If you don't stop and look at what's controlling your soul," I replied, "it will have its way with you. But if you look, you will find freedom. As Jesus said, 'You shall know the truth, and the truth shall make you free' (John 8:32). But first, the truth may make you miserable!"

Looking honestly at your heart is no distraction. In fact, it puts you in touch with reality.

One of the most profound theologians of all time, John Calvin, wrote, "Without knowledge of self, there is no knowledge of God."[9]

Self-knowledge always points us beyond ourselves. When we explore the mysteries of our lives—our hopes and fears, our darker and lighter sides, our place in the scheme of things—we begin to think of the bigger questions and seek the deeper answers. The self, the personal, profound dimension of the soul, takes on a deeper dimension. And so, the writer of Proverbs exhorts us, "Keep your heart with all vigilance; for from it flow the springs of life." (Proverbs 4:23, RSV). Caring for your soul is one of the most practical steps you can take to become more effective in all your relationships and other undertakings.

God's redemptive promise fuels your courage to take this journey from soul neglect to spiritual vitality. When you finally see yourself in the mirror of truth, the Lord begins to stir in you dreams of the astonishing hope and freedom he promises.

Chapter 3
Vital Signs of a Healthy Soul

The Paris Opera House, best known through Andrew Lloyd Webber's musical *Phantom of the Opera*, sits on three acres of land. Four-fifths of the theater exists backstage, with more than seventeen stories, seven of which lie below stage level. The stables for the opera horses still exist.

And yes, there is a monument to La Carlotta.

The facility also has a real subterranean lake, more accurately a reservoir, that served as the famous haunt of the phantom described in the novel by Gaston Leroux. The opera house designer created the reservoir because it needed a deep basement for its substage but discovered an unexpectedly high level of groundwater. To deal with this problem the architect, Charles Garnier, designed a double foundation to protect the superstructure from moisture. His plan incorporated a water course and an enormous concrete cistern (cuvee) that both relieved the pressure of the external groundwater on the basement walls and served as a reservoir in case of fire.[10]

This reservoir, seven stories beneath the building, forms an essential part of the structural design. Operators use it as ballast, raising or lowering the water level to support varying weights of different scenes on stage.[11]

Ciceri, the opera's chief designer from 1824-1847, recreated the eruption of Vesuvius on stage using real stones! Can you imagine the weight? Any other wooden structure would have collapsed. But just as the ocean can support the great weight of a ship, so the lake helped support excessive strain on the stage. The brilliant backstage design ensured the enormous onstage success.

I see here two fascinating parallels to our spiritual lives:

- Much of our life lies backstage.

- What we do backstage maximizes or limits our on-stage effectiveness.

What Supports Your On-Stage Life?

Our soul is like the lake below the stage. What an intriguing metaphor. We all possess an inner reservoir meant to be filled continually with the living water of Christ:

If anyone is thirsty, let him come to me and drink. Whoever
believes in me, as the scripture has said, 'streams of living water
will flow from within him.' By this he meant the Spirit whom
those who believed in him were later to receive (John 7:37-38
NIV).

This backstage reservoir supports the fluctuating weights and stresses
that strain the public stage of our lives. To remain effective, we must
continually replenish the reservoir. Too often, however, our personal
reservoir runs dry. Much like physical dehydration, we may not even
notice the dryness until we hit a crisis.

The prophet Jeremiah describes our problem this way: "Thus
says the Lord, '. . . my people have committed two evils: they have
forsaken me, the fountain of living waters, and hewed out cisterns for
themselves, broken cisterns, that can hold no water'" (Jeremiah 2:13,
RSV). God's response here sounds more sad than angry.

It saddens God, not only that we have allowed our reservoir to run
dry, but also because we have turned away from him, the only source
of living water. God grieves our foolishness in forsaking the care of
our hearts.

When I was in seminary, my wife Sarah, and I lived in a cottage where
the water was supplied by a well and stored in a small holding tank. If
we showered too long, the tank drained, and then *look out!* It would
start spewing rust and gunk drawn from the bottom of the tank.

When you drain your spiritual tank and somebody turns on your
faucet once too often, the rust, grit, and sludge of your soul spew out
instead of streams of living water. God calls us to discover the strategy
for releasing those streams of living water that the Holy Spirit
supplies within and through us.

Our goal is overflow. An overflowing soul reflects the vital signs of a healthy soul.

In his classic commentary *The Song of Songs* (*Song of Solomon*),
Bernard of Clairvaux also speaks of our souls as reservoirs:

> The (one) who is wise, therefore, will see his life more as a
> reservoir than a canal. The canal simultaneously pours out what

it receives; the reservoir retains the water until it is filled, then discharges the overflow without loss to itself... Today there are many in the church who act like canals, the reservoirs are far too rare.... You must learn to await this fullness before pouring out your gifts, do not try to be more generous than God.[12]

Our goal is overflow. An overflowing soul reflects the vital signs of a healthy soul.

Signs of Spiritual Vitality

The symptoms of soul neglect help diagnose our spiritual condition. But what about spiritual health? What does that look like?

We measure our physical health by basic criteria called vital signs: heart rate, blood pressure, temperature, and respiration rate. All of these, taken together, reveal our physical condition.

The soul, likewise, has vital signs by which we measure spiritual health and symptoms of soul disease. So, how do you know if you have a healthy soul? What does spiritual vitality look like in the "dailies" of life? Let's consider five characteristics of spiritual vitality.

The Five Vital Signs of Spiritual Health Are:

- God's pace redeems our time.
- God's presence fills our hearts.
- God's perspective renews our minds.
- God's power strengthens our wills.
- God's purpose directs our steps.

1. GOD'S PACE REDEEMS OUR TIME

There are no shortcuts to health—physical or spiritual. Getting healthy and staying healthy take intentional time and effort, focused on doing the right things well. If we don't take the time, we won't see the changes we know the Lord wants for us.

There are no shortcuts to health—physical or spiritual.

One of the congregations I served described our ministry as "meeting people at the intersection of busy and stressed out." People passing through this intersection endure many close calls and suffer many collisions. Discovering the power to take back your calendar is one of the joys of soul care.

If we don't take the time, we won't see the changes we know the Lord wants for us.

God's word presents clear direction for how the Lord wants us to steward the time entrusted to us. Pace is not about time management but about life stewardship. We are not living on borrowed time. We are living on bought time (see 1 Corinthians 6:19-20).

Our Lord has redeemed us from a life of frantic futility. We *can* be delivered from bondage to worldly desires that drive overcommitment.

The spiritual implications of my use of time often surprise me. "If you want to see a person's priorities," we often hear, "check their bank statement." We might also say, "If you want to understand a person's motivation, look at their schedule."

The psalmist gives an intriguing insight into our time.

> "...all the days ordained for me were written in your book before one of them came to be" (Psalm 139:16, NIV).

This passage does not mean God has written a detailed script dictating every moment of our lives. Rather, these verses assure us of God's gracious care for us in every moment of life. That's not fatalism but faith.

We are not living on borrowed time. We are living on bought time.

We can improve this dimension of our spiritual lives through what I call Pathways to God's Pace. These pathways equip you with three practical disciplines for making the most of your time: Redeem Your Time; Enjoy Sabbath Rest; Celebrate Sacred Milestones.

2. GOD'S PRESENCE FILLS OUR HEARTS

Spirituality, simply put, means experiencing God with us in all aspects of life.

The symptoms of soul neglect trace their roots to the loss of our assurance of God's presence. When we forget God, neglect God, or doubt our connection to God, our spiritual energy drains away. We fall prey to spiritual depression and boredom. We fail to keep our priorities in order, and we find ourselves indifferent to spiritual things and vulnerable to our weaknesses.

God does not limit his presence to expressly spiritual activities, such as worship, prayer, and Bible study. True spirituality seeks to discern God's presence and the Holy Spirit's activity in *all* of life's experiences: our relationships, health, career, schooling, finances, politics, and recreation, to name some of the major areas.

We must not compartmentalize life into "spiritual" and "nonspiritual" or "sacred" and "secular." *Every* facet of life is shot through with glory. And every part of our life cries out for redemption.

Our sense of God's presence is rarely vivid. God may bless us with specific occasions in which he seems almost tangible to us, but most often God's presence seems more like our vital organs. While we know they sustain our lives, we remain mostly unaware of their moment-by-moment function. We can, however, exercise spiritual disciplines to make us more aware of and more sensitive to the movement of God in and around us. We root our "soul life" in our relationship with God, not in techniques or gimmicks. It all begins with Christ in us.

God does not reward us with his love at the finish line for an impressive race. The Lord gives his love at the starting line. We win even before the race begins! That is how we run with joy and freedom.

Living daily in grace means telling ourselves every morning and throughout the day:

> I am accepted.
> I am loved.
> I am called today to live in the power of the Lord.
> Nothing good I can do today will make God love me more.
> No sin or failure will make God love me less.

This second vital sign of a healthy spiritual life can grow stronger through what I call the Pathways to God's Presence. These pathways include three practical disciplines for experiencing God's presence, moment by moment: Preview, Review, and Prayer.

3. GOD'S PERSPECTIVE RENEWS OUR MINDS

A dear friend of mine, whom I'll call Karen, nearly always seems happy. Her cheerfulness and good humor refresh everyone who meets her. After knowing her for a while, I asked, "Are you always this cheery?"

"Not always," she replied. She then told me of her painful divorce. She had lived with intense financial pressure as she cared for her four children, at the same time having to deal with the emotional pain of her husband's betrayal.

"But I don't see any trace of bitterness!" I marveled.

"One morning, soon after the divorce became final," she replied, "I was praying, and the thought came to me that God is watching out for me. God will never betray me. So, I decided I just wasn't going to let the pain of the past steal my joy!"

A wonderful smile crossed her face—and in that moment, I saw real faith. Our outlook on life depends very much on our "in-look."

Our outlook on life depends very much on our "in-look."

More than any other factors, our attitude and perspective shape how we respond to and interact with life. If our hearts have grown parched, we often see only dryness in life. If the assumptions of this world have captured our minds, we will see little to inspire hope and joy in the middle of hardship. So, how do we change?

Spiritual vitality springs from the artesian well of a renewed mind. "Do not conform any longer to the pattern of this world but *be transformed by the renewing of your mind,*" God tells us (Romans 12:2, NIV, italics added). Because we have both God's resources and the indwelling Holy Spirit, we have great power to deal with life's difficulties.

Spiritual maturity comes as God replaces worldly assumptions with biblical truth, a truth that directs our steps daily. This truth must not only permeate our thinking but must also percolate through our hearts and behavior.

The spiritual disciplines connected to this vital sign enable us to move beyond a sterile, intellectual study of God's written word into a dynamic encounter with the Living Word, Jesus Christ. In the process, we learn to think about life with the mind of Christ (see 1 Corinthians 2:16).

Harry Blamires, the British theologian and literary scholar, challenges us to think Christianly:

> To think secularly is to think with a frame of reference bounded by the limits of our life on earth: it is to keep one's calculations rooted in this-worldly criteria. To think Christianly is to accept all things with the mind as related, directly or indirectly, to man's eternal destiny as the redeemed and chosen child of God.[13]

This third vital sign of a healthy spiritual life can grow stronger through what I call the Pathways to God's Perspective. These pathways feature three practical disciplines for renewing your mind: Bible Study, Meditation, and Spiritual Input.

4. GOD'S POWER STRENGTHENS OUR WILLS

One of the greatest deterrents to spiritual growth is our tendency to draw power from our human assets instead of relying on the Lord. Like Lot, we look at the lay of the land and choose the fertile places the world offers us, not realizing they may harbor Sodom and Gomorrah (see Genesis 13:10). We more readily find spiritual power when, like Abram, we freely accept a "lesser land" overflowing with the promises of God (see Genesis 13:14-18).

Our assumptions about power are central to our spiritual health. If we don't settle the source and use of our power with ourselves and with God, we will likely become its victims or its abusers. Spiritually speaking, power means having the resources and ability to pursue and achieve godly goals; to maintain our convictions and standards in the face of both subtle challenges and direct opposition; and to influence individuals, groups, and relational networks (systems) for godly purposes.

What is your power base? What assets do you rely on for security and advancement? Do you depend on your ability with words? Your influence with others? Your comforts and pleasures? Your material resources? Your athletic prowess? Your artistic talent? Your business savvy? We all have carefully cultivated power reserves.

The goal in spirituality is to detach ourselves from our own power resources so that we can tap into God's infinite power. This doesn't mean we ignore or eliminate the natural powers we possess, but we make them subservient to the Lord.

The disciplines of fasting, solitude, and silence are commonly called disciplines of detachment, meaning that they detach us from the world. I consider such a designation incomplete.[14]

Simply detaching from the world doesn't help us much. It's like taking off dirty clothes but having nothing clean to put on. In fact, we detach from the world *so that* we can attach to the Lord. We detach from the world to receive from God the power we once sought from the world. We deny our natural appetites to re-orient ourselves to the rich resources we find in God.

We detach from the world so that we receive from God the power we once sought from the world.

Far from robbing us of joy and pleasures, these disciplines help us to pursue and maintain our spiritual maturity, our personal energy, and our joy as God's people. Rather than restricting our freedom, they give us pathways to freedom. They not only help us deny our fleshly nature, but help us tap into God's energy for daily life.

This fourth vital sign of a healthy spiritual life can grow stronger through what I call the Pathways to God's Power. These pathways include three practical disciplines for tapping into God's power by stepping back from the world's power sources: Fasting, Silence, and Solitude.

5. GOD'S PURPOSE DIRECTS OUR LIVES

Spiritual disciplines show us the value of withdrawing from activity for a brief time so we can be equipped to live, work, serve, and play to the fullest. Spiritual disciplines are means, not ends.

Jesus modeled a rhythm of involvement and withdrawal. He often followed his creative teaching and compassionate ministry with times of solitude and prayer. Jesus' prayer and solitude fueled his ministry, and his ministry shaped his prayer and solitude.

Spiritual vitality bears fruit in our lives and brings fruit to the world around us. We cultivate Christ's character in our daily activities and interactions. We engage with the fellowship of our brothers and sisters in Christ for mutual instruction and support. We reach out to the world to continue Christ's work at all times and in all places.

Spiritual disciplines show us the value of withdrawing from activity for a brief time so we can be equipped to live, work, serve, and play to the fullest.

God calls us to live in ways that make others curious. We remind the world that God exists and that following him makes a difference.

This final vital sign of a healthy spiritual life can grow stronger through what I call the Pathways to God's Purpose. These pathways include three practical disciplines to help you live as Jesus' apprentice in everyday life: Character, Community, and Calling.

The Lord has much for us to do to bring the world to a redeeming knowledge of himself. But to do this, we must be connected to God, filled with the mind of Christ, and empowered by the Holy Spirit. We cannot accomplish what God intends in any other way.

Vital Signs of a Healthy Soul

1 GOD'S PACE REDEEMS OUR TIME

If we don't take the time, we won't see the changes we know the Lord wants for us. Discovering the power to take back your calendar is one of the joys of soul care.

2 GOD'S PRESENCE FILLS OUR HEARTS

Spirituality, simply put, means experiencing God with us in all aspects of life. The symptoms of soul neglect trace their roots to the loss of our sense of God's presence. When we forget God, neglect God, or doubt our connection to God, our spiritual energy drains away. True spirituality seeks to discern God's presence and the Holy Spirit's activity in all life's experiences. We must not compartmentalize life into "spiritual" and "nonspiritual" or "sacred" and "secular." Every facet of life is shot through with glory. And every part of our life cries out for redemption.

3 GOD'S PERSPECTIVE RENEWS OUR MINDS

More than any other factors, our attitude and perspective shape how we respond and interact with life. If the assumptions of this world have captured our minds, we will see little to inspire hope and joy in the middle of hardship. Spiritual vitality springs from the artesian well of a renewed mind. "Do not conform any longer to the pattern of this world but *be transformed by the renewing of your mind*" (Romans 12:2, NIV, italics added). Because we have both God's resources and the indwelling Holy Spirit, we have great power to deal with life's difficulties. Spiritual maturity comes as God replaces worldly assumptions with biblical truth, a truth that directs our steps daily.

4 GOD'S POWER STRENGTHENS OUR WILLS

One of the greatest distractions to spiritual growth is our tendency to draw power from our human assets instead of relying on the Lord. Our assumptions about power are central to our spiritual health. Spiritually speaking, power means having the resources and ability to pursue and achieve godly goals; to maintain our convictions and standards in the face of both subtle challenges and direct opposition; and to influence individuals, groups, and relational networks (systems) for godly purposes. The goal in spirituality is to detach ourselves from our inadequate worldly power resources so that we can tap into God's infinite power. This doesn't mean we ignore or eliminate the natural powers we possess, but that we make them subservient to the Lord.

5 GOD'S PURPOSE DIRECTS OUR STEPS

Spiritual disciplines show us the value of withdrawing from activity for a brief time, so we get equipped to live, work, serve, and play to the fullest. Spiritual disciplines are means, not ends. Jesus modeled a rhythm of involvement and withdrawal. Spiritual vitality bears fruit in our lives and brings fruit to the world around us. We cultivate Christ's character in our daily activities and interactions.

Chapter 4

Understand the Process of Spiritual Growth

Spiritual growth is not about information but transformation. It is not automatic but requires intentional effort.

I grew up practicing the typical "quiet time" of reading the Bible and prayer. I read through the entire Bible in a year a few times (yep, I often stalled at Leviticus but would press on). I also used several daily Bible reading resources. But I wanted *more*. It often felt like a duty, and I wanted the delight described in the Psalms.

Then I got a copy of Richard Foster's *Celebration of Discipline*.[15] Quite literally, it changed my life. It reshaped my soul. I began to practice the disciplines, broadening my repertoire of spiritual disciplines beyond Bible study, prayer, and journaling. I began to feel refreshed and energized.

I gave the book to a few friends who had expressed interest in spiritual growth. Their reactions puzzled me.

"Interesting," they would say, "but I can't really get into the disciplines."

About ten years later, Dallas Willard published his breakout book, *The Spirit of the Disciplines*. I had a similar experience of renewal reading it. He covered much of the same ground as did Foster but with additional philosophical and theological insight.

Again, I gave the book to friends. Again, I failed to anticipate their reactions.

"Interesting," they would say, "but it's a bit too deep for me."

Do you think less of my friends (or less of me for having such friends)? The more I thought about their reactions and the more I spoke with these truly committed disciples, the more I learned what they *really* wanted.

Then I did a class on spirituality with Dr. Roberta Hestenes for my Doctor of Ministry degree at Fuller Theological Seminary. And there I had an insight that changed everything for me.

Looking back, I noted that Foster grouped his disciplines using the categories of "Inward, Outward, and Corporate." He thought of them in terms of *where* the disciplines applied. Willard, by contrast, framed his disciplines in the categories of abstinence and engagement, detachment and attachment.[16] He presented them in terms of their orientation toward life in this world (for instance, we practice solitude to "abstain/detach" from human interaction, while we worship to "attach/engage" with God). But both their paradigms seemed to miss something important.

As a preaching pastor, I continually focus on application. I always ask, "What does this biblical truth, idea, or practice look like in real life?"

Trying to identify what seemed missing in the approaches of both Foster and Willard, I compiled a list of their disciplines in one column, along with a few of my own, while in another column I evaluated each discipline in terms of the result(s) it was supposed to produce in our lives. Finally, I grouped the disciplines together by results.

Suddenly, I "got it." I saw how the disciplines described by Foster, Willard, and others could be "translated" into practical applications for developing fulfilling spiritual experiences in five key categories:[17]

- God's pace for my life
- God's presence throughout the day
- God's perspective on life
- God's power for daily living
- God's purpose and fulfilling my call.

(I know the five "P's" can seem cheesy. Just smile and pass it off as a preacher thing.)

I showed this framework to my friends and they also "got it." *The disciplines are not about the activities themselves, but about the results they produce in our lives.* We don't exercise and work out just to fill time. We work out to get healthier, to feel better, to increase our energy and strength.

The disciplines are not about the activities themselves, but about the results they produce in our lives.

I am not criticizing Foster and Willard; I consider them my mentors. I include them among the most influential teachers of spirituality in recent generations. They have blessed millions of readers, including me. I feel deeply grateful for their wisdom and insights.

Still, I have found that focusing on the results of the disciplines has helped me shape "soul plans" tailored more specifically to individuals' spiritual needs and personalities. This focus on results has helped free men and women from feeling overwhelmed by the variety of disciplines. Instead, they focus on one or two that will refresh and energize them at a particular season in their life. This simple change has helped them move from information to transformation, from being stuck to feeling motivated.

How Does Your Soul Change?

I am no fan of New Year's resolutions. Too often they become mirrors of failure.

Think of all the projects you've begun that lie waiting to be finished. Think of all the books (physical books, if you read those!) with white flags of surrender halfway through (you call them bookmarks). Think of your to-do lists that should really be called "You still haven't gotten this done?" lists. How many things get added and never crossed off? How many lists do you have? I even have lists of my lists.

Our failure to follow through makes us reluctant to start something new.

We want to know how to get beyond an initial burst of enthusiasm. How do we translate that initial, impulsive commitment, often driven by the emotion of the moment, to sustained commitment?

In other words, how do we get beyond our good intentions?

Growth Is Natural—Almost!

Every living thing grows, seeking its greatest potential. Growth tends to happen involuntarily at the physical level. Living things grow naturally. Nothing within a tree says, "That's enough for now. No more leaves!"

While physical limitations clearly affect growth, the energy of life naturally seeks to overcome those limitations. Despite the second law of thermodynamics, which in my simplistic understanding says, "Everything tends toward disorder" (just look at your desk or bedroom), God has put a life force within creation that nudges living things toward growth.

The human heart, mind, and spirit, however, do not grow involuntarily. God created human beings to play a conscious role in their own development.

While other animals move by instinct, God created humans to engage actively in their development. God wants us to make choices that bring us into partnership with him. The classic biblical text on this idea is Philippians 2:12-13:

> Work hard to show the results of your salvation, obeying God with deep reverence and fear. For God is working in you, giving you the desire and the power to do what pleases him. (NLT)

Or consider this translation:

> ...continue to work out your salvation with fear and trembling, for it is God who works in you to will and to act in order to fulfill his good purpose. (NIV)

We will remain spiritually underdeveloped unless we take responsibility for our own growth. As in physics, order requires energy.

If people don't learn to read, they will not automatically develop the ability. If people don't hear or study a language other than their native tongue, they won't automatically be able to speak it. Likewise, if a person doesn't seek the things of the Spirit and the kingdom of God, those things won't appear automatically.

The first step toward change? Accepting that it will take intentional effort.

But not all intentional effort is effective.

Inadequate Strategies for Change

When we finally take seriously our responsibility for spiritual growth, more than likely we will try what we've always tried before, even if it doesn't work. If we are to live up to and even beyond our great expectations, however, we must recognize five inadequate strategies for growth.

THE FAILURE OF INSPIRATION

We probably all know the euphoria of a retreat or conference experience. We leave inspired and ready to change: "This time, I'm going to do it! Things will be different." As we descend from the mountain top to the valley, however, our enthusiasm fades.

Inspiration is both wonderful and necessary. It expands our vision, energizes us, motivates us, stirs our imagination, and gives us ideas and hope. But that intensity eventually fades. If you don't have a plan to channel inspiration's energy, it will dwindle.

Inspiration is like fireworks: they're bright for the moment, but you can't read by them. Inspiration is good for a jump start, but it does not supply the continual source of inner power we need.

THE FAILURE OF GUILT

We could call this the failure of condemnation. We are all too familiar with the "shoulds" that strike, like whips on a back already scarred and burdened.

Spirituality, wrongly pursued, can generate feelings of guilt and a tone of legalism. We can falsely suppose these disciplines are about performance that impresses God. Instead, we must realize that such disciplines encourage us to be impressed by God. These disciplines make us available to receive God's imprint on our hearts and minds.

These disciplines make us available for the Lord to receive God's imprint on our hearts and minds.

It's easy to get things wrong here. Paul reminds us how God's law, meant for good, in fact brought death:

> The old way, with laws etched in stone, led to death, though it began with such glory that the people of Israel could not bear to look at Moses' face. For his face shone with the glory of God, even though the brightness was already fading away (2 Corinthians 3:7 NLT).

The law, without the Holy Spirit enabling people to live in a holy way, brought knowledge of sin but no power to change. The same can be said of any "spiritual" activity. Any strategy will fail if guilt weighs us down, blocking the flow of grace.

The spiritual disciplines are not about meeting legal requirements. We can't legislate love. Think of the difference between compliance and commitment:

- Compliance is grudging obedience given out of compulsion and duty.

- Commitment is joyful engagement based on mutual vision and value.

THE FAILURE OF WILL POWER

I also call this the failure of perspiration. Will power has two main problems.

First, because will power emphasizes human effort, it is an unreliable source for change due to our fallen condition. Think of your promises to diet, to read the Bible and pray daily, to do a random act of kindness, to control your temper. How are these working for you?

Or think about Peter's bravado at the Last Supper:

Simon Peter asked, "Lord, where are you going?"

Jesus replied, "You can't go with me now, but you will follow me later."

"But why can't I come now, Lord?" he asked. "I'm ready to die for you."

Jesus answered, "Die for me? I tell you the truth, Peter—before the rooster crows tomorrow morning, you will deny three times that you even know me" (John 13:36-38 NLT).

Or think of the disciples' experience in Gethsemane:

Then Jesus returned to the disciples and found them asleep. He said to Peter, "Couldn't you watch with me even one hour? Keep watch and pray, so that you will not give in to temptation. For the spirit is willing, but the body is weak!" (Matthew 26:40-41 NLT)

Finally, think of Paul's vulnerability when he admits:

So, the trouble is not with the law, for it is spiritual and good. The trouble is with me, for I am all too human, a slave to sin. I don't really understand myself, for I want to do what is right, but I don't do it. Instead, I do what I hate (Romans 7:14-15 NLT).

Quite simply, human will power is inherently inadequate to supply the continuing energy required for spiritual change. "We have this treasure [of the gospel] in jars of clay," says Paul (2 Corinthians 4:7 NIV). Our will power is clay-based.

Human will power is inherently inadequate to supply the continuing energy required for spiritual change.

Second, will power alone doesn't tap the full range of emotional and spiritual resources we have in Christ. It has too narrow a focus. It also tires, like an overused muscle.

Change happens when the *whole person* remains engaged. If inspiration is like fireworks, then will power is like a flashlight with a dying battery—the light slowly fades and eventually goes out.

THE FAILURE OF WAITING FOR CIRCUMSTANCES TO CHANGE

If we rely on outward circumstances, we surrender our lives to forces beyond our control. Most often these forces do not obey God or God's purposes. I call this the "When/Then Syndrome."

A teenager says, "When I get out of the house, then I'll…"

A student says, "When I finally finish my degree, then…"

A young adult says, "When I finally find the right person to share life with, then…"

An employee says, "When I get a better job.…"

A middle-aged person says, "When I finally gain financial independence.…"

Very soon, you "when/then" your life away. God created us in his image to exercise responsible partnership with him, despite our circumstances.

THE FAILURE OF EXPECTING IT TO JUST HAPPEN

I sometimes call this "laissez-faire" spirituality or "waiting for the feeling." Too many live by the creed that, "if it's going to happen, it will happen naturally."

If I am supposed to read the Bible, I will feel inspired to read the Bible. And when I do read it, I will have great insights and good feelings.

If I am supposed to pray, I will want to pray and find it meaningful.

If I am supposed to be a middle school counselor for the youth group, I will feel excited about being a middle school counselor for the youth group.

But feelings tend to follow behavior. We cannot wait to *feel* like doing something positive. As with inspiration, feelings are not a reliable source for spiritual fuel. Act first, then feelings may follow.

Act first, then feelings may follow.

God honors us by entrusting us with the responsibility for our own spiritual growth. Echoing the principle of Philippians 2:12-13 (see above), Paul wrote to his disciple, Timothy:

Instead, train yourself to be godly. "Physical training is good, but training for godliness is much better, promising benefits in this life and in the life to come." This is a trustworthy saying, and everyone should accept it. (1 Timothy 4:7-9 NLT)

Don't get me wrong. While all these strategies can play a useful, albeit limited, role in our lives, they cannot supply the energy we need nor can they sustain our transformation "from one degree of glory to another" (2 Corinthians 3:18, NRSV).

So then, if these strategies aren't adequate, what is?

Inadequate Strategies For Change

1 ### THE FAILURE OF INSPIRATION

Inspiration is good for a jump start, but it cannot supply the continual source of inner power we need. If you don't have a plan to channel inspiration's energy, it will dwindle away.

2 ### THE FAILURE OF GUILT

You could call this the failure of condemnation. We can wrongly suppose these disciplines lead to performance that impresses God. Instead, we must realize that these disciplines allow us to be impressed by God, making us available for the Lord to imprint his character on our hearts and minds.

3 ### THE FAILURE OF WILL POWER

Human will power is inherently inadequate to supply the continuing energy required for spiritual change. Countless examples in scripture illustrates will power's shortcomings. Will power has too narrow a focus. Change happens when the whole person is engaged.

4 ### THE FAILURE OF WAITING FOR CIRCUMSTANCES TO CHANGE

If we rely on outward circumstances, we surrender our lives to forces beyond our control. This strategy makes personal action conditional on outward circumstances. People victimize themselves, trapped in the "When/Then Syndrome" of waiting for *when* something else will happen so that *then* they will care for their inner lives.

5 ### THE FAILURE OF EXPECTING IT TO JUST HAPPEN

This strategy takes a "laissez-faire" approach to spirituality, believing that "if it's going to happen, it will happen naturally." It doesn't. We cannot wait to feel like doing something positive. Act first, then feelings may follow.

Chapter 5

Develop Your Vision for Spiritual Growth

We're all being shaped, every day. The question is: What's shaping *you*?

Most followers of Jesus lead subnormal Christian lives, nowhere close to experiencing all the good things made possible by Jesus's death. We seem to have accepted the idea, "well, that's just the way things are."

But again, I return to the truth: *Jesus did not die so we would stay the same.* While I introduced this concept in the first chapter, now it's time to develop it.

Only a holy discontent with our mediocre experience will motivate us to seek a new vision of what God wants for us.

The Primary Motivation for Spiritual Vitality

Spiritual change begins when a vision for a better life—a great life, the life we've always wanted—captivates us. A vision for the life God intends for us in Christ.

One amazing verse inspires and convicts me at the same time:

> And all of us, with unveiled faces, seeing the glory of the Lord as though reflected in a mirror, are being transformed into the same image from one degree of glory to another; for this comes from the Lord, the Spirit (2 Corinthians 3:18 NRSV).

From one degree of glory to another? Yes, from one degree of glory to another. I'm not sure that I've experienced the first "degree," let alone moved to another degree and on to another.

Spiritual change begins when a vision for a better life—a great life, the life we've always wanted—captivates us.

God's goal for our lives is no less than our being conformed to the image of Christ. The Holy Spirit shapes us from within, sharing with us more and more of Christ's glory. This glory is not the unique glory inherent in the Triune God. God will not, cannot share *that* glory with another (see Isaiah 42:8; 48:11). This glory refers to the restoration and development of the glory originally intended for humanity as created in God's image (see Genesis 1:26-28).

Jesus became flesh, lived with us, died for us, rose from death, and poured out the Holy Spirit upon us so we could be "re-imaged" to reflect the nature of true children of God. I know, this is deep theology. Some want to keep it simple, but our failure to go deep has resulted in shallow lives.

If we want to succeed in any area of life, we must go deep. Chefs go deep into the chemistry of cooking. Musicians go deep into music theory. Contractors go deep into building codes. Jesus' followers *must* go deep—and when they do, they will bring up a staggering catch they never anticipated (see Luke 5:4-7).

We progress in the glory-to-glory process by cultivating Christ's character and conduct through intimate fellowship with God. We live in power by depending completely on God. The spiritual life is not simply a matter of imitating Christ but of forming Christlikeness within us.

The spiritual life is not simply a matter of imitating Christ but of forming Christlikeness within us.

Christ's glory is now ours through faith in him. Paul speaks of this as "the mystery that has been kept hidden for ages and generations but is now disclosed to the saints . . . the glorious riches of this mystery, which is *Christ in you, the hope of glory*" (Colossians 1:26-27, NIV, italics added).

Our problem is not information, but motivation. And what's the key to self-perpetuating motivation?

Vision.

Receive Your Defining Vision

His brother always had been a bit of a dreamer. If someone new came along, he was among the first to investigate. This time, Andrew felt sure he'd found The One.

"Come on, Simon," Andrew insisted, "I'm not fooling this time. He's The One!"

Simon walked out to meet the man, but before he could say anything, the stranger began speaking to him: "So, you are

Simon, son of John? I have a new name for you. I'm going to call you Cephas" (which means "the rock").

"Now," Jesus continued, "come with me."

Simon looked at the man for quite some time without speaking. A new name? Only a father could change a name! *What could this man see in me*, Simon wondered, *that would make him call me that?* One thing for sure: Simon Peter would stick with him until he could figure it out[18] (see John 1: 35-42).

Jesus' renaming of Simon as "Peter" provides one of the most vivid examples of vision as the key to faith, growth, and life. Why did Jesus give Simon the name Cephas (or Peter), "the rock?" Not to describe Simon as he was, but to hold out the hope of what Simon would become, through Jesus' touch.

Why didn't Jesus rename all the disciples? We aren't told. But what Jesus did with Simon, he does with all of us. The book of Revelation holds out the hope that the Lord has a new name for each of us (see Revelation 2:17). What new name might the Lord give you?

Peter's new name became his defining vision, although he didn't change suddenly. Through time and trials, along with the infilling of the Holy Spirit on Pentecost, Peter became a rock. Jesus' promise formed Peter into a building block in "the foundation of the prophets and the apostles" on which the Lord's church stands (see Ephesians 2:19-22).

Picture *Now* What Will Be

God often uses vision to lead his people to redemption:

- The vision of a new nation, through which all nations of the earth would be blessed, drew Abram from the comfort of his homeland to the land of God's choice (see Genesis 12:1-3).

- The vision of worshiping the true God in freedom and prosperity carried Moses and the Israelites through the wilderness to the Promised Land (see Deuteronomy 8:7-10).

- The vision of a glorious temple for worshiping and honoring God guided David's life in his later years (see 1 Chronicles 29).

- The vision of a world that needs to hear the good news of Jesus Christ fueled the mission of the early church (see Acts 1:6-8).

Vision means looking with the eyes of the Holy Spirit to see who we are to become and how we are to live in Christ. Vision can also describe the clear perception of a destination or goal that we greatly value.

George Barna wrote, "Vision for ministry is a clear mental image of a preferable future imparted by God to His chosen servants and is based upon an accurate understanding of God, self, and circumstances." Barna continued:

> The objective is not to acquiesce to a preordained future but *to create the future*. The vision is the means to define the parameters within which the future will emerge. Realize that the future is not something that just happens; it is a reality that is created by those strong enough to exert control over their environment. The future is not a "done deal" waiting for response. The future belongs to God and through Him to those who are driven to shape it (italics added).[19]

Take special note of Barna's assertion that the purpose of vision is *to create the future*.[20]

His statement jars us loose from a complacent resignation to "our lot in life." Barna challenges us to give God the opportunity to open our eyes to a life that is more, much more, than we ever imagined. This is what Paul meant when he wrote, "Now all glory to God, who is able, through his mighty power at work within us, to accomplish infinitely more than we might ask or think" (Ephesians 3:20 NLT). Men and women captivated by great visions attempt great things for God.

Vision means looking with the eyes of the Holy Spirit to see who we are to become and how we are to live in Christ.

Henrietta Mears, a uniquely gifted teacher at Hollywood Presbyterian Church from 1928 through 1963, sparked vision in many of her students. She would often say, "There is no magic in small plans. When I consider my ministry, I think of the world. Anything less than that would not be worthy of Christ, nor of his will for my life."[21]

This conviction explains the bold dream of a young couple in Miss Mears' class, Bill and Vonette Bright. They dreamed of beginning a Christian ministry on college campuses across the nation, and for generations Campus Crusade for Christ was ranked among the premier vehicles for university outreach and discipleship worldwide.[22]

Vision pictures something *now* as it will be. Through meditation on God's word, prayerful dialogue with the Lord, and examining our hearts, we see we were made for something *more*—and this longing to be more stirs us to action.

What Does a Life of Glory Look Like?

Do we appreciate the unspeakable privilege that is ours in Christ Jesus? I confess I neglect my privilege as Jesus' follower, or too often I take it for granted.

Most of us have no clue what living in "ever-increasing glory" would look like for us. In fact, such a concept can demotivate and discourage us, presenting an ideal that intimidates us because we do not understand it.

Remember back in the first chapter where I wrote, "Picture a life where joy carries you through the day and laughter comes as naturally as breathing"? There I described the primary elements of my vision of what following Jesus looks like for me. That vision has energized me spiritually and empowered me for life and ministry through some very difficult times.

What does your vision of following Jesus look like for you? How can it energize you spiritually and empower you for life and ministry, even through difficult times?

Guidelines to Picture God's Best for Your Life in Christ

Once a compelling vision captures your mind and heart, you will discover the motivation to take the next steps. Your desire will stir you to intentional action.

If you don't yet have a compelling vision that motivates you to action, follow the seven simple steps below to get you on the road toward discovering God's best for you.

PREPARE

Schedule ten to twenty minutes when you can be alone and uninterrupted. Sit at a desk or someplace where you can write comfortably. Have ready your journal or several pieces of blank paper and a pen. Or, use an appropriate feature of your mobile device to make notes and adapt these suggestions for it.

CENTER AND FOCUS

Start this time with prayer and a favorite passage from Scripture. If you don't have a favorite, consider Psalm 139, which expresses confidence in God's plan for your life. Be still and open your heart and mind to the Lord.

NAME YOUR STRUGGLES AND YOUR DESIRES

Take a sheet of blank paper and draw a line from top to bottom, dividing the page into two columns. At the top of the left-side column write "My Struggles." At the top of the right-side column write "My Desires."

Under "Struggles," list those things you wish you could change about your attitude, thoughts, and behavior. In these aspects, you have primary control and responsibility for yourself.

Under "Desires," list the characteristics you sense Jesus most wants for you. These excite you, encourage you, motivate you. This is the kind of person you hope to become.

Do not take time to edit; just write as much as you can for each one. Do not censor yourself; you will have time later to revise and edit. The primary goal is to get your thoughts on paper.

Take five to ten minutes to fill in both columns, as best you can.

LOOK FOR PATTERNS AND SIMILARITIES

Take the next five minutes to look for similar ideas within each column. You might circle them in different colors to link them. Or you may want to combine them into one phrase.

Then look for connections between the columns, drawing lines to link them. You might link "financial stress" under struggles with "trusting God for everything" under your desires. Think of this as moving from A to B. A represents your current condition of spiritual immaturity and inexperience and B represents the person Jesus is calling and empowering you to become.[23]

MAKE A ROUGH DRAFT OF YOUR DESIRED VISION

On a new sheet of paper or in your journal, write sentences or bullet points that describe particulars of the life you've always wanted in Christ. You likely will add to your draft over the coming days, weeks, and even months. Keep it handy.

COMMIT YOUR VISION TO THE LORD

John wrote, "And this is the boldness we have in him, that if we ask anything according to his will, he hears us. And if we know that he hears us in whatever we ask, we know that we have obtained the requests made of him" (1 John 5:14-15, NRSV). I'm certain that being changed to Jesus' likeness from one degree of glory to another is God's will for all of us. Your vision provides your initial grasp of your "one degree of glory to another." Joyfully, confidently, boldly, offer it to the Lord!

READ AND PRAY THROUGH YOUR VISION EVERY DAY

Begin every morning by reading your vision. Read it aloud. Yes, it may sound a bit grandiose at first. But remind yourself that Jesus died to make these changes possible through the power of the Holy Spirit working within you.

Also read your vision before going to bed. Marinate in the power of the gospel changing your life in tangible ways.

Even if it's a very rough draft, just getting a few ideas down tends to stir up many more ideas—and it gives energy. Remember, discipline ignited by vision changes us. Discipline gets the vision off the page and into our lives, where it blooms, grows, and changes us forever.

Discipline: The Link Between Desire and Achievement

We've all heard the phrase, "If you keep doing what you're doing, you'll get what you've got." We could rephrase it to say, "If you keep neglecting what you need to do, you'll keep missing what you want." Or more positively, we might say, "If you start doing what you need to do, you'll get what you've always wanted."

Which has contributed most to your lack of success:

- not knowing the right information
  or
- not doing what you know?

My greatest problem is my failure to do what I already know. My goal in this book includes not only presenting new information on the nature of spiritual growth, but also practical instruction on how to pursue the process of spiritual growth. How do we unlock the energy to do what we already know to do?

Vision shows us our God-inspired, Jesus-purchased, Spirit-empowered destination. Discipline taps the energy reserves stored within the soul to make that vision a reality.

Vision is like a travel brochure with lush descriptions of my destination. Discipline provides the transportation and resources to get there.

Vision is the why. Discipline is the how.

Discipline, as an end in itself, is as dry as dust. It is just plain hard work. But discipline attached to a vision is fire that fuels light and life.

We must learn to live for our vision, not our undisciplined impulses.

Returning to the image of our inner well or reservoir, discipline keeps the water flowing in consistently.

Discipline Brings Freedom

Many of today's most successful athletic coaches tell their players, "You can choose the pain of discipline or the pain of regret." Discipline means freedom from regret, one of the most discouraging attitudes in life. One simple sentence has helped me keep pursuing spiritual discipline: "Discipline weighs ounces; regret weighs tons."[24] Discipline frees, while regret imprisons.

> The trained athlete has the greatest freedom in any contest.

> The trained musician has the greatest freedom in performance.

> The disciplined students have the greatest freedom in their studies.

Disciplined Jesus-apprentices have the freedom to face life unafraid, confident that they can trust God. They join with God in developing the skills and resources that sustain them, no matter the circumstances.

Discipline produces the freedom to face life with confidence. Discipline develops "spiritual reflexes" before you need them. When Joe Frazier reigned as the world heavyweight boxing champion, he revealed something of his own personal philosophy of life. "You can map out a life plan or a fight plan," he said, "but when the action starts, you're down to your reflexes. That's where your road work shows. If you cheated on that in the dark of the morning, you're getting found out now under the bright lights."[25]

In one of my first snow skiing lessons, my instructor said, "A muscle needs to repeat an action about two hundred times to remember what it's supposed to do. The idea of practice is to build muscle memory. Do it right, again and again, and your muscles will gain the habit you want. You'll begin to react without effort, without even thinking. If you've learned the wrong way, however, it will take even more repetition for your muscles to unlearn the bad habit and develop the right one."

Discipline produces the freedom to face life with confidence.

Spiritual discipline develops soul memory. We develop spiritual reflexes to respond to life in God's way. We discipline ourselves to develop soul memory in normal times so that we'll be equipped for the times of high demand or deep crisis. That is the way to thrive in Jesus.

Guidelines: Picture God's Best For Your Life In Christ

1   PREPARE

Schedule ten to twenty minutes when you can be alone and uninterrupted. Sit at a desk or someplace where you can write comfortably. Have ready your journal or several pieces of blank paper and a pen. Or, use an appropriate feature of your mobile device to make notes and adapt these suggestions for it.

2   CENTER AND FOCUS

Start this time with prayer and a favorite passage from scripture. Psalm 139 expresses confidence in God's plan for your life. Be still and open your heart and mind to the Lord.

3   NAME YOUR STRUGGLES AND YOUR DESIRES

Take a sheet of blank paper and draw a line from top to bottom, dividing the page into two columns. At the top of the left-side column write "My Struggles." At the top of the right-side column write "My Desires."

Under "Struggles," list those things you wish you could change about your attitude, thoughts, and behavior. In these aspects, you have primary control and responsibility for yourself.

Under "Desires," list the characteristics you sense Jesus most wants for you. These excite you, encourage you, motivate you. This describes the kind of person you hope to become.

Do not take time to edit, just write as much as you can for each one. Do not censor yourself. You will have time later to revise and edit. The key thing is to get your thoughts on paper.

Take five to ten minutes to fill in both columns, as best you can.

4   LOOK FOR PATTERNS AND SIMILARITIES

Take the next five minutes to look for similar ideas within each column. Circle them in different colors to link them.

Or combine them into one phrase.

Look for connections between the columns, drawing lines to link them. For example, a person might link "financial stress" under struggles with "trusting God for everything" under desires. Think of this as moving from A to B, where A represents your current condition of spiritual immaturity and inexperience, and B represents the person Jesus died to make possible.

5   MAKE A ROUGH DRAFT OF YOUR DESIRED VISION

On a new sheet of paper or in your journal, write sentences or bullet points that describe particulars of the life you've always wanted in Christ. You likely will add to your draft over the coming days, weeks, and even months. Keep it handy. Even if it's a very rough draft, just getting a few ideas on paper will tend to stir up many more ideas—and it gives energy.

6   COMMIT YOUR VISION TO THE LORD

"And this is the boldness we have in him, that if we ask anything according to his will, he hears us. And if we know that he hears us in whatever we ask, we know that we have obtained the requests made of him" (1 John 5:14-15 NRSV). I'm certain that being changed to Jesus' likeness from one degree of glory to another is according to God's will. Your vision provides your initial grasp of your "one degree of glory to another." Joyfully, confidently, boldly, offer it to the Lord.

7   READ AND PRAY THROUGH YOUR VISION EVERY DAY

Begin every morning by reading your vision. Read it aloud. Yes, it may sound a bit "grandiose" at first. But remind yourself that Jesus died to make these changes possible through the power of the Holy Spirit working within you. Also read your vision before going to bed. Marinate in the power of the gospel changing your life in tangible ways.

Part Two

Pathways to Spiritual Vitality

Pathways to God's Pace for Living

Pathways to God's Pace for Living
Redeem Your Time | Enjoy Sabbath Rest | Celebrate Sacred Milestones

Pathways to God's Presence with Us
Preview | Review | Prayer

Pathways to God's Perspective
Bible Study | Meditation | Spiritual Input

Pathways to God's Power
Fasting | Silence | Solitude

Pathways to God's Purpose for Our Lives
Character | Community | Calling: Daily Call and Vocational Call

Chapter 6
Redeem Your Time

When I give myself permission to live at a holy pace, many problems almost take care of themselves.

- Problems born of irritability diminish because I gain relief from feeling pressured.

- Problems born of poor decisions lessen because I don't force myself to hurried action based on inadequate information and insufficient prayer.

- Problems born of not trusting God are less frequent because I stop believing that everything depends on me.

When I lighten up on my activities and pace, I find hope again. Having margin in my schedule makes it far more possible for peace to flourish in my life.

Do you want to be kind to yourself and to others? If so, understand that living at God's pace is one of the most practical ways to accomplish it.

Over-Booked, Under-Graced

Life is full. We have so many responsibilities, so many options and so many distractions clamoring for our attention that we quickly become over-booked but under-graced.

Life gets especially full when we try to maximize all the available opportunities for our family and significant relationships, for our studies, our work, our play, our well-being, and our call to serve the Lord. We fear missing out on something special, so we cram more and more into our schedules.

We are over-booked but under-graced.

In the rush to experience as much as we can, however, we miss those factors that bring peace, perspective, and meaning into our lives. How can we confront and break "the tyranny of the urgent"?[26] We do so when we align our time with God's values. Although this alignment takes work to implement, it is worth the effort and even the frustrations of failure.

Grace takes time. To experience peace takes time. To let God love you takes time. To let go and trust God takes time. If you want to break free from the time crunch, watch your heart, not your watch.

To break free from the time crunch, watch your heart, not your watch.

What Controls Us?

We never get the impression that Jesus rushed. In fact, Scripture never portrays God as rushing, except in that beautiful portrait of the running father in the Parable of the Prodigal son (see Luke 15:20).

By contrast, rushing, busyness, and time stress seem to be the normal condition for most of us. How can we change such deep-rooted but destructive habits?

As we've already seen, the journey to spiritual vitality begins with awareness and assessment. One symptom of soul neglect is "Losing Control Over Life's Routine." The only remedy is to pause and discern the reasons for our rushing. Once we can name the forces that control our time and life decisions, we can intentionally choose how to respond and change.

Spiritual vitality comes when we practice the disciplines in ways that enable us to partner with God in becoming more like Christ. One of the most significant passages on time anywhere in Scripture appears in Ephesians 5:15-20:

> Be careful then how you live, not as unwise people but as wise, making the most of the time, because the days are evil. So do not be foolish but understand what the will of the Lord is. Do not get drunk with wine, for that is debauchery; but be filled with the Spirit, as you sing psalms and hymns and spiritual songs among yourselves, singing and making melody to the Lord in your hearts, giving thanks to God the Father at all times and for everything in the name of our Lord Jesus Christ (Ephesians 5:15-20 NRSV).

To be filled with the Holy Spirit is like accepting an apprenticeship from a master craftsman. We long to sit at the feet of a master.

We gladly invest the long hours and the strenuous effort required because we know we will learn from the best. What makes all the difference for us isn't our management of time, but God's management of us.

It isn't our management of time, but God's management of us that makes all the difference.

Guidelines for Redeeming Your Time

Allow me to suggest eight steps to help you better schedule and manage your time. Redeeming your time not only makes you more efficient, but it also opens up whole new vistas of deeper spirituality that enable you to become more like Jesus.

PREPARE

Plan this initially as a weekly exercise. When you look at each day in light of a week and a month, and even from a longer perspective, you will have a larger, more useful framework for decision-making.

Schedule twenty to thirty minutes when interruptions seem less likely. Have your calendar/schedule available, along with your journal and/or blank paper for notes. You can make notes on your computer or mobile device if you prefer. Sit in a place where you can easily spread out your materials and write.

To see the "big picture," I suggest using a larger format paper calendar (8 ½ x 11, for example) that shows an entire month. I prefer to write my appointments in pencil to make it easier to note changes to my schedule. It's easy to transfer the schedule to the calendar on your computer or mobile device.

PRAY

Since "the days are evil" (Ephesians 5:16), we exercise spiritual authority in redeeming our time. Acknowledge God's gift of every moment and invite the Holy Spirit to give you wisdom to fill your time for God's glory and your joy in Christ.

LIST YOUR PRIORITIES, PROJECTS, AND APPOINTMENTS

Make three lists.[27]

First, list your "Urgent and Important" priorities for the week and for each day.[28]

Second, list your "Important but not Urgent" priorities for the week and for each day.[29]

Third, list your "to do's," appointments, meetings, and projects that you need to consider in the coming days and week.

SCHEDULE YOUR PRIORITIES

Select a reasonable number of items from your three lists and estimate the amount of time each one will require. Then schedule time for them on specific days during your current week. Schedule the important things first, then fill in other matters around them. Don't just prioritize your schedule; schedule your priorities.

Be patient as you juggle your different commitments. You may initially feel frustrated because you have too many urgent commitments crowding out the important. That's normal. Over time, you will adjust your schedule to align with your priorities.

PRAY OVER YOUR SCHEDULE[30]

Commit your planning to the Lord, humbly acknowledging God's ultimate control. As you gain confidence and expertise, try to broaden your planning to include larger blocks of time. Include times for a personal retreat morning or day to give special, focused attention to strengthening your spiritual life and vitality.

MONTHLY

List the projects, appointments, and plans you want to accomplish in the next thirty days. Knowing what you know now, schedule them into your calendar.

QUARTERLY

List the projects, appointments, and plans you want to accomplish in the next ninety days. Knowing what you know now, schedule them into your calendar.

ANNUALLY

Include vacation times and a time to evaluate your year.

At first, it may seem like a monumental task to be intentional about stewarding your time. It may feel something like the massive energy required for a rocket to break free from earth's gravity. Once free, however, that rocket soars and easily adjusts its movement. By redeeming your time, you become that rocket.

Number Your Days

In his book, *How to Get Control of Your Time and Your Life*, Alan Lakein presents six of the most common factors that determine people's use of time:[31]

> *Habit.* We have routines and activities that we no longer evaluate; we just do them. Even though the activity may no longer have meaning, we keep doing it anyway.
>
> *Others' Demands.* We all know "the squeaky wheel gets the grease." Others' priorities can fill our schedule, regardless of their legitimacy.
>
> *Escapism.* We daydream about all we could do instead of accomplishing something.
>
> *Impulse.* On the spur of the moment, we suddenly decide to do something—but inadequate preparation and poor timing often bring disappointing results.
>
> *Default.* We neglect to act, and instead we allow others to decide for us.
>
> *Conscious Decision.* We take responsibility for choosing the best course of action and then we go to work to accomplish it.

Lakein writes that while the first five factors may not be wrong, "if you aren't satisfied with the payoff from those decisions, more conscious efforts are called for. How tempting it is in difficult situations to drift, dream, or drown...there is an alternative...you can decide."[32]

Psalm 90:12 says, "Teach us to number our days, that we may gain a heart of wisdom." We count what we value. We count our collections, our money, our relationships, and our accomplishments. We count our years of marriage, of friendship, and of service. Moses advises us to count our days. My friend Tim Hansel wrote,

> I once read a thought-provoking article titled, "If You Are 35, You Have 500 Days to Live." Its thesis was that when you subtract the time spent sleeping, working, tending to personal matters, hygiene, odd chores, medical matters, eating, traveling, and miscellaneous time-stealers, in the next thirty-six years you will have roughly the equivalent of only five hundred days left to spend as you wish. No wonder the Psalmist advised, "So teach us to number our days that we may apply our hearts to wisdom."[33]

You are closer than you think to a new and better way of living. When you realize you have a choice about your time, you can tap into God's power to help you redeem the time he has given you.

Redeem Your Time by God's Power

To redeem means to "buy back," "to liberate," "to repurpose." We redeem time when we reinvest our seconds, minutes, hours, days, months, and years for God's glory and our joy.

We don't kill time; we fill it with life. We redeem our time when we appreciate each day as a gift given by God:

> You saw me before I was born.
>> Every day of my life was recorded in your book.
> Every moment was laid out
>> before a single day had passed (Psalm 139:16 NLT).

We don't kill time. We fill time with life.

These verses do not mean God has a script for every moment of our lives. They give us a poetic expression of God's intimate involvement in our daily lives. They express the promise of God's presence, not fatalistic determinism. I picture God writing a holy journal or diary of my life experience, like many parents do as they record the experiences of a newborn.

Scripture teaches us to confront the reality of our mortality. We swim in the sea of time, only vaguely aware of the shores of eternity beyond the sea. But time in this world has an expiration date. When we get serious about spiritual growth, we must pay careful attention to our time:

> Seventy years are given to us!
> Some even live to eighty.
>
> But even the best years are filled with pain and trouble;
> soon they disappear, and we fly away...
>
> Teach us to realize the brevity of life,
> so that we may grow in wisdom (Psalm 90:10-12 NLT).

Scripture teaches us to confront the reality of our mortality. Time in this world has an expiration date.

Redeeming your time means examining your use of time and energy in light of God's purpose and our limitations. Ask yourself, "Why do I say yes to the things that I agree to do?"

- Describe your healthy, legitimate reasons.

- Describe any unhealthy reasons.

- When do you say yes at the expense of healthy boundaries and priorities?

- What unexamined assumptions or uncontrolled desires may influence your decisions?

- How might the expectations of others control your use of time?

- What determines your schedule?

- What activities get the most attention? Why?

- Where do you find energy and motivation?

- When do you ignore your soul desires because of "more urgent" demands?

The greatest lie is that we don't really control our time. While I will admit that many necessities impose obligations and responsibilities on us, a thoughtful analysis of our time reveals many hours available every week for soul, heart, and mind care. If you won't make the time, you won't make the connection.

Be Kind to Yourself

When I began to pay more careful attention to my schedule, I realized how hard I tend to push myself. I don't take enough breaks. I schedule far too many appointments without sufficient time to rest between them. I undertake too many projects to complete in a "normal" 40 – 50 hour work week. I am my own worst boss.

The Lord isn't a harsh taskmaster. I now understand Jesus' invitation to rest, to take on his yoke, as an invitation to lead a sustainable life at a godly pace.

Maximizing life means enjoying rest as well as work. It means savoring life's pleasures as well as fulfilling life's responsibilities:

It is in vain that you rise up early
    and go late to rest,

eating the bread of anxious toil;
    for the Lord gives sleep to his beloved (Psalm 127:2 NRSV).

Be realistic in what you can accomplish! What needs to be done now? What can wait? Don't keep pushing ahead at the expense of your rest, self-care, and relational priorities. If you make sacrifices for some projects, try to schedule recovery time. Plan "buffer days" between major time commitments. Break the tyranny of time by aligning your time with God's values.

Time is a heart issue. While many books on time management suggest techniques and principles for being more efficient and more effective with our time, our use of time ultimately reflects our values, stated or unstated. To break free from the time crunch, watch your heart, not your watch.

Guidelines: Redeeming Your Time

1   PREPARE

Schedule twenty to thirty minutes weekly. Use a paper
calendar that shows an entire month, or work from the
calendar on your computer or mobile device if you prefer.
After completing the exercise, you can transfer the schedule
to your mobile device or computer calendar system.

2   PRAY

Take spiritual authority, requesting God's wisdom to fill your
time for his glory and your usefulness.

**3   LIST YOUR PRIORITIES, PROJECTS, AND
APPOINTMENTS**

List your "Urgent and Important" priorities for the week
and for each day. List your "Important but not Urgent"
priorities for the week and for each day. List your "to
do's," appointments, meetings, and projects that need to be
considered in the upcoming days and week.

4   SCHEDULE YOUR PRIORITIES

Schedule a reasonable number of items from both lists into
your week before you make any additional commitments or
take on any more work.

5   PRAY OVER YOUR SCHEDULE

Make sure to bring God into your time management.

6   BROADEN YOUR PLANNING

Include monthly, quarterly, and annual projects,
appointments, and plans.

Chapter 7
Enjoy Sabbath Rest

I am grateful I began my Christian life learning that Sabbath time was about spiritual health and physical refreshment, not legalism. In stark contrast to the Pharisees' burdensome approach to Sabbath-keeping, Jesus' teaching reminded us that God gives the Sabbath as a gift. "The Sabbath was made to meet the needs of people," Jesus insisted, "and not people to meet the requirements of the Sabbath" (Mark 2:27 NLT).

In high school I kept the Sabbath by not doing homework on Sundays. I would occasionally read books for assignments, but I made the effort to get my papers and other assignments done before Sunday.

I continued that practice throughout college and seminary.[34] I experienced Sunday as a day of freedom to worship and to respond to whatever opportunities came my way. I enjoyed lunch or dinner with friends, went on walks, played games, played guitar, or just relaxed and read. Sunday became an oasis. My experience confirmed a basic principle of time: work expands or contracts to fill the time allotted.[35]

I am sad to confess that the responsibilities of adulthood brought me far more struggles with Sabbath rest. Before I knew it, my commitment to a day of rest eroded. I began to drift on the current of busyness and soon got caught in the rapids of exhaustion.[36]

Unless we rest consistently, we will be spiritually drained continually.

For good reason, God commanded his people to stop working one day a week. Unless we rest consistently, we will be spiritually drained continually.

Activity Addiction Exacts a Cost

We pay a heavy price for our addiction to activity. We may fail to realize the negative impact until it's too late. Our 24/7, always-on lifestyle can lead to burnout and even stress-related illness or death. Our choices, often around our use of time, hurt us. "Hurry sickness" and emergency living wear on our souls. Thomas Merton names our hurried lifestyle "frenzy's violence":

> To allow one's self to be carried away by a multitude of conflicting concerns, to surrender to too many demands,

> to commit one's self to too many projects, to want to help
> everyone in everything is to succumb to violence. Frenzy
> destroys our inner capacity for peace. It destroys the
> fruitfulness of our work, because it kills the root of inner
> wisdom which makes work fruitful.[37]

We often feel uncomfortable taking time off because we fear the
consequences. The U.S. Travel Association explored the trend of
American workers foregoing vacation time with its "Project: Time
Off initiative." A 2018 survey[38] of 1,303 American workers whose jobs
featured paid time off revealed the underlying reasons why so many
of us sacrifice our hard-earned vacation days. Consider the top reasons
these workers claimed they left vacation time unused (respondents
could cite more than one reason):

- Fear of returning to a mountain of work (40%)
- The belief that nobody else could do the job (35%)
- Inability to afford taking time off (33%)
- Fear of being seen as replaceable (22%)
- To show greater dedication to the company and the job (28%)

In some cases, workers can be their own worst enemies. They suffer
from what Roger Dow, president and CEO of the U.S. Travel
Association, calls a "work martyr complex."[39]

Our high tolerance for misery erodes our spiritual vitality.

When Jesus' followers resist taking time off weekly for rest and
refreshment, they pay an extremely high price. Our high tolerance for
misery erodes our spiritual vitality.

Break Free from Activity Addiction

Two scriptural principles break the spell of activity addiction. You
could think of one as the stick and the second one as the carrot that
motivate the proverbial donkey. The first one, the wakeup call of
disillusionment, provides the stick. While we think our activity will
ensure our security, both life and scripture teach us that our anxious

striving for security is pointless. God instructs us instead to fully rely on him.

> Unless the LORD builds the house,
>> those who build it labor in vain.

> Unless the LORD guards the city,
>> the guard keeps watch in vain.

> It is in vain that you rise up early
>> and go late to rest,

> eating the bread of anxious toil;
>> for he gives sleep to his beloved (Psalm 127:2 NRSV).

> I am the vine; you are the branches. Those who abide in me and I in them bear much fruit, because apart from me you can do nothing (John 15:5 NRSV).

The second principle, the carrot, appears in the Lord's invitation to rest with him. Jesus promises that we learn best when we yoke ourselves to him in rest:

> Come to me, all you that are weary and are carrying heavy burdens, and I will give you rest. Take my yoke upon you and learn from me; for I am gentle and humble in heart, and you will find rest for your souls. For my yoke is easy, and my burden is light (Matthew 11:28-30 NRSV).

Or, as the late Eugene Peterson wrote in this often-quoted Bible translation *The Message*, "Learn the unforced rhythms of grace. I won't lay anything heavy or ill-fitting on you. Keep company with me and you'll learn to live freely and lightly."

Our over-emphasis on personal responsibility and our under-appreciation of God's grace both drive us to exhaustion—and we think we're being virtuous! That's the saddest part.

Guidelines for Enjoying Your Sabbath Rest

Five simple guidelines for enjoying your Sabbath rest can begin to revolutionize your walk with God. If you feel tired, drained, and without energy, start here.

AFFIRM SABBATH REST AS GOD'S GIFT TO RESTORE YOU

David's best-known psalm gives a convincing testimony of divine restoration:

> The Lord is my shepherd, I shall not want.
>> He makes me lie down in green pastures;
>
> he leads me beside still waters; [or *waters of rest*]
>> he restores my soul [or *my life*] (Psalm 23:1, NRSV-additional wording is mine).

ASK YOURSELF SOME CRUCIAL QUESTIONS:

- When do I give God time to reach me?
- When am I available to God?
- Do I expect God to bless me on the run?
- When am I free to relax with no thought of other responsibilities?

Soul disciplines are not about getting God's attention, but about getting us to pay attention to the Lord.

SCHEDULE A 24-HOUR PERIOD FOR A PERSONAL/FAMILY SABBATH

Take a day, from sundown to sundown, when you do none of your ordinary work activity. The Israelites based their Sabbath tradition on the biblical account of creation that repeatedly says, "it was evening and it was morning, one day" (Genesis 1:5, 8, 13, 19, 23, 31). For this reason, the Jewish Sabbath begins at sundown Friday and ends with sundown Saturday.

Since the vast majority of Christians celebrate Sunday as their Sabbath[40], they could celebrate their Sabbath from Saturday evening through Sunday evening. Because I work weekends, Thursday evening to Friday evening has turned out to be my best time for Sabbath.

Abstain from all your ordinary work activities (paid or unpaid). Try to have everything you need for the coming twenty-four hours. Avoid your workspace. Shut off text, email, and social media notifications so they don't distract you. And if you miss something, don't fret. Just get what you need and get back to Sabbath-time.

Many suggest that, in our common five-day work week (is that still the norm?), we distinguish Sabbath from a day off that we fill with chores and errands. I find this distinction very helpful.

Be ready to feel uncomfortable the first few times you try this! Give yourself grace. After a few times, you will actually crave this time for relief and re-focus.

DEVELOP A LIST OF SABBATH-FRIENDLY ACTIVITIES

Choose activities that refresh your spirit, renew your relationships, bring joy and relaxation into your life, and let you rest. Many people have a bucket list of activities they want to experience in their lifetime; I suggest a Sabbath list of activities that renew you. They could include:

- Reading blogs or books that encourage your spiritual growth.

- Extended hikes or similar activities with friends and/or family.

- Agenda-free time, when you simply pray, "Lord, you know what I need. Please bring that into my life in these hours."

This is not selfish time but self time. Your Sabbath time will positively affect all other time.

MAKE WORSHIP WITH GOD'S PEOPLE A PRIORITY

Sabbath has both personal and community aspects. Sabbath includes renewing your relationship with the Lord in the fellowship of believers as well as rest and refreshment for yourself. How often do you normally attend in-person worship services? If your answer is something other than weekly, what is getting in the way? What could you eliminate to make worship a priority?

BE FLEXIBLE WHEN NECESSARY

We all have times when necessity disrupts our schedule. So, we adjust. Don't feel guilty. God isn't keeping score. Keep Paul's perspective: "Don't let anyone condemn you for what you eat or drink, or for not celebrating certain holy days or new moon ceremonies or Sabbaths. For these rules are only shadows of the reality yet to come. And Christ himself is that reality" (Colossians 2:16-17 NLT).

Experience the Blessings of Sabbath Rest

Sabbath rest reminds us that our first priority is to worship and imitate our Creator God. The Ten Commandments present God's design for the abundant life, and the fourth commandment (on keeping the Sabbath) provides the primary rationale for the critical importance of this day:

> Remember to observe the Sabbath day by keeping it holy. You have six days each week for your ordinary work, but the seventh day is a Sabbath day of rest dedicated to the Lord your God. On that day no one in your household may do any work. This includes you, your sons and daughters, your male and female servants, your livestock, and any foreigners living among you. *For in six days the Lord made the heavens, the earth, the sea, and everything in them; but on the seventh day he rested. That is why the Lord blessed the Sabbath day and set it apart as holy* (Exodus 20:8-11 NLT, italics added).

The Sabbath principle is rooted in creation. As creatures created in God's image, we imitate God in both work and rest:

> Then God looked over all he had made, and he saw that it was very good! And evening passed and morning came, marking the sixth day. On the seventh day God had finished his work of creation, so he rested from all his work. And God blessed the seventh day and declared it holy, because it was the day when he rested from all his work of creation (Genesis 1:31-2:3 NLT).

God did not rest to recover from fatigue. God ceased creating because his work of creation was complete and ready for enjoyment with his image-bearers. God rested at the consummation of creation to savor the joy and satisfaction of the very good creation he had made. As God's representatives, given dominion over creation, we serve God's purposes in all we do. That includes honoring God's model of six days of work and one day of rest.

We will always have unfinished business. Since we never get completely done, we must accept the divinely ordained limits within which we can truly live. God's strict enforcement of Sabbath-keeping had its roots both in God's honor and in our limits. Even the work of building the tabernacle was to cease on the Sabbath.[41]

Few books on the Sabbath are more profound than Abraham Joshua Heschel's book *The Sabbath: Its Meaning for Modern Man*. Heschel writes:

> Six days we wrestle with the world, wringing profit from the earth; on the Sabbath we especially care for the need of eternity planted in the soul. The world has our hands, but our soul belongs to Someone Else.[42]

He also wrote:

> Six days we live under the tyranny of things of space; on the Sabbath we try to become attuned to holiness in time, a day on which we are called...to turn from the results to the mystery of creation; from the world of creation to the creation of the world.[43]

Heschel reminds us that we are not beasts of burden who rest so we can work harder. We rest to remind us that we are meant for more than this world. He calls the Sabbath both a "cathedral in time" and a "palace in time."

Sabbath rest reminds us to rely on our Almighty God for daily and eternal deliverance.

It feels jarring to think about the defiant Sabbath-breaker put to death for this high-handed sin (see Numbers 15:30-36). We must realize, however, that ignoring the Sabbath brings the slow death of the individual spirit and the demise of the spiritual health of the community.

Sabbath rest reconnects us with God in fellowship and worship. Sabbath rest reminds us to rely on our Almighty God for daily and eternal deliverance. In fact, the re-presentation of the Ten Commandments in Deuteronomy 5 cites another reason for Sabbath observance: Sabbath reflects God's grace in delivering his people:

> Remember that you were once slaves in Egypt, but the Lord your God brought you out with his strong hand and powerful arm. That is why the Lord your God has commanded you to rest on the Sabbath day (Deuteronomy 5:15, NLT).

Think of the Sabbath as a weekly sign posted in the middle of life to remind us that God has delivered us in Christ and will continue to care for and guide us. On the latter idea, Hebrews 4:9-10 tells us the Sabbath also points ahead to the goal of history:

> So then, a Sabbath rest still remains for the people of God; for those who enter God's rest also cease from their labors as God did from his (NSRV).

Sabbath loosens the grip of earthly responsibilities so we can take hold of our eternal hope. Sabbath rest also expresses our trust in the Lord. Candidly, I often feel reluctant to rest because I feel I must do as much as possible. As a pastor, I have always felt responsibility to do all I can for the Lord, all the time. I also have a variety of interests combined with a significant amount of energy. As a result, I keep pushing because I want to do so much . . . and I feel like I can. But that's not helping my spiritual health.

Sabbath loosens the grip of earthly responsibilities so we can take hold of our eternal hope.

You see the problem, right? It comes down to trust—or more accurately, a lack of trust—in God. My friend Dave Rhodes warns us about the "arrogance of unlimited capacity." We don't recognize our limits.[44] I am guilty of this when I cheat on taking a full day off. It doesn't seem like a problem . . . for a while. And then it hits: I feel blue and blah. I can't concentrate. I have little interest in much of anything. At times, I don't even have the energy to do the activities that normally renew me, like playing guitar or golfing.

Sabbath-keeping is like staying hydrated. In one of my blog posts, I reflected on the adage, "Drink before you're thirsty." That's the key to both physical hydration and spiritual hydration.[45]

Pride says, "God needs my work." Sabbath says, "I sincerely trust God to do what needs to be done."

Pride says, "I must work to prove my sincerity to God." Sabbath says, "God wants *me* far more than my work."

When we acknowledge our limits, we make room for God's limitless power. Sabbath cultivates our trust in God, awakens our appreciation for God's goodness, and infuses our lives with God's graciousness. God gives us Sabbath rest to rekindle our worship, to renew our spirits, to refresh our minds, to relax our bodies, and to reestablish our priorities.

Enjoy the Lord and the good gifts of Sabbath rest!

Guidelines: Enjoying Sabbath Rest

1 AFFIRM SABBATH REST AS GOD'S GIFT TO
RESTORE YOU

Sabbath rest is not about getting God's attention, but about
paying attention to God.

2 SCHEDULE A 24-HOUR PERIOD FOR A
PERSONAL/FAMILY SABBATH

Make it from sundown to sundown when you do none of
your ordinary work activity. Use this time for anything other
than your primary activities. Try to have everything you need
for the coming twenty-four hours. Avoid your workspace.
Shut off text, email, and social media notifications.

3 DEVELOP A LIST OF SABBATH ACTIVITIES

Include activities that refresh your spirit, renew your
relationships, bring joy and relaxation into your life, and
let you rest. This is not selfish time but self time, and it will
positively affect all other time.

4 MAKE WORSHIP WITH GOD'S PEOPLE A PRIORITY

Sabbath has both personal and community aspects. Sabbath
includes renewing our relationship with the Lord and God's
people, as well as rest and refreshment for ourselves.

5 BE FLEXIBLE WHEN NECESSARY

When necessity disrupts your schedule, adjust without feeling
guilty.

Chapter 8
Celebrate Sacred Milestones

God loves a good party.

To the surprise of many, celebration is a spiritual discipline. Far from denying pleasure and relaxation, our Lord graciously invites us to set aside special times to savor his gifts, remember his grace, and affirm his goodness. God called his people to form their lives around times of celebration whenever they recalled and re-experienced God's grace and power breaking into their lives.

God's pace for living includes *all* aspects of time. The Lord paired the daily rhythm of night and day and the weekly rhythm of work and Sabbath with an annual cycle of feast days and festivals. These feasts and festivals celebrated God's deliverance and God's provision for his people. Our journey to spiritual vitality means redeeming time by restoring holidays to their original "holy days" of meaning and joy.

Our journey to spiritual vitality means redeeming time by restoring holidays to their original "holy days" of meaning and joy.

Jewish theologian Abraham Heschel wrote,

> "The Bible is more concerned with time than with space. It sees the world in the dimension of time. It pays more attention to generations, to events, than to countries, to things; it is more concerned with history than geography... Judaism teaches us to be attached to holiness in time, to learn how to consecrate sanctuaries that emerge from the magnificent stream of a year."[46]

Spiritual health cherishes the milestones of life.

Remember and Relive Sacred Milestones of Deliverance

In true worship and celebration, remembering is more than commemoration of an event in salvation history. Remembering makes it *real*. "By immersion in its recollection the praying people relive, participate in, and in a symbolic way make real the past events."[47]

The Israelites truly relived their nation's nomadic wandering through the wilderness whenever they celebrated the Feast of Booths, as they basically "camped out" in temporary structures. Celebration is a whole-person experience. That's why we often visit a special location or decorate a place to create an atmosphere appropriate to the occasion. Food and drink fuel the joy. Stories often get told to delight adults, educate children, and awaken the holy imagination of those who relive the remembered experience. Celebrations thrive through intentional effort, thoughtful preparation, and luxurious surrender to the experience.

Israel's history provides an instructive model for us. The Lord designated five specific days and two specific weeks for holy days, forbidding the people from working during those periods. They made special offerings and enjoyed special meals in honor of the Lord.[48]

In the spring of each year, the Day of Passover and the subsequent Festival of Unleavened Bread lasted eight days. This feast celebrated the Exodus, God's powerful deliverance of his people from Egypt.

The unleavened bread spoke vividly of the urgency required to escape the tyranny of Egypt. The Israelites had no time for the yeast to rise. Leaven (yeast) later became a symbol of the sin that keeps God's people in bondage. The bitter herbs God instructed the people to consume reminded them of the bitter taste of toil under Egyptian slavery, while the slain lamb pointed to the cost that had to be paid for their redemption.

This annual celebration reminded them of everything God had done to liberate them from worldly bondage. The Lord called the Israelites to live in an entirely new way, to shine among the nations as a light pointing to God's way to freedom. When times were good, the people needed the annual celebration to remind them that God was the basis for their freedom. When times were bad, the annual celebration reminded them that God hadn't forgotten them (see Exodus 2:24).

Take Time to Celebrate God's Provision

The Day of Atonement and the subsequent Feast of Shelters (also called "Booths") took place in the fall of each year, lasting eight days. The feast celebrated God's provision for the people in the wilderness, on the way to the promised land.

The people were to offer the fruit of their harvest during a festival that delighted in God's goodness. Think of it as something like a huge campout, with the people living in makeshift shelters, "to remind each new generation of Israelites that their ancestors had to live in shelters when I rescued them from the land of Egypt. I, the LORD, am your God" (Leviticus 23:43, NLT). Living in these shelters for a week changed the celebration from a cerebral ceremony to a vivid immersion in experiential learning, especially potent for the children. The past came alive. The celebration proclaimed that the God of Might, who acted powerfully in the past, was the same Mighty God who could act powerfully in their lives.

The people annually renewed their commitment to trust God. As they recalled the pillar of cloud that guided the Israelites by day and the pillar of fire that guided them by night, celebrants committed themselves to continue to seek God's guidance and protection.

Guidelines for Celebrating Sacred Milestones

The feasts and festivals of Israel's history provide patterns for framing our spiritual experiences. Use the following guidelines to create your own personal celebrations of God's work in your life.

CELEBRATE YOUR EXPERIENCES OF DELIVERANCE

When has the Lord helped you in specific ways? What's your Passover?

Your Passover represents those special times when you experienced freedom from a specific problem, victory over a particular need, or an open door into a new relationship or opportunity. It may be the first day of sobriety in any area of life. It may be your recognition of a special sacrifice someone made for your sake. Whatever it is, celebrate your deliverance!

Make a list of the things that once held you captive and burn it or tear it into pieces to be thrown away. You might want to make a special offering or sacrifice (anonymously or not) to help someone on their own road to freedom.

A journal provides a record of God's work in your life. When the Lord works in your life, you think you'll always remember it, but far too often, you forget. Keeping a journal and periodically reviewing it can reawaken your faith.

CELEBRATE YOUR EXPERIENCES OF GOD'S PROVISION

When did Jesus Christ become more than a name to you? When was your Day of Atonement?

When it comes to conversion, some people are like light switches while others are like rheostats (dimmers). Some know exactly when they put their faith and trust in Jesus Christ as Savior and Lord—it was the moment the light went on, like a switch. Others cannot pinpoint an exact date and time, but they know they love the Lord. The light shines, but they can't say exactly when the switch flipped to "on." They are more like the rheostat being turned up gradually.

Celebrate either the exact date of your salvation or pick an appropriate date as your spiritual birthday. Have a special meal and invite friends to join you. Share your story of faith and make specific prayer requests for the coming year.

In addition to the time when you came to faith in Jesus, when have you experienced God's provision? Your Feast of Shelters represents those special times when God gave you shelter from the storms and trials of life. You might celebrate God's provision of a job or career. Or a special provision of money when you were in need. Or it might be the provision of a friend, or a ministry, or an opportunity to serve that has brought great satisfaction.

CELEBRATE THE SACRED MILESTONES OF YOUR SPIRITUAL JOURNEY

Take time to search Scripture and to review your story to highlight those special sacred milestones that have shaped your life. Be as creative as you like. For instance, you might have a Nehemiah day when God laid a burden on your heart that led you to a new commitment (see Nehemiah 1). Or perhaps you want to celebrate your Pentecost when the Holy Spirit became real to you in a new way (see Acts 2).

Of course, you also want to commemorate your special life events, such as birthdays, marriages, and deaths of loved ones. Those are the three "biggies" in life. How can you celebrate them intentionally as a witness to your faith?

CELEBRATE JESUS' LIFE THROUGH THE CHRISTIAN YEAR

In addition to celebrating sacred milestones based on Israel's feasts and festivals, and on our own sacred milestones, we can also relive the mighty acts of God in the celebration of the Christian year.

The Christian year commemorates the major events of Christ's life. The Western church's observance of the Christian year[49] begins with *Advent*. Advent is the four-week season designed to prepare for celebrating Christ's coming. It not only looks back to Christ's first coming, but also looks forward to when the Lord will come again. The spiritual season of Advent remembers God's promises of a savior and God's provision of hope, love, joy, and peace. We enter the anticipation of God's plan to send a savior. We also cultivate expectation as we look forward to Christ's return.

Christmas celebrates Jesus' birth, the defining event of human history. Christmas lights can symbolize Jesus as the Light of the World, overcoming the darkness of spiritual winter. Christmas banquets can express our joy in feasting on Jesus as the Bread of Life. The giving and receiving of gifts, recalling the gifts of the wise men celebrated at Epiphany, display God's generosity and our response to the greatest gift of all.[50]

Lent is the second primary season of the Christian year; it begins with Ash Wednesday and concludes with Holy Week.[51] This forty-day period commemorates Jesus' forty days in the wilderness and Israel's forty years in the wilderness. During Lent, we give serious attention to the condition of our spiritual lives, to reordering our priorities, and to forsaking temptations. Fasting is commonly practiced during Lent.[52]

Ash Wednesday, which begins Lent, is named for the practice of placing ashes on the forehead (usually in the sign of a cross) at the start of the forty days. In biblical symbolism, ashes speak of our mortality ("ashes to ashes, dust to dust") and grief. They remind us both of our mortality and of our repentance.

Holy Week (also called Passion Week), which concludes Lent, begins with Palm Sunday and includes Maundy Thursday, Good Friday, and Easter. The dilemma of these days is how to respond appropriately to their intensity and importance. The four Gospels devote nearly one-third of their content to this week alone!

Obviously, we cannot hope to relive all that occurred in such a short time. Still, our worship moves through the paradoxical praise of Palm Sunday, the tension of intimacy and betrayal of Maundy Thursday, the agony of Good Friday, and the ecstasy of Easter.[53]

Easter is also called Resurrection Sunday. Easter recalls the shock and joy of the resurrection. Jesus' resurrection quite literally changed everything! This is the highest feast day of the year and should be celebrated with great joy.[54]

Pentecost marks the birth of the church with the outpouring of the Holy Spirit.

In the weekly recitation of worship and the annual cycle of the Christian year, we find new strength and wisdom for our lives as we relive the life of our Lord and call attention to how God continues to work among his people.[55]

Time is transformed when we form our schedule around our faith. Peace marks our days as pressure dissolves. Margin magnifies grace, and Sabbath rest becomes an oasis for refreshment and connection. Seasonal celebrations fuel our faith and gratitude.

Allowing God's pace to redeem our time opens the doors to spiritual vitality. Time serves us, instead of us serving it. Time becomes a tool for our flourishing rather than a tyrant inhibiting our growth. The exercise of spiritual disciplines helps us to thrive as we move ever deeper into the abundant life Jesus died to make possible.

Guidelines: Celebrating Sacred Milestones

1   **CELEBRATE YOUR EXPERIENCES OF DELIVERANCE**

When have you seen God's grace helping you in specific ways? What's your Passover? Your Passover represents those special times when you celebrate your deliverance. Review your journal to compile a list of things that held you captive and then burn that list or tear it into pieces to be thrown away. Make a special offering or sacrifice (anonymously or not) to help someone else on their road to freedom.

2   **CELEBRATE YOUR EXPERIENCES OF GOD'S PROVISION**

When did Jesus Christ become more than a name to you? When was your Day of Atonement?

Celebrate either the exact date of your conversion or an appropriate date you pick as your spiritual birthday. Have a special meal and invite friends to join you. Share your story of faith and make specific prayer requests for the coming year. Your Feast of Shelters represents those special times when God gave you shelter from the storms and trials of life.

3   **CELEBRATE THE SACRED MILESTONES OF YOUR SPIRITUAL JOURNEY**

Highlight those special spiritual experiences that have shaped your life. Be as creative as you like. You can also celebrate your special life events (such as birthdays, marriages, and deaths of loved ones) in ways that witness to your faith.

4   **CELEBRATE JESUS' LIFE THROUGH THE CHRISTIAN YEAR**

In addition to celebrating sacred milestones based on Israel's feasts and festivals, and on our own sacred milestones, we can also relive the mighty acts of God in the celebration of the Christian year.

Pathways to God's Presence with Us

Chapter 9
Preview

Pondering our experience of God's presence often leaves us disappointed. We expect goosebumps (or "chicken skin," as I've heard some say). We expect emotion and inspiration. We expect immediate answered prayers and dramatic evidence of God's power.

And often we feel let down. The saying, "Expectation is an appointment with disappointment," applies here.[56]

Yes, I know Moses had the burning bush. Ezekiel had the spinning wheels, Isaiah had the overwhelming vision of God high and lifted up, and Daniel fell on his face, trembling, at the sight of awesome things to come. Those experiences all accompanied their calls. Day in and day out, however, most of us have a low-key experience of our connection to the Lord.

God's presence is more like a great friendship than a private state dinner with the Queen of England. A true friend is available, present, easy. That relationship is not necessarily emotional, but it is reliable. Presence is about trust, not emotion. God is trustworthy. God keeps his promises.

The starting point for recognizing God's presence is developing spiritual awareness.

God Gives Us Spiritual Sight

One of our great problems in contemporary culture is our inability to pay attention. We all know about Attention-Deficit/Hyperactivity Disorder (ADHD) that affects some. But a new phenomenon called Continuous Partial Attention (CPA) threatens us all.

CPA is the process of trying to pay simultaneous attention to multiple sources of incoming information, but at a superficial level. Linda Stone coined the term in 1998. She writes, "We want to connect and be connected. We want to effectively scan for opportunity and optimize for the best opportunities, activities, and contacts, in any given moment. To be busy, to be connected, is to be alive, to be recognized, and to matter."[57]

We pay continuous, partial attention in an effort not to miss anything. Ironically, in so doing, we often miss or devalue the most important connections.

Jacob Received Spiritual Sight

Isaac's son, Jacob (the younger twin of Esau) felt consumed by his dream of "success." He had deceived and gotten the best of his brother and father at every turn. Jacob had wrangled Esau's birthright in a swap for a meal of stew (Genesis 25:27-33), and he had hustled his father, Isaac, to secure the blessing due Esau (Genesis 27).

Jacob's dream of success soon turned into a nightmare. He had to run for his life in fear of his enraged older brother—and that's when God gave him a very different sort of dream:

> As he slept, Jacob dreamed of a stairway that reached from the earth up to heaven. And he saw the angels of God going up and down the stairway. At the top of the stairway stood the LORD, and he said, "I am the LORD, the God of your grandfather Abraham, and the God of your father, Isaac… I am with you, and I will protect you wherever you go. One day I will bring you back to this land. I will not leave you until I have finished giving you everything I have promised you."
>
> Then Jacob awoke from his sleep and said, "Surely the LORD is in this place, and I wasn't even aware of it!" (Genesis 28:12-16 NLT)

Instead of the dream of his own achievements—climbing his deceiver's ladder of success—Jacob discovered God's ladder! But he almost missed it.

We are blinded when we try to do things in our own way. Think about your own experience for a moment. How have you worked to establish yourself, only to find all your efforts have backfired?

God's revelation opens our eyes. God's word comes to us, not necessarily in a dream, but through the Bible, through a message in a sermon, in a song, a book, or when a friend says something arresting.

Elisha's Servant Received Spiritual Awareness

A fascinating account of God giving spiritual sight occurs in 2 Kings 6. Elisha's servant went outside as usual one morning and felt stunned and terrified to find the area surrounded by the horses and chariots of Israel's enemy Aram (modern-day Syria). The Aramean king had laid siege to the town because he knew the prophet Elisha somehow was learning and disclosing Aram's plans to ambush the king of Israel.

Elisha's servant panicked. When he hurriedly informed his master, Elisha responded, "Don't be afraid! For there are more on our side than on theirs!"

I wish I could have seen the puzzlement on the servant's face as he counted those on his side: "One (himself), two (Elisha), but where are the others???"

The servant had seen God do many mighty acts through Elisha, but this time he had evaluated the situation and his resources by worldly standards. And his limited perspective blinded him to the truth. Worldly standards are deceptive and far from reliable in what they seem to promise:

> Some nations boast of their chariots and horses,
>> but we boast in the name of the Lord our God
>> (Psalm 20:7 NLT).

> Don't count on your warhorse to give you victory—
>> for all its strength, it cannot save you (Psalm 33:17 NLT).

> At the blast of your breath, O God of Jacob,
>> their horses and chariots lay still (Psalm 76:6 NLT).

Elisha did not want to leave his servant in the dark, so he prayed: "O Lord, open his eyes and let him see!" The Lord did open the young man's eyes, and when he looked up, he saw the hillside around Elisha filled with horses and chariots . . . of *fire*. Prayer broke through the servant's unbelief and opened his eyes to God's powerful protection.

The discipline of Preview gives spiritual sight as we pray through our day, visualizing the Lord in everything we do.

The Power of Visualizing God's Presence at Work

Years ago, I led a weekly Bible study of men in the congregation I served in Old Greenwich, Connecticut. We met in the early morning, and then the men caught the train to Grand Central Station in New York City.

One morning, a man I'll call Jim suggested we change from meeting in the morning to meeting at noon for lunch in midtown Manhattan one time each month. I said I would certainly consider the idea, but wondered why he wanted to make the shift.

"This study is really helpful," Jim began, "but to be honest, by the time I get to my office, I have pretty much forgotten what we studied and discussed. I have a feeling that if I had an appointment for a Bible study on my calendar midday, I'd think more about God throughout that day."

Jim's comment about his calendar sparked an idea. After we discussed his proposal, I said, "Let's do something different for our closing prayer. Get out your calendars (this took place before mobile phones). Take some time to pray over each of your appointments and 'to do' lists. Picture the Lord with you in every situation. After you pray, put a cross, a Bible verse, or any idea that comes to you in prayer by that appointment or 'to do' item. Then, when you look at your schedule during the day, you will think of the Lord and this prayer time."

Jim called me that evening. He couldn't wait to tell me about a situation he had prayed over. That day he had planned to terminate an employee he really liked. He had recruited this man, which made his decision especially difficult.

"As I previewed that situation," Jim reported, "nothing specific came to mind, except that the Lord would do something about that situation that day."

When Jim had arrived at his building (following his commute from our Bible study), he stepped into an empty elevator, something quite uncommon at that time of day. Just then he heard a familiar voice call out, "Can you hold the elevator, please?"

It was the employee Jim had prayed about.

Once they were alone in the elevator, the man asked, "Can we meet later this morning?"

Jim had planned to ask him the same question, so he said, "Sure. What about?"

"Just something I want to discuss," he said.

The man came to Jim's office at 10:30 a.m., as planned.

"Jim, this is really hard to admit," the man said, "but it's not working for me to stay here. I don't want to disappoint you, but I am not a good fit here. So, I'd like to suggest a plan of action; but before I do, can I share something?"

Jim, by then on the edge of his seat, replied, "Of course."

"I've been wrestling with this for a few days now," the man continued. "When I prayed this morning, I asked the Lord for help. I said that I would take it as a sign that I should go ahead and speak with you if we got on the same elevator alone. You can imagine how I felt when that happened!"

Jim gulped.

"So, I'd like to give you my resignation," the man added, "but I'd like to ask you to consider giving me up to six weeks to wrap up things here and start my search on my own time. Would that be OK?"

Jim replied, "I agree with you that it hasn't worked as we both hoped. Yes, I'll give you up to six weeks. Now, let me tell you a story..."

Cultivate Spiritual Awareness Through the Discipline of Preview

That day with my men's Bible study group, I stumbled onto what I call the discipline of Preview. I have not heard of anyone else suggesting this spiritual discipline, but it may be a common idea.

Preview is a discipline of anticipation, seeing our days as ordered by God. We view our meetings as divine appointments, and our projects as opportunities for God to work through us. We approach our studies, work, interactions, and activities as assignments in God's kingdom. We also see our scheduled recreation as re-creation, savoring God's goodness.

In short, we learn to bring the Lord into every moment and aspect of our lives, listening for his direction, discerning his presence, and depending on him in all things. We live the wisdom of Philippians 4:8, 9:

> And now, dear brothers and sisters, one final thing. Fix your thoughts on what is true, and honorable, and right, and pure, and lovely, and admirable. Think about things that are excellent and worthy of praise. Keep putting into practice all you learned and received from me—everything you heard from me and saw me doing. Then the God of peace will be with you (NLT).

Guidelines for the Discipline of Preview

Five simple guidelines will help you to preview your day, asking the Lord to walk through the day with you, every step of the way.

SCHEDULE FIFTEEN MINUTES AT THE START OF THE DAY WITH YOUR BIBLE, JOURNAL, AND CALENDAR

> "Listen to my voice in the morning, Lord.
>
> Each morning I bring my requests to you and wait
>   expectantly" (Psalm 5:3 NLT).

The value of practicing this discipline at the start of the day is that it sets the tone for everything you will encounter. You can also preview the next day in the evening. You might consider copying your schedule into your journal so you can easily write the thoughts and ideas that come to you in this process.

ASK THE LORD TO REDEEM THE TIME GIVEN YOU TODAY

We've already contemplated God's call to redeem the time entrusted to us in the section on Pathways to God's Pace for Living. "Make the most of every opportunity in these evil days," says Ephesians 5:16 (NLT). "Live wisely among those who are not believers and make the most of every opportunity," says Colossians 4:5 (NLT).

Preview builds God's call to obey into our schedule. We offer our day as a sacrifice to the Lord (Romans 12:1 NIV). We also develop a sense of expectancy and anticipation as we prepare to move into the day. Several prayers help me come to the Lord with expectation. The first two are my own prayers:

> "Lord, give me what you want to give me this day."
>
> "Lord, give me what you want me to give others today."

I pray a third prayer adapted from Benedict of Nursia, the founder of the Benedictine Order:

> Gracious Father, give me diligence to seek you and wisdom to find you today. May my ears hear your voice, my eyes see your goodness, and my tongue proclaim your name as I commit my life to pleasing you.[58]

FOCUS ON TODAY'S PLANS ONLY

Jesus told us, "Don't worry about tomorrow, for tomorrow will bring its own worries. Today's trouble is enough for today" (Matthew 6:34 NLT).

We experience God's presence when we are present in the present moment.

We have this moment only. We experience God's presence when we are present in the present moment.

INVITE JESUS TO WALK WITH YOU THROUGH YOUR DAY

Jesus also promised, "And be sure of this: I am with you always, even to the end of the age" (Matthew 28:20 NLT). The writer of Hebrews reaffirmed God's promise originally given in Joshua 1:5: "God has said, 'Never will I leave you; never will I forsake you'" (Hebrews 13:5 NIV).

Dallas Willard asks, "How would Jesus live your life if he were you?"[59] In a similar vein, ask yourself, "How would I live this day if Jesus were physically present with me?"

Who will you see? What projects will you work on? What appointments do you have? What difficult situations will you face? What are you looking forward to doing?

Bring all these, one by one, to the Lord, picturing the Lord literally present with you. Bathe these situations in prayer. See the Lord alongside you in conversations, meetings, and activities. How will you interact with others in light of Christ's presence in, with, and through you?

Write in your journal any insights or ideas that come to you. Ideas and options will come to mind that you had never even considered. I cannot count the number of times the discipline of Preview has given me ideas for solving problems, for handling difficult issues, even for new activities to do with our family that had never occurred to me.

Names of people may come to mind who you hadn't thought about for some time. Write them down and try either to call, text, email, or mail them a simple note. It is a powerful blessing for someone to hear, "You came to mind as I was praying this morning. Just want you to know I care."

SURRENDER YOURSELF AND YOUR PLANS TO THE LORD

James says:

> Look here, you who say, "Today or tomorrow we are going to a certain town and will stay there a year. We will do business there and make a profit." How do you know what your life will be like tomorrow? Your life is like the morning fog—it's here a little while, then it's gone. What you ought to say is, "If the Lord wants us to, we will live and do this or that" (James 4:13-15 NLT).

Let the counsel of James guide your discipline of Preview. Make your primary goal being available to God. We make our best plans when we yield to God's sovereign direction of our lives. We trust the Lord to bring divine appointments and even interruptions[60] to us throughout the day. When we do this, we enter our day with a refreshing sense of anticipation and expectancy. It's like holy prospecting as we mine our day to discover God's presence.

The Phone Call

Preview is one of the most practical disciplines available to help us develop our sensitivity to the spiritual reality always around us. Our experience may not be as dramatic as that of Elisha and his servant, but it can be as real.

I practice the discipline of Preview throughout the day, especially when I face a problem, an interruption, or a difficult meeting. When I have a difficult phone call to make, I often preview the conversation. I try to script it with Christ. I ask, "Lord, what do you want me to say and how do you want me to say it? Lord, give me the opening line. How do I start this conversation?"

I once called a woman who had directed strong criticism toward a staff member. I procrastinated calling because I didn't want to face the anger I thought would come. When I could delay no longer, I took a few minutes to preview the conversation in prayer.

As I pictured Jesus making the call, I knew—I'm not sure how, but I just knew—that she was having a very difficult time that very day.

I switched gears from calling as a supervisor who had to deal with a complaint to being a pastor calling a person in need.

"I can't believe you called today," she said to me. "This is one of the worst days of my life. I never thought it would be this bad." She proceeded to tell me her ex-husband was getting remarried that day, and that her grown children all were attending the ceremony, leaving her desperately alone.

Preview is one of the most practical disciplines available to help us develop our sensitivity to the spiritual reality always around us.

We talked and prayed, then as the conversation neared its end, I mentioned her concern about a staff member.

"Well, I think we can work things out," she said, "I overreacted, with all that's been going on emotionally these past few months. I'll give him a call next week."

Words cannot express the power of God in that phone call. I shudder to recall my own hard feelings and frustration as I had contemplated calling her. None of that changed until I took time to preview the conversation prayerfully with the Lord.

Spiritual vitality comes from living moment-by-moment in the awareness of Jesus Christ by the power of the Holy Spirit. Spiritual vitality puts us in touch with life in Christ and brings the touch of Christ's life into the world.

Spiritual vitality means breaking free from distractions, seeing through deceptions, and discerning God's movement in our lives and in the world around us. The Lord opens our eyes to see the ordinary as extraordinary and the extraordinary as ordinary.

Guidelines: The Discipline of Preview

1   SCHEDULE 15 MINUTES AT THE START OF THE DAY WITH YOUR BIBLE, JOURNAL, AND CALENDAR

Copy your schedule into your journal so you can easily write the thoughts and ideas that come in this process.

2   ASK THE LORD TO "REDEEM THE TIME" GIVEN YOU TODAY

I use at least three prayers to help me come to the Lord with expectation:

"Lord, give me what you want to give me this day."

"Lord, give me what you want me to give others today."

"Gracious Father, give me diligence to seek you and wisdom to find you today. May my ears hear your voice, my eyes see your goodness, and my tongue proclaim your name as I commit my life to pleasing you."

3   FOCUS ON TODAY'S PLANS ONLY

We experience God's presence when we remain present in the present moment.

4   INVITE JESUS TO WALK WITH YOU THROUGH YOUR DAY

Picture the Lord literally present with you in conversations, meetings, and activities. Write any insights or ideas that come to you in your journal. Ideas and options will come to mind you had never considered.

5   SURRENDER YOURSELF AND YOUR PLANS TO THE LORD

Make your best plans and remain available to the Lord, trusting the Lord to bring divine appointments to you throughout the day.

Chapter 10
Review

If you begin your day by previewing situations to become aware of God's presence throughout the day, it makes sense to "close the loop" and consider how the day went. You asked the Lord to guide you, so what happened? How did God show up? Too often, we pray and then move on, as if nothing will change. The discipline of Review trains us to look back at our day to discern God's presence and provision. We also want to take note of the ways God worked that we didn't anticipate.

The people of ancient Israel built review into their songs, their prayers, and their worship. God gave the Passover feast to his people to remind them, every year, of his mighty works (Exodus 12:12). This discipline formed the basis for *all* their annual festivals.

David's review of past deliverance gave him the confidence to endure present difficulties. When he faced death at the hands of the Philistines, the Lord delivered him. In response, David composed this psalm:

> I sought the LORD, and he answered me,
>   and delivered me from all my fears.
>
> Look to him, and be radiant;
>   so your faces shall never be ashamed.
>
> This poor soul cried, and was heard by the LORD,
>   and was saved from every trouble.
>
> The angel of the LORD encamps
>   around those who fear him and delivers them
>   (Psalm 34:4-7 NRSV).

When you review what the Lord has done in you, through you, and for you that day, you get a heightened sense of his intimate involvement in your life. It's a great way to kick up your own spiritual vitality several notches.

Look Back to See God's Fingerprints on Your Day

In her book, *The God Hunt*, Karen Mains talks about "God Hunt Sightings." Karen writes, "The God Hunt is choosing to recognize God anytime he intervenes in our everyday life."[61] She lists four categories:

- Any obvious answer to prayer
- Any unexpected evidence of God's care

- Any help to do God's work in the world
- An unusual linkage or timing

We could add to these categories the times when we have sensed God's "nudge" (or divine whisper) to pray for someone, to write a letter, make a call, and so on. A God Hunt Sighting is like a holy game of hide-and-seek. We're looking for God—and God wants to be found. People may call these situations "coincidences," but we call them "God-incidences."

David's review of past deliverance gave him the confidence to endure present difficulties.

When I came home from church one day, one of our sons, Tim, said, "Dad, I had a God Hunt Sighting today!" He told me that he'd had a problem getting to soccer practice that day. Since we have one daughter and three sons, all of whom were active in school and sports, we sometimes had schedule conflicts that made us feel more like air traffic controllers than parents. Neither Sarah nor I could drive Tim to practice that day, so he rode the mile on his bike. But when he arrived at the school practice field, he saw no one there. Then he remembered: the practice had been moved to a venue across town!

As Tim wondered what to do, the mother of another soccer player drove into the lot. She knew soccer practice was scheduled for a different location, but she thought some of the boys might have forgotten. She put Tim's bike in her van, drove him to practice, and then brought him home after practice. Sarah and I had no idea about the change. Tim smiled ear to ear as he finished his story: "The Lord didn't leave me alone at the playground. I got a ride across town!" What could have been just another irritation and a coincidental solution in a boy's ordinary day had become a window through which Tim saw God working.

What would our churches be like if all of us cultivated such sensitivity and thanksgiving? How would it change *your* life if you looked for God both before you encountered situations and then once again when those situations had passed? How would this discipline affect your overall outlook on the challenges, irritations, and small victories of each day?

Review and The Prayer of Examen

This discipline of Review (paired with Preview) is like the prayer of examen. Prayer has many facets, such as the common format of Adoration, Confession, Thanksgiving, and Supplication (A.C.T.S.), but there are many other types of prayer. The prayer of examen is a type of soul-searching prayer that takes us more deeply into the awareness of God's working and of our need.

THE EXAMINATION OF CONSCIOUSNESS

The first aspect of the prayer of examen is the examination of consciousness. We prayerfully review our day to discover how God has been present to us throughout the day and how we have responded to his loving presence.[62] We learn how to begin to pay attention to (become conscious of) God's work in our lives and around us. We ask several questions:

- How did I see God work today?

- How responsive was I to God's "nudges"?

- How often did I pray for specific situations or needs?

- How often was I unaware of the Lord?

THE EXAMINATION OF CONSCIENCE

The second aspect of the prayer of examen directs our attention to those areas that need cleansing, purifying, and healing. Again, we ask several questions:

- When did I let God, myself, and/or others down today?

- When did I miss opportunities to show God's love in word and in practical ways?

- Where do I need God's touch to heal a hurt or help me forgive?

Review Extended Times of Your Life

The discipline of Review is valuable not only for reflecting at the end of the day, but also for identifying God's touch in your life over longer periods of time.

If you keep a journal, going back to read your previous entries can remind you of how God worked. That reminder strengthens your faith and confidence. You can also harvest your journal for insights and lessons God has taught you.

Many of us already review the old year when we approach the new year. We ask, "What have I accomplished? What seeds have been planted for the future?" Review a challenging season of your life to discern God's presence and direction and to capture the lessons you learned.

Guidelines for Review

The following four short guidelines will help you to make the most of your time of Review.

SET ASIDE FIVE TO FIFTEEN MINUTES AT THE END OF THE DAY

Take your Bible, journal, and calendar and use them in quiet reflection to help you walk back through your day.

WRITE IN YOUR JOURNAL THE HIGHLIGHTS AND LOWLIGHTS OF THE DAY

Our family has used the terms "peaks and pits" to describe the events of the day. You could also call them the high times and the hard times. You may have time for only one or two. Go with the one or two that energize and instruct you. Don't get bogged down in a catalog of all that happened that day, or this discipline will become a heavy burden. Answer two primary questions:

- Where did I see the hand of God today?

- Where did I have a hard time seeing the hand of God today?[63]

Pray and reflect over the situations or incidents you have highlighted.

As you pray, focus on three primary actions: thanksgiving, confession, and instruction. Take time to thank God for his care and provision. Confess and release your sin and regret. Then ask, "Lord, what were you trying to teach me today?"

PREPARE YOUR MATERIALS FOR THE NEXT MORNING

Since we view Review as a discipline paired with Preview, do what you can at night to make it easier to get started in the morning. Most of us have a difficult time getting up and going at our morning disciplines. If we cannot find our Bible, journal, or calendar, we most likely will say, "Oh, forget it!" and go back to bed or on to other matters.

What About When We Don't Feel God's Presence?

We cannot talk about God's presence without acknowledging the reality of feeling God's absence. We often feel spiritually alone, especially in one of three situations.

WHERE DOES GOD GO WHEN I GO WRONG?

When we are guilty of some wrongdoing, or we feel guilty, it usually seems as though God has left us. God is not truly absent in such times, though our sense of positive connection has been disrupted.

If you are, in fact, guilty of some sin, then you can deal with it through confession and repentance. Don't interpret a sense of absence as God's rejection. When David sinned terribly, he described God's hand as "heavy upon" him. God was *very* present in a misery-producing way (see Psalm 32:4)! David spoke of losing the joy of his salvation, but of not losing his salvation itself (see Psalm 51:12). Your immediate sense of fellowship may be disrupted, but you are never left alone.

If guilt feelings plague you that seem to have no foundation in actual sins of commission or omission, take time to explore those feelings. If the feelings are unfounded, you can find release by speaking truth to yourself and identifying Satan's lies about you. Writing about it in a journal can help you rediscover God's grace and presence. I encourage people to begin simply by writing a letter to Jesus.

"Dear Jesus, where are you? The last time I remember being with you was . . ."

After reflecting on this, continue by completing this statement: "Ever since I have felt I lost touch with you..."

Those who learn to reflect on these matters often find a sense of God's presence returning to them sometime in the process.

WHERE IS GOD WHEN MY WORLD CAVES IN?

We wrestle honestly with doubts about God's goodness and love when we experience life's heartache and pain. I have been continually instructed and encouraged by faithful people who witness to God's nearness when life steals what they value most.

Ted, who lost his teenage son in a freak accident, told me several years later, "The Lord is good. It still hurts when we think of Tim but walking with Christ has made it clear." Ted's simple, profound words, accompanied by his tears, testify to his his experience of "the love of Christ that surpasses knowledge" (Ephesians 3:19 NRSV).

At times like these, our best response is to cry out to God, clinging to the hope that we forged in better days. This was the strategy of the psalmist in Psalm 42:

> As a deer longs for flowing streams,
>   so my soul longs for you, O God.
>
> My soul thirsts for God,
>   for the living God.
>
> When shall I come and behold
>   the face of God?
>
> My tears have been my food
>   day and night,
>
> while people say to me continually,
>   "Where is your God?"
>
> These things I remember,
>   as I pour out my soul:
>
> how I went with the throng,
>   and led them in procession to the house of God,
>
> with glad shouts and songs of thanksgiving,
>   a multitude keeping festival.
>
> Why are you cast down, O my soul,
>   and why are you disquieted within me?
>
> Hope in God; for I shall again praise him,
>   my help and my God.
>
> My soul is cast down within me;
>   therefore, I remember you (Psalm 42:1-6 NRSV).

We are wise to be gentle, humble, and compassionate with ourselves and with others in times of crisis and depression. Parker Palmer, who traveled through a deep, long valley of depression, advises us to renounce a "fix it" mentality:

> One of the hardest things we must do sometimes is to be present to another person's pain without trying to "fix" it, to simply stand respectfully at the edge of that person's mystery and misery. Standing there, we feel useless and powerless, which is exactly how the depressed person feels.[64]

Scripture's affirmations greatly encourage me:

> The LORD is close to all who call on him, yes, to all who call on him in truth (Psalm 145:18 NLT).

> For God has said, "I will never fail you. I will never abandon you" (Hebrews 13:5 NLT).

WHERE IS GOD IN LIFE'S ROUTINE?

Sometimes we simply don't sense God's nearness. We remain faithful, but our hearts feel wooden. It's all ordinary, very ordinary.

In the normal process of spiritual growth, we move through the initial "infatuation phase" of spiritual life to the maturity of walking by faith, not by feelings. I once heard a counselor say, "No marriage really grows until the infatuation gets knocked out of it." By that, she meant couples need to move beyond the idealization both of a person and of the relationship and on to the practical realities of routine, hard work, persistence, failure, disappointment, adjustment to life-as-it-is, and to the person as-he/she-is.

God wants our faith, character, and lifestyle to mature so we don't depend on good feelings. Often the people who sense God's presence most are those who know him least! The Lord is merciful to new Christians who often need an extra emotional boost. But as we grow, the Holy Spirit weans us off the security of "feeling close to God" so we learn to be people of power and conviction, with or without the emotional support.

This doesn't mean we'll never feel close to God again; only that the Lord doesn't want us so dependent upon the emotional high. This is precisely where the discipline of Review plays a practical, even vital role in developing our awareness of God's presence.

As you practice the simple discipline of Review, you will learn to recognize the ways God's grace, presence, and power are woven throughout each day. You will remember and savor those special moments, too quickly forgotten. They nourish stronger faith. I think this is one aspect of what David meant when he wrote,

> Be angry, but sin not; commune with your own hearts on your beds and be silent. Offer right sacrifices and put your trust in the Lord (Psalm 4:6 NRSV).

God is at work in *everything*. The disciplines of Preview and Review teach us to anticipate God's presence in daily life. This is more than making prayer requests and tracking the answers. Preview and Review heighten our awareness of God's activity in our lives. We train ourselves to discern God's presence even in situations where it surprises us or appears in a different form than we had expected.

As we become more aware of God's presence in our everyday lives, we become conscious participants in Jesus' continuing ministry in this world.

Guidelines: Review

1 **SET ASIDE FIVE TO FIFTEEN MINUTES AT THE END OF THE DAY**

Use your Bible, journal, and calendar to walk in quiet reflection back through the day.

2 **WRITE IN YOUR JOURNAL THE HIGHLIGHTS AND LOWLIGHTS OF THE DAY**

Don't get bogged down in a catalog of all that happened that day, or this discipline will become a heavy burden. Ask yourself, "Where did I see the hand of God today?" and "Where did I have a hard time seeing the hand of God today?"

3 **PRAY AND REFLECT OVER THE SITUATIONS OR INCIDENTS YOU HIGHLIGHTED**

As you pray, focus on three primary actions: thanksgiving, confession, and instruction.

4 **PREPARE YOUR MATERIALS FOR THE NEXT MORNING**

In order to take advantage of the momentum generated by Review to support the discipline of Preview, do what you can at night to make it easier to get started in the morning.

Chapter 11
Prayer

Lois Main returned to her home in her little town following a three-day spiritual retreat. She felt eager to share the new insights she'd gained, especially about prayer.

The next day, Sunday, she awakened feeling strangely depressed. She attributed it to the letdown after her retreat. But when she went to church, she met other women who felt the same way. One woman said, "It feels as if there are children in trouble."

The odd feeling stayed with the women throughout the day. That night, at evening services, they continued to pray for whatever caused this mysterious sense of urgency. They didn't leave church until after midnight.

Lois went home but couldn't fall asleep. Was God trying to tell her something?

The ominous feeling grew stronger. Then, she seemed to hear God speaking insistently to her, "Pray for the people [of this town] . . . get out and pray for my children. *Now*."

"Yes, Lord." She dressed and went out into the starlit night. She began walking down all the streets of the town, praying, "O Lord, protect the people; watch over the children." She walked past the shopping plaza, the pharmacy, the jewelry store, the inn.

At 5:30 a.m., Lois slipped back into bed for a few moments' rest, feeling that she had done what God had asked her to do.

Soon, the town awoke and began its Monday morning activities. Little did the townspeople realize what lay ahead for them that day. At 4:42 that afternoon, May 2, 1983, an earthquake struck their city— Coalinga, California—with such force that nearly every building lay in ruins afterward.

A *Guideposts* article reported, "At the Coalinga Hospital, the doctors geared up for an expected onslaught of victims. Instead of an onslaught, however, only 25 people came—and most of them with minor injuries. The most severe casualty was a man with two broken legs. Not one life was lost!"[65]

In the days that followed, Lois learned that two other women also had received the urgent message, "Pray for my people." They, too, had left their beds to pray through the town.

God had heard their prayers.

Prayer is our essential connection with God, but our prayers grow dull when we approach them merely as a duty. God intends prayer to be an actual conversation with our heavenly Father who loves us, waits to hear from us, and has much to say to us . . . if only we will apply ourselves to listening.

Even as newborns move through developmental stages, learning to talk and interact, so we move through several developmental stages of prayer. The process doesn't look the same for everyone, but all of us can experience at least three stages of prayer.

Stage One Prayer: Monologue

As new believers, we think of prayer as "talking to God," with the emphasis on "to." Prayer at this level is a one-sided conversation. We inform God of our needs or of the needs of others. We may take a few moments to thank the Lord, but requests drive our prayer. We also are inclined to instruct the Lord as to how he might best answer our prayers!

At some point, our monologue prayer moves beyond being request-driven. We begin to include fewer self-focused subjects in our communication with God. We see this broader concept of prayer most clearly in the Lord's Prayer.

Jesus taught us the Lord's Prayer not only as a specific text to be recited, but also as a model for expanded prayer. The Lord's Prayer is the greatest prayer known to humanity. These few words span the spectrum of divine purpose and human concerns. They sweep from the majesty of God in heaven to the earthly details of daily bread. The Lord's prayer upholds the highest ideals while recognizing the realistic obstacles of human temptations and failure. It searches us, instructs us, inspires us, and empowers us to become all God intended us to be.

THE LORD'S PRAYER

Meditating on the specific elements of the Lord's Prayer (Matthew 6:9-13, NKJV) leads into rich, new avenues of conversation with the Lord. Insights come when we slow down and consider each word and phrase.

"Our Father in heaven."

Jesus begins his prayer by affirming our identity as God's children, by faith. We celebrate and stand secure in our relationship with the Giver of Life. If your father or mother has failed you, you can be "re-parented" by the Lord. God is eager to be in fellowship with you and care for you.

Not only is God close enough to care, God is also great enough to help.

Archbishop Trench says, "We must not conceive of prayer as overcoming God's reluctance, but as laying hold of his highest willingness."

Not only is God close enough to care, God is also great enough to help. God's resources and power are unlimited by time, by space, or by any other earthly constraints or human failings.

Reflect: What limits have I put on God that hinder my prayer and weaken my faith?

"Hallowed be your name."

God's honor is our highest calling. In prayer, we worship God with our lips and our lives. We ask not only, "What would Jesus do?" We also ask, "How will my thoughts, words, and deeds make people curious about God's greatness and goodness?"

Reflect: How does my lifestyle honor God's name?

"Your kingdom come. Your will be done on earth as it is in heaven."

Jesus came to reclaim this rebel world and re-establish God's Kingdom (see Mark 1:15). His preaching of God's truth dispelled the lies of evil. His healing reversed the consequences of the curse. And his casting out demons demonstrated his power over Satan (see Matthew 4:23). God's Kingdom agenda determines our agenda. What does God's Kingdom look like in our context? How would it look in my family? School? Workplace? Neighborhood? Congregation?

Reflect: Have I surrendered my agenda so that I can eagerly pursue God's agenda?

"Give us this day our daily bread."

God is ready to provide whatever we need this day, including our practical needs. My faith grows as I remember how God provides for us. Where God guides, God provides.

Where God guides, God provides.

Reflect: What do I need today?

"And forgive us our debts, as we forgive our debtors."

God's grace shown to us must show through us to others. Forgiveness means, in part, "I surrender my right to hurt you back."[66] If my hands are full of bitterness, they are closed to God's mercy. If I hold fast to grudges, I cannot take hold of God's grace.

Reflect: Whom do I need to forgive? To whom do I need to confess?

"And do not lead us into temptation but deliver us from the evil one."

God protects and guards our lives. We commit ourselves to God's care, equipping ourselves with the full armor of God for the spiritual battle of each day (see Ephesians 6:10-18).

Reflect: Where does opposition keep me from the full experience of God's grace and the full implementation of God's plans? Release God's power into those areas.

"For yours is the kingdom and the power and the glory forever. Amen."

The Lord's prayer circles back to where it began, focusing on God's glory and coming kingdom.

A person praying at Stage One can have a vital prayer life. The Lord is merciful, often answering such prayers in wonderful ways. But prayer at this stage remains incomplete in terms of developing our sensitivity to God's presence.

Stage Two: Dialogue

We enter a deeper level of prayer when we realize that God wants prayer to be a dialogue, a two-way exchange of thoughts and ideas. In other words, prayer includes listening to God.

The thought of listening prayer makes some nervous. It seems so subjective, and we can all cite stories about people who claim, "The Lord told me…"

We are wise to be cautious. People who have taken their experience as authoritative over Scripture have done much damage. We don't want to be presumptuous. We don't want to compromise the sole authority of the Bible. We don't want to be led astray.

Yet the testimony of God's people in the Bible and across the centuries insists that God communicates with them in prayer. We must take listening seriously when we consider God's call to Abram, Jacob's dream of a ladder, the boy Samuel hearing God call his name, and the people hearing the Father say of Jesus, "This is my Son, whom I love; with him I am well pleased" (Matthew 3:17 NIV).

George Muller, noted for his intense prayer life in support of the Bristol orphanage, said, "The most meaningful time of prayer is the fifteen minutes after I say 'Amen.'"

My mom, Lillian, was going through a time of emotional turmoil. My dad traveled a great deal on business, and Mom felt the weight of some family challenges, intensified by her loneliness. Dad called every night, but that couldn't make up for his absence.

"I was praying in the dining room one evening while you boys were in bed," Mom told me, "Then I felt a hand on my shoulder. I knew it was the Lord. He said, 'I am with you, Lillian. It will be all right.' That moment changed my life. Even though things didn't get easier right away, God's presence gave me new strength."

Mom felt very reluctant to share that story for many years. While she knew her experience was real, she feared people would not accept it. But when she told me, I knew it had really happened. And when I have told her story to others, it has moved many others to relate similar experiences.

Whenever we wonder if some touch of the Lord was real or a product of our imagination, it helps to ask:

- Did the experience bring glory and honor to the name of the Lord?

- Did the experience express truth consistent with God's word and the experience of God's people?

- Did the experience bear fruit in faith (belief) and faithfulness (behavior)?

Early in my walk of faith, I felt skeptical about this possibility, but several of my own experiences convinced me God still communicates with us in prayer. One of my most vivid examples came in a time of prayer with a group led by a man I didn't know well. I had asked for prayer and as the group got ready to pray, Gary said, "Doug, we've never met before, and this doesn't usually happen to me, but I keep thinking I am to read you the opening verses of Isaiah 43. To be honest, I have no idea what is in Isaiah 43, but would you mind if I read it?"

His words stunned me. I had spent the entire previous week memorizing Isaiah 43:1-5! How could Gary have known? Some would write this off as a coincidence. I know, however, that when I take time to humble myself and listen, experiences like this happen.

Listen to the cry of your heart for the nearness of Abba Father! Feel the longing of your heart for a divine touch. And don't be afraid to expect God's personal communication with you.

Guidelines for Listening Prayer

Use the following six guidelines to help you listen for God's voice as you pray.

QUIET YOURSELF

You may find this easier after your initial prayer. Some people begin prayer by listening, while others share their requests first. No set formula exists.

Quiet your mind. Focus on God, perhaps as if God were sitting across from you. If distracting thoughts intrude—such as errands you need to run—jot them down and forget about them (more on this later). If you have learned some helpful techniques for relaxing your mind and body, use them to make yourself still.

ASK, "LORD, IF YOU WERE TO SAY ANYTHING TO ME RIGHT NOW, WHAT WOULD YOU SAY?"

We give God our expectant attention. I often start writing in my journal, using my name as if the Lord were speaking to me personally: "Doug, I love you. I am ready to encourage you…"

WRITE THE THOUGHTS THAT COME

Have your journal open, or your computer journal file or a note-taking feature on your mobile device ready to write the ideas that come to mind. A word, phrase, or sentence may come. You may think immediately of a passage of Scripture. Write these down, open your Bible, and read the verses around the passage that came to mind. Keep in mind that God can speak to us in ways other than an audible voice.

IF YOU HEAR NOTHING, CONSIDER A FEW POSSIBLE FACTORS

Perhaps your thoughts remain too active. Write down all the thoughts, ideas, projects, problems swirling in your mind. You decrease their distracting energy when you write them out.

Perhaps you may not want to hear God because of some personal struggle, and you fear what God may say. Focus on verses such as, "God is love, and those who abide in love abide in God, and God abides in them... There is no fear in love, but perfect love casts out fear; for fear has to do with punishment, and whoever fears has not reached perfection in love. We love because he first loved us" (1 John 4:16-19 NKJV).

Sometimes our enemy, the devil, has a high interest in jamming the signals. Prayer not only connects us with the Lord, but also brings us into the realm of spiritual warfare. Pray against distraction by saying, "This is a private conversation! In Jesus' name, I forbid you to eavesdrop."

IF YOU STILL HEAR NOTHING, RELAX, AND ENJOY THE STILLNESS

Trust that God is present in the silence. Rest in his grace, mercy, and peace. God is pleased that you are simply choosing to spend time with Him.

TEST AND APPLY WHATEVER YOU HAVE HEARD

By "test," I mean to check your spirit to see if what you heard and experienced harmonizes with Scripture and the wisdom of holy common sense. Does it evidence the fruit of the Spirit, bringing love, joy, and peace?

Stage Three: Unceasing Prayer

Barry, a high school student, walked up to me after church one day and said he needed help understanding what he called "the most discouraging passage of Scripture" he'd ever read. I silently prepared myself for a discussion on election (such as Romans 9) or the fear of losing our salvation (such as Hebrews 6) or our call to "Be perfect, therefore, as [our] heavenly Father is perfect" (Matthew 5:48).

It took me aback when Barry said, "It's 'Pray constantly'" (1 Thessalonians 5:17, RSV). Barry put his dilemma succinctly: "If I do what this verse says, I'll never get anything else done. And if I try to do the things I have to do, like study algebra and chemistry, I can't be praying all the time!"

Some people might contend that this verse merely sets a high ideal and we shouldn't take it literally. They might paraphrase it, "Do your best to pray often, any time of day." I once tended to follow this interpretation myself, but I have begun to see that we have ways to develop a habit of ongoing prayer that move us closer to the ideal.

Enriching our God-talk starts with noticing our self-talk. We usually speak aloud at the rate of 150-200 words per minute, while our "inner conversation" speeds along at the rate of approximately 1,300 words per minute![67] According to much research, up to 80 percent of our self-talk is negative.[68] Self-talk, for good or ill, shapes our thoughts, feelings, and behavior.

Wisely stewarding our self-talk leads to spiritual and mental health. Our attitudes change for the better when we exchange negative self-talk—such as "I always fail," "I'm just no good," "I might as well give up"—for positive affirmations such as, "I am loved by God," "In God's strength I can do whatever he calls me to do," and "God will enable me to keep going." Prayer drives useless, empty, even destructive self-talk from our minds.

With practice, we can learn to redirect our inner chatter into inner prayer. Like a friendly conversation that roams over a landscape of topics, nothing is off limits with the Lord.

Guidelines for Unceasing Prayer

To help you move closer to the scriptural directive to pray without ceasing, you may find the following six guidelines useful.

BECOME AWARE OF YOUR SELF-TALK

What subjects most often swirl through your mind? Note the pattern of topics and the sources that influence your inner conversation. How much is negative and pessimistic? How much is positive and hopeful? How much is just plain chatter?

Far from judging yourself, you work to become aware so you can constructively influence your thoughts. One author exhorts us to "transform your inner critic into your inner coach."[69]

IMAGINE YOUR SELF-TALK AS A CONVERSATION WITH THE LORD

How could you include your faith and spiritual desires in your self-talk? I began to influence my self-talk by discussing my projects and meetings with the Lord as I prepared for them: "Lord, here's what I'm thinking… what do you think?" I then proceed with my preparation and sometimes new ideas or changes come to mind.

Whenever you face an opportunity or problem, a choice, or a decision, simply ask, "Lord, what do you want me to do? What's best here?" Continue to listen, then do what seems best.

INVITE THE LORD TO MAKE HIS THOUGHTS YOUR THOUGHTS

Our thoughts do not hold us captive, making us into helpless victims. Paul says, "we take every thought captive to obey Christ" (2 Corinthians 10:5 NRSV). You can take charge of your thinking.

God's word is like a fruitful seed, like rain that brings life, like a sword (or even a scalpel) that cuts through lies and deception. It shines brightly to illumine your path.

REWRITE YOUR NEGATIVE CONVERSATIONS

Some negative thoughts plague us. Criticisms and hurtful comments replay over and over in our minds. Did you know you can record new messages over those negative ones? Instead of telling yourself, "I'll never change," hear the Lord say, "My power in you can change your life." Instead of "I'll never measure up," hear, "I accept you as you are." What power we can tap!

BRING EVERY THOUGHT TO GOD

Nothing is off limits with God. If it bothers you, it bothers God. If something seems too shameful, too proud, too selfish, remember, it doesn't surprise God. Bringing those thoughts to God opens you up to the possibility of transformation. Trust God to be the most gracious counselor and friend you've ever had. God doesn't condemn your candor. God invites your honesty. The old cliché works for me: "The One who knows us best loves us most."

CREATE REMINDERS TO WEAVE PRAYER THROUGHOUT YOUR DAY

Some people set hourly (or more frequent) notifications. Others put a sticker on their phone or on their screen as a reminder. What gets your attention? Make it playful, not burdensome.

What About Distractions and Wandering Thoughts?

When we begin a more intentional prayer discipline, we often find our devotional time suddenly filled with thoughts of things to do, things we forgot to do, and things we know we shouldn't do.

Henri Nouwen compares this experience to that of a person who, after years of living with open doors, suddenly decides to shut them. The visitors who formerly entered the home whenever they wanted will start pounding on the shut doors, wondering why they can no longer enter. Only when they realize that they are not welcome do they gradually stop coming.[70] In the same way, we can reduce unwelcome thoughts in our prayer time.

As you persist in disciplined prayer, fewer and fewer distractions present themselves. In addition to persistence, keeping paper and pencil handy to write down any significant thoughts can also relieve you of the tension and fear of forgetting.

I used to think that prayer meant coming to God to get what I wanted. Now, I realize prayer means coming to God to receive what he has for me.

Guidelines: Listening Prayer

1   QUIET YOURSELF

Focus on God, maybe as if he sat across from you. Write down distracting thoughts and put them aside.

2   ASK, "LORD, IF YOU COULD SAY ANYTHING TO ME RIGHT NOW, WHAT WOULD YOU SAY?"

Be still and pay attention to any thoughts that arise.

3   WRITE THE THOUGHTS THAT COME

Write the Scriptures, words, phrases, or sentences that come to mind.

4   IF YOU HEAR NOTHING, CONSIDER A FEW POSSIBLE FACTORS

Perhaps your thoughts are still too active. Focus on the stillness, perhaps on your breathing. Perhaps you fear what God may say. Focus on verses such as, "God is love... There is no fear in love, but perfect love casts out fear" (1 John 4:16-19 NKJV). Perhaps there is spiritual opposition. Pray against distraction.

5   IF YOU HEAR NOTHING, RELAX, AND ENJOY THE STILLNESS

God is present. Rest in God's grace, mercy, and peace.

6   TEST AND APPLY WHAT YOU HAVE HEARD

Does it evidence the fruit of the Spirit, bringing love, joy, and peace? Does it honor the Lord?

Guidelines: Unceasing Prayer

1   BECOME AWARE OF YOUR SELF-TALK

What subjects most often swirl through your mind? Become aware so you can constructively influence your thoughts.

2   IMAGINE YOUR SELF-TALK AS A CONVERSATION WITH THE LORD

Include your faith and spiritual desires in your self-talk: "Lord, what do you want me to do? What's best here?" Continue to listen, then do what seems best.

3   INVITE THE LORD TO MAKE HIS THOUGHTS YOUR THOUGHTS

We are not helpless victims held captive by our thoughts. Take charge of your thinking. Welcome God's word as a fruitful seed, like rain, like a sword that cuts through lies and deception, like a light to illumine your path.

4   REWRITE YOUR NEGATIVE CONVERSATIONS

Replace the negative self-talk that plagues you. Let the Lord's gracious voice drown out enemies and critics.

5   BRING EVERY THOUGHT TO GOD

Nothing is off limits with God. God is the most gracious counselor and friend you've ever had. "The One who knows us best loves us most."

6   CREATE REMINDERS TO WEAVE PRAYER THROUGHOUT YOUR DAY

Set hourly (or more frequent) notifications. Put stickers in strategic places as reminders. Make it playful, not burdensome.

Pathways to God's Perspective

Chapter 12
Bible Study

God's word is alive! We not only read God's word, but God's word reads us.

I always love—and laugh— telling the story about an American Bible Society distribution campaign in Zimbabwe years ago.[71] One recipient responded with great antagonism.

"If you give me that New Testament," the man told Gaylord Kambarami, the General Secretary of the Bible Society of Zimbabwe, "I will roll the pages and use them to make cigarettes!"

"I understand that," Kambarami replied, "but at least promise to read the page of the New Testament before you smoke it." When the surprised man agreed to the unusual request, Gaylord gave him the New Testament.

Many years later the General Secretary attended a Methodist convention in Zimbabwe. The platform speaker suddenly spotted him, pointed him out to the audience, and said, "This man doesn't remember me, but fifteen years ago he tried to sell me a New Testament. When I refused to buy it, he gave it to me, even though I told him I would use the pages to roll cigarettes. I smoked Matthew, and I smoked Mark, and I smoked Luke. But when I got to John 3, verse 16, I couldn't smoke anymore. My life was changed from that moment!"

The cigarette-smoking antagonist had become a full-time church evangelist, devoting his life to showing others the way of salvation he had found in God's word. A person totally uninterested in religion was transformed when he read God's word. That's the power of Scripture!

As the rain and the snow
  come down from heaven,

and do not return to it
  without watering the earth

and making it bud and flourish,
  so that it yields seed for the sower and bread for the eater,

so is my word that goes out from my mouth:
  It will not return to me empty,

but will accomplish what I desire
  and achieve the purpose for which I sent it.

You will go out in joy
and be led forth in peace;

the mountains and hills
will burst into song before you,

and all the trees of the field
will clap their hands.

Instead of the thornbush will grow the juniper,
and instead of briers the myrtle will grow.

This will be for the Lord's renown,
for an everlasting sign,
that will endure forever (Isaiah 55:10-13 NIV).

Why, then, do so many of us seem unaffected by Bible study? It happens because we read the Bible without encountering the living Lord. We haven't learned how to move from content to engagement. We accumulate facts without experiencing faith.

Spiritual vitality results from approaching Bible study with the tools of meditation.

Christian tradition encourages two primary approaches to meditation: cognitive and contemplative. Both have biblical roots and have won practitioners throughout church history. We'll explore cognitive meditation in this chapter and contemplative in the next.

I have no desire here to add yet another method to the many Bible study systems already available. I want to help you take *any* method to the next level by asking, "How can Bible study *change* me? How can study refresh me, encourage me, renew me? How can the Bible lift me from a blah spiritual life?"

Meditate on God's Word

Throughout the Scriptures we find the exhortation to meditate.

This book of the law shall not depart out of your mouth; you shall meditate on it day and night (Joshua 1:8, NRSV).

… their delight is in the law of the LORD, and on his law they meditate day and night (Psalm 1:2, NIV).

The Hebrew word for "meditate" literally means "muttering," as in reading a passage to yourself aloud quietly, thoughtfully. We say the words over and over, as when struck by a new idea.

Meditation focuses on a single thought or concept, turning it over and over in our mind. We view it from as many angles as possible. The goal is not to gather a quantity of facts but to go deeper for understanding.

Think of looking at the night sky. At first, we notice only a few stars. As our eyes adjust, and with patient attention, more and more stars come into view. In meditation, we give the time and attention necessary to see more and more stars. We ponder the word of God, allowing the Holy Spirit to reveal the riches of his wisdom—far more than simply surveying the material for content.

Cognitive Meditation

This first level of meditation engages our active thinking, using the analytical part of our brain and consciousness. We concentrate on words and their meanings and examine the logical sequence of thought.

I define cognitive meditation as exploring God's written word by the power of focused reasoning to give us a deeper understanding of its meaning for our lives.

This approach echoes study, but emphasizes letting a specific phrase in God's word speak to the heart. It takes study beyond observation to in-depth pondering.

Guidelines for Cognitive Meditation

Allow me to suggest five guidelines to help you meditate on Scripture using a cognitive approach.

PRAY

Since the Holy Spirit inspired the Bible (see 2 Timothy 3:16), we rely on the Holy Spirit to give us understanding. This prayer is not an empty ritual. It not merely a formality. In prayer we acknowledge our readiness for God to address us. Prayer reminds us that the Bible is no ordinary book and that, through it, we have the privilege of interacting with the living Lord.

The psalmist prayed, "Open my eyes, that I may behold wondrous things out of thy law" (Psalm 119:18, RSV). Theologians call this a prayer for illumination, asking God to bring light to our understanding. Prayer asks God to shed his light on our pathway. And so, we pray, "Lord, speak to me through your word. Give me ears to hear your voice, eyes to see your truth, a mind to learn it, and a heart to obey it."

SELECT A BRIEF VERSE OR PASSAGE THAT ATTRACTS YOUR ATTENTION

Pick a Scripture that interests you because of a specific problem you have or because you feel some text promises rich insight. You could also select a particular word, phrase, or verse that jumps out at you from your regular Bible reading. Some suggested passages are Psalm 103, Colossians 1:15-20, or Romans 8:18-30.

SAY OR WRITE IT SEVERAL TIMES UNTIL YOU "HAVE IT" WITHOUT HAVING TO LOOK AT IT

I always feel surprised when I copy something word for word, because I usually notice something I missed in reading. My eyes seem to skip words until I write them down. Writing the verse or phrase helps it take root in your mind. Don't get distracted by the surrounding verses. Focus on this single thought.

REFLECT DEEPLY

Look at your passage, word, or verse, in as many ways as possible. You might rephrase, or paraphrase, the verse in your own words. Eugene Peterson's *The Message* shows how Scripture can capture not only the actual words translated but the contemporary meaning in a way that brings God's word alive.

Consider Psalm 1:2, "I will meditate on God's word both day and night." Explore those words "day" and "night."

Day: I will take God's word into my activities and responsibilities to guide my behavior, to influence the way I make decisions and treat others. The Lord is with me all day. So, how will Scripture guide me in my specific duties and appointments today?

Night: I will rejoice in God's faithfulness through this day. I will remember what God taught me today. I will take comfort that God's word covers the disappointments of the day, assuring me of forgiveness as I confess the sins of the day. I will meditate on the light of God's word as I enter the darkness of night…

Picture as many ways as possible that God's word could apply to the routine activities of your day and evening.

You may also want to do some basic study of the verse, such as defining a term using a Bible dictionary or checking a confusing concept in a commentary. The emphasis should be on your own reflection on God's word, but a commentary, study Bible note, or other resource can be very useful in stimulating fresh thoughts and insights. They can contribute invaluable information to overcome our limited understanding of the culture and context of biblical times.

WRITE IN YOUR JOURNAL WHAT COMES FROM YOUR MEDITATION

You can either journal as you meditate or summarize your experience and the insight you received after you've completed your meditation. I prefer to write as I go because it helps keeps me focused.

Writing preserves your learning and experience. Over time, your notes accumulate, and you discover trends in the Lord's teaching for you. You can also go back and relive the experiences, recalling lessons that have helped you move forward.

Cognitive Meditation Renews Our Minds

Paul's exhortation in Romans 12 provides the most hopeful and helpful insight into spiritual change:

> Do not conform to the pattern of this world but be transformed by the renewing of your mind. Then you will be able to test and approve what God's will is—his good, pleasing, and perfect will (Romans 12:2 NIV).

Empowered by the Spirit, we think our way into a new manner of living.

God transforms our thinking to change our lives. Repentance means, literally, to change your mind about something. Empowered by the Spirit, we think our way into a new manner of living.

A common model for understanding our emotional responses is known as the ABCs of an Emotion.[72] Cognitive behavioral therapy uses this model to clarify how our perception affects our reaction. We need to pay attention to three key factors:

A: Activating event
What happens to us.

B: Belief system about the event
What we think about what happened.

C: Consequent emotion
How we feel about what happened.

When something happens (A), what you believe about it and how you interpret it (B) affects how you will feel (C).

EXAMPLE #1: INCORRECT BELIEF SYSTEM

Activating Event ❯	Belief System ❯	Consequent Emotion
I send an email, but you do not respond	I believe you're ignoring me	Anger and resentment

I become frustrated, angry, and even resentful by the event of an unanswered email because of what I believe about what happened. At this point, I have no direct information about what really happened, but I assume the recipient is ignoring me or is too busy for me.

How do you think I will feel when I learn that the recipient never got the email because it went into "junk" or "spam," or because it was mis-addressed? Learning the email never arrived causes a very different response:

EXAMPLE #2: CORRECT BELIEF SYSTEM

Activating Event ❯	Belief System ❯	Consequent Emotion
I send an email, but you do not respond	I learn that my email went to spam	Not upset

Meditation renews our minds by releasing us from false beliefs.

A similar process happens with our faith. If we respond to disappointment by believing God is apathetic or even cruel (like the wicked servant in Matthew 25:24), we will likely miss the blessings of God's mercy and grace. If we believe, however, that God works in all situations, we will most often discover treasures of grace, mercy, and peace. Meditation renews our minds by releasing us from false beliefs.

Learn to Live with an Eternal Perspective

We tend to view our lives from a very short-sighted perspective. We focus on immediate success, immediate relief, and immediate results. Our problem? Life doesn't work that way. It's about the long journey.

If we live for today alone, we will behave far differently than if we see our actions in the light of eternity. If we rely only on the resources we can perceive with our senses, we will respond far differently than if we look confidently to God's provision.

Cognitive meditation trains us to see life in view of things both seen and unseen, and of things eternal as well as those past and present. An eternal perspective not only develops knowledge about God and the things of faith, but it views all of life as if we were "seated with Christ in the heavenly places" (see Ephesians 2:6 and Colossians 3:1).

"A mind that is stretched by a new experience can never go back to its old dimensions," said Oliver Wendell Holmes. Spirituality is truly a stretching process. But God wants to do more than stretch our minds; he wants to change us from the inside out, moving beyond "do this" and "don't do that" to literally make new our minds.

Learn What God's Really Like

Most people develop their ideas about God from hearsay, hurt, and heresy. The best way to know God's true nature is by reading and studying God's story.

Scripture teaches very clearly, for instance, that the Lord is not always angry and vengeful (a common misconception based on a few difficult passages from the Old Testament). Instead, the words of Psalm 103 comfort and encourage us:

> The Lord is like a father to his children,
>   tender and compassionate to those who fear him.
>
> For he knows how weak we are;
>   he remembers we are only dust (Psalm 103:13-14 NLT).

We revise our puny images of God as we study the nature and acts
of God as revealed in Scripture. We meet the Lord of creation, the
judge of the flood, the compassionate deliverer of the exodus, the
patient sustainer of the wilderness wanderers, the founder of David's
royal line, the inspirer of prophets, the incarnate God-with-us Jesus,
the Holy Spirit empowering the early church, the coming King.
We break free from our ignorant prejudices as study and cognitive
meditation correct our misconceptions.

See Through the Deceptions of Worldly Thinking

I spoke with a man who had recently come to know Christ. As I took
him through a one-on-one Bible study, he said, "I really don't understand what is happening to me. I am starting to see things I never saw
before and think about things I never even cared about before."

That, in its simplest form, is evidence of the mind of Christ being
formed in a new believer. He was discovering a different way to
approach life. He had begun revising his priorities and finding a
significant measure of freedom from problematic thought habits.

A renewed mind does not guarantee the effortless expression of daily
Christian thinking. Paul addressed exactly that problem in Corinth,
a problem we still experience today: believers who are stunted in
their thinking.

In his book, *The Christian Mind,* Harry Blamires sounds a call to
engage in the rigorous discipline of learning to "think Christianly"
while living in a secular culture.

> The Christian mind has succumbed to the secular drift with
> a degree of weakness and "nervelessness" unmatched in
> Christian history. It is difficult to do justice in words to the
> complete loss of intellectual morale in the twentieth-century
> Church. One cannot characterize it without having recourse
> to language which will sound hysterical and melodramatic.
> There is no longer a Christian mind. There is still, of course,
> a Christian ethic, a Christian lifestyle, and a Christian

spirituality… But as a thinking being, the modern Christian has succumbed to secularization.[73]

John Stott recalled the time Billy Graham addressed some six hundred ministers. Graham said that if he had his ministry to do all over again, he would study three times as much as he had. "I've preached too much and studied too little," Graham declared. He later told Stott of a statement by Donald Barnhouse: "If I had only three years to serve the Lord, I would spend two of them studying and preparing."[74]

Guidelines: Cognitive Meditation

1   PRAY

Ask the Holy Spirit to give you understanding of the text he inspired. The psalmist prayed, "Open my eyes, that I may behold wondrous things out of thy law" (Psalm 119:18, RSV). Pray, "Lord, speak to me through your word."

2   SELECT A BRIEF VERSE OR PASSAGE THAT ATTRACTS YOUR ATTENTION

Pick a Scripture that interests you or a particular word, phrase, or verse that "jumps out" at you from your regular Bible reading.

3   SAY OR WRITE IT SEVERAL TIMES UNTIL YOU "HAVE IT"

Writing the verse or phrase helps it take root in your mind. You may notice words you skipped over as you were reading.

4   REFLECT DEEPLY

Look at your passage, word, or verse in as many ways as possible. Read your passage in multiple translations using a Bible app or online Bible. Rephrase, or paraphrase, the verse in your own words. Picture as many ways as possible that God's word could apply to the routine activities of your day and evening.

5   WRITE IN YOUR JOURNAL WHAT COMES FROM YOUR MEDITATION

Writing helps keeps you focused and preserves your experience and lessons learned.

Chapter 13
Meditation

As we gathered for prayer one Sunday evening after I had taught on contemplative meditation, Nicole asked if she could speak. Here's her story from that night:

> Several weeks ago, God began to do something in my life when Doug led us through a meditation on Jesus' healing of the paralytic in Mark 2. Remember how we were asked to picture ourselves in Capernaum, with the crowds coming to Jesus and the paralytic being carried by his friends? Well, I saw myself as the paralytic on the stretcher. When we got up on the roof, however, a whirlwind came along, like a tornado, and swept me up, out of reach of my friends. I was terrified and wanted to get back to earth, but I couldn't. I kept reaching down, trying to grab Julie's hand—she was one of the friends who was carrying me—but we couldn't touch.
>
> When the meditation time ended, I was still in the air! I was deeply troubled by this experience. I've only been coming to church for several months now, and I really don't know much about Christianity. I decided I needed to talk to one of the pastors, so I met with Dr. Ernie Bradley on staff here. He took time to answer my questions and explained the way of salvation through Jesus Christ. I wanted time to think about this, so I didn't make any decision at that time.
>
> Tonight, when we began to sing, I immediately saw myself back in Capernaum, hovering in the air above the roof with my friends! Then, as we sang "Amazing Grace," it all made sense. My friends grabbed my hand and lowered me to the roof, then into the presence of Jesus. He told me I'm forgiven and free!

What a joy to hear Nicole's testimony of coming to faith in Jesus Christ! The whole group burst into tearful applause at the power of God. It delighted and amazed me that God had used a meditation I had assumed was for more mature Christians as the means of bringing about a new spiritual birth!

Contemplative Meditation

Research on brain function has helped us understand that the brain has two primary jobs. The analytic functions, rooted in the left hemisphere of the brain, are balanced by the intuitive functions of the right hemisphere. [75]

In the intuitive mode, we view things in terms of their completeness instead of in separate parts. We see how things link together, how they make sense as a whole. This type of thinking is visual and symbolic, connected to stories, art, the physical body, and movement.

Spiritual vitality unlocks both our cognitive and our intuitive powers through meditation.

The vast majority of Christians in the West approach their faith from the perspective of the analytical, left-brain perspective. We emphasize ideas, methods, principles, and concepts. We strive for good information and content. And while these are right and good, they are incomplete.

God created us with multiple means to perceive and experience life. Spiritual vitality unlocks both our cognitive and our intuitive powers through meditation.

We've already considered cognitive meditation, so in this chapter we will explore contemplative meditation. I define contemplative meditation as encountering the living Lord through God's written word by the power of the God-given faculty of imagination.

Scripture comes alive when we use our God-given ability of imagination.

Imagination plays a central role in any vital experience of meditation. "Our lives are dyed the color of our imaginations," said an ancient philosopher.[76] Our imaginations help us solve problems in creative ways, uncover new possibilities, and even experience aspects of life as vividly as if they were occurring at the time. Scripture comes alive when we use our God-given ability of imagination.

One key to using our imagination is to involve all our senses as we approach a biblical passage. If you imagine yourself with Jesus at the feeding of the five thousand, see the crowds and visualize the setting. Hear the noise, smell the fragrances and odors, feel the grass as Jesus invites you to sit. Taste the bread and the fish.

Such a creative exercise opens aspects we'd normally never consider. The impact of the miracle becomes more impressive. Envision the huge crowd. Look at all the bread. What an amazing provision! The boy's gift seems more touching; he did what he could and watched the Lord work.

In a contemplative meditation, we move through a series of steps in dialogue with the verse. Because of this "conversation" with the biblical text, contemplative meditation is also called "discursive" meditation (or dialogical meditation). The left brain remains engaged but does not dominate.

Guidelines for Contemplative Meditation

Nicole's experience, related at the beginning of this chapter, happened in response to a guided contemplative meditation that I led on Mark 2. It followed this outline, which I use both personally and in leading groups.[77] Biblical stories are rich sources for meditation because storytelling naturally engages your imagination.

SELECT A PASSAGE

Ask the Holy Spirit to guide your selection of a passage for meditation. Selections from the Gospels, especially encounters with Jesus, and the parables, are often the most fruitful starting places. Pick a passage that seems to address an issue you want to bring to the Lord.

PREPARE PHYSICALLY

The condition of our body affects the way we take in information. We will meditate most effectively if we relax and consciously rid our bodies of tension.

One relaxation method many people find effective is to sit upright on a firm chair and relax your body from the feet up. Consciously tense and relax a few muscles at a time. Begin by extending your right leg and pointing your toes up so that your foot is perpendicular to your leg. Hold the tension for ten seconds, then relax and return to a normal position. Breathe in deeply as you tense the muscles and breathe out slowly as you relax them. Do this with the other leg, then with each arm, then clench and release each hand. Finally, hunch your shoulders and relax them, then do neck rolls. Breathing is one of the most important facets of relaxation. Take deep breaths from the diaphragm (without lifting your shoulders) and expel them easily, counting to ten. This oxygenates the blood, refreshing the body.

FOCUS AND CENTER YOUR THOUGHTS

Someone has called this "the recollection of the scattered self." Turn your full attention to the Lord and his word. Offer simple prayers or repeat short Scriptures such as, "The Lord is near to all who call upon him, to all who call upon him in truth" (Psalm 145:18, RSV), or "Open my eyes, that I may behold wondrous things out of thy law" (Psalm 119:18, RSV). I also offer the prayer I noted in a previous chapter, "Lord, give me what you want to give me in this time." You can even repeat a single word such as Lord, hope, peace, or trust.

REFLECT

Read the passage a few times so you know the content. Then imagine the scene vividly in your mind. Picture the physical aspects of the passage: the air, the temperature, time of day, smells, textures, tastes, appearances of people, objects around, landscape . . . involve all your senses. Be *there*.

And then, reflect on the material. What is happening in this situation? Why? What does the environment feel like? What are people saying?

ENTER INTO AN IMAGINARY CONVERSATION

Select one person in the situation with whom to dialogue. You may give an open invitation to the crowd, or you may want to talk to a bystander or a main character or even to Jesus. Often you will feel an attraction to one character.

Write a short paragraph in the first person, as if this character were speaking. For example, in meditating on Mark 2, you might begin with this journal prompt, "I, the paralytic, wondered if life would ever interest me again. . ."

Imagine having a conversation with this character. Ask questions and listen. What fears do they express? What concerns weigh on their hearts? What do they think as they encounter Jesus?

CONCLUDE YOUR MEDITATION

Gradually return to your current situation. You may picture yourself walking from the dusty streets of Jerusalem onto a road near your location. Then complete your journey to where you are.

DEBRIEF

Consider the insights gained from your meditation. Evaluate images and symbols and the messages they may communicate. Remember Nicole calling a pastor to help her sort out the whirlwind and her inability to "make the connection" with her friends? You may write, draw a picture, or write a poem or song to summarize the meditation.

A Syrian Commander Meets a Hebrew Prophet

The best way I know to give you a clear concept of what I mean is to present one of my own meditations. The following is my meditation on the story of Naaman with Elisha, based on 2 Kings 5.

Naaman, a Syrian commander and political enemy of Israel, suffered from leprosy. His wife's maid, a young Israelite girl, told Naaman's wife about Elisha, the prophet, who could cure Naaman. Naaman therefore visited Israel to seek healing.

Elisha's servant told Naaman, "Go and wash in the Jordan seven times, and your flesh shall be restored, and you shall be clean" (2 Kings 5:10, RSV). Naaman grew very angry, first of all, because the prophet didn't see him personally, but merely sent a servant. Second, Naaman considered this a ridiculous prescription for healing.

In my meditation, following a time of relaxation, I prayed, "Lord, let me enter the river with Naaman. Show me what he might have experienced." Here is what I imagined as Naaman's experience.

> **Naaman:** I, Naaman, great among men but horrible to look at, was caught in the profound dilemma of great achievement in the world and living death in my body. I was an angry, bitter man. I had won great victories in war but was being defeated by the wretched battle waging within me. The ache! Always, ". . . but he is a leper." To be admired and detested . . .

> **Doug:** Naaman, when did your quest begin?

> **Naaman:** My body was broken, but my spirit—No. That Jewish girl offered me hope. I had tried many remedies, but nothing worked. This girl spoke of a prophet in Israel. This time I could hear.

Doug: I know the history. Is there more you have to tell me?

Naaman: You've heard it before but be patient to receive much more than you've read.

I wanted a show; God wanted to be glorified.

I gathered my impressive resources. God demanded my brokenness.

I wanted to earn; God wanted to give freely.

I wanted to boast; God wanted silence.

Doug: Tell me about your experience as you went through each of the seven dips into the Jordan River.

Naaman: Have you ever played blindman's bluff? You feel so silly as people watch you stumble…

I stepped into the water with resignation. I left hope and fear on the bank.

The first dip overwhelmed me with the physical sensation of the water, the miry bottom, the flow of my robes with the current. The coldness and smell. The muted noises in my ears. I felt as if I would never get through six more. Why couldn't it stop now?

Up—a breath of air. I dare not open my eyes. Warm sun. Dripping. A different silence on the bank. Down.

The second dip. Will this never end? Home, wife, the maid, the king. This seems so silly.

Up. Breath. Dare not open eyes. Down.

The third dip. Why did Elisha tell me to do this? How did he know that asking me to do this was hardest of all? I'm a man! A warrior!! Can I receive? Be passive? Allow the water to flow over me?

Up. Breath. I still do not open my eyes. I'm aware of water swirling around my waist, my legs feel the current. I am still. Silent. The water is moving. I have no control except whether to go under or come up.

A stirring on the bank comes to my ears. I have been up a long time. They probably think I've given up. They fear my wrath.

My back is to them. If they could see my… smile.

The fourth dip. Awareness of the flow of the stream and its subtle, gentle, continual power. It is the master. It could carry me away, but I could never carry it.

Carry away the rage and fear. Fear. Flotsam. My eyes are shut.

Up. Breath. Three times to go. Awareness fills me. I am drawing life from the water. Down.

The fifth dip. Carry away pride. Pride, Pride, Pride. I dare to open my eyes under water. I can see nothing but a murky brown. Then I note the diffusion of warm, bright light.

Up. Breath. Two more times. Anxiety is silenced, but excitement remains. "Be not afraid. You will be clean."

The sixth dip. I am at home in the river. Its current is like a familiar caress. It washes me. It washes me. Again, I open my eyes, under water. I feel as if my whole body were eyes opening to see life again. They've been shut too long.

Up. Breath. Deep, delightful breath. Thank god. God? God?? God! God.

One more dip. I thought I would never come to this point. Time and transformation.

The seventh dip. The embrace of life. The embrace of God. God's presence cleansed the leprosy of my heart. It was joy to be submerged in Elisha's God. To die and be buried in the waters. Only in this way does new life come. My skin tingles as if spices had been rubbed all over me.

Up very slowly. Eyes open to behold, first, the land of God. Then I look at my hands.

A laugh of joy escapes, breaking open the silence like an alabaster flask of perfume. I am clean!! Tears. Tears. Holy joy.

I stand for a long time. Precious communion with Elisha's God. My God? Yes, *my* God.

The stirring on the bank claims my attention. I turn, and love sweeps over me.

"Look! I am clean!"

Oh, that they had each been healed…

Blessed be the Lord God Almighty because he has washed me and made me clean.

Doug: Thank you. Praise God.

Naaman: This cleansing is yours. Remember it. Share it with others. Celebrate it. Yield to the purifying water and fire of the loving Spirit.

Doug: I am grateful. Thanks be to God.

When I completed this meditation, I felt as if I had truly witnessed God at work. My mind was alive to his presence. My heart had awakened with new hope for my own healing and growth. I thought how, like Naaman, I had been too proud to humble myself for healing and reconciliation with God.

As I encountered the living word through prayerful imagination, I saw the process of transformation that we can all experience. Like Naaman, we all pass through baptismal experiences. I don't mean the literal ritual of baptism, but immersions into suffering and trials that can strip away the leprosy of our souls.

Naaman showed me the process of conversion. A person travels a journey from fear and resistance (often hidden behind pride) to confusion, to awareness, to openness and acceptance, and to celebration in the new life that only God can give.

The power and clarity of the dialogue surprised me. Creative artists know the sense of receiving something they didn't create. I had a sense that God had given me a legitimate insight into the transformation of Naaman. Of course, I knew this was not literally Naaman speaking from the grave! That would be heresy and folly of the most serious order (see Deuteronomy 18:9-13).[78] Still, I had a clear sense that the Spirit had taught me by bringing added dimensions to the written word.

My meditation on Naaman may a seem a bit elaborate or literary. But that's not the point. Your meditation may have simpler dialogue and descriptions. We are not being judged or evaluated on our writing abilities. We are engaging imaginatively with God's word.

God gives us the ability to project ourselves into different settings to experience God's word in a fresh way. God created art and beauty and music and imagination to give greater depth and breadth to our lives. When we neglect or disparage them, we limit ourselves to a partial taste of the banquet that is ours in Christ.

Our Lord waits for us to acknowledge and practice the gift of meditation so that its holy power can awaken our worship, increase our joy, and motivate us to greater obedience.

Guidelines: Contemplative Meditation

1   ### SELECT A PASSAGE

Ask the Holy Spirit to guide your selection of a passage for your meditation. Select an encounter with Jesus from the Gospels or other stories that attract your attention.

2   ### PREPARE PHYSICALLY

We will meditate most effectively if we consciously rid our bodies of tension and relax. Sit upright on a firm chair and relax your body from the feet up. Concentrate on your breathing, taking a few deep breaths and slowly exhaling.

3   ### FOCUS AND CENTER YOUR THOUGHTS

Turn your full attention to the Lord and his word. Pray or repeat short Scriptures. My personal prayer is, "Lord, give me what you want to give me in this time." You can even repeat a single word such as Lord, hope, peace, or trust.

4   ### REFLECT

Read the passage a few times so you know the content. Then imagine the scene vividly in your mind. Involve all your senses. Be there. Ask yourself, "What is happening in this situation? Why? What does the environment feel like? What are people saying?"

5   ### ENTER INTO CONVERSATION

Select one person in the situation with whom to dialogue. Write a short paragraph in the first person, as if this character were speaking. Talk to the person. Ask questions and listen.

Conclude your meditation.

Gradually return to your current situation.

6   **DEBRIEF**

Consider the insights gained from the meditation. Evaluate images and symbols and the messages they may communicate. You may write, draw a picture, or write a poem or song to summarize the meditation.

Chapter 14
Spiritual Input

Ideas energize us, feeding the mind and soul. The right idea can result in a life changed for the good forever.

In addition to Scripture, our Christian tradition has a rich heritage of thinkers who instruct and motivate. The Lord wants us to feed our minds and hearts intentionally with spiritual input from a vast array of Christian resources.

God has blessed every generation with women and men who have followed the advice given to Moses "You shall write…" (Deuteronomy 27:2-3 NRSV). Moses recorded not only God's law, but the experiences of God's people.

Paul wrote, "Now these things which happened to our ancestors are illustrations of the way in which God works, and they were written down to be a warning to us who are the heirs of the ages which have gone before us" (1 Corinthians 10:11, J. B. Phillips).

We are thinking people and feeling people. We focus and move forward in faith when a message touches both our hearts and minds.

We live in a time rich with resources to instruct and inspire our faith. I'll consider many such resources, beginning with spiritual reading as a model for how we can more intentionally interact with materials designed to nurture spiritual vitality.

Spiritual Reading

Booksellers know that contemporary consumers tend to buy books for five reasons:

- *Felt need* — The reader has some need that the book promises to meet.

- *Favorite author* — Whatever this author writes, a large audience wants it.

- *Controversy* — Takes a stand on some cultural or theological issue, or other raging controversy.

- *Entertainment* — Just fun to read; most fiction falls into this category.

- *Intrigue* — Meets none of the other criteria but has such an intriguing title and theme that it attracts a wide audience.[79]

We read for many reasons. We read to learn. We read to relax. And we read for inspiration. Spiritual reading falls into this third category.

The primary goal of spiritual reading is not content, but impact. We read until we encounter one thought that awakens special interest. Spiritual reading goes deep, not broad.

Think of the difference between reading a news article and reading a love letter. We quickly scroll through the article and then move on. We read a brief love note, however, again and again. We care about the content, but we crave the sense of presence and emotional connection it inspires. This is how we must read God's word. And this is how we derive the most benefit from the writing and insights of other believers.

The primary goal of spiritual reading is not content, but impact.

When we read in this way, we savor the message, prayerfully letting the words soak into our minds. We read to put us in touch with the Lord. The classic expression of this discipline comes from Baron von Hugel (1852-1925), a Roman Catholic layman who served as a spiritual director to many individuals:

> That daily quarter of an hour, for now forty years or more, I am sure has been one of the greatest sustenances and sources of calm for my life…I need not say that I would not restrict you to only one quarter of an hour a day. You might find two such helpful. But I would not exceed the fifteen minutes at any one time; you would sink to ordinary reading if you did.[80]

We often think (incorrectly) that connecting with God takes a long time. Maybe you've heard the quote from Martin Luther: "I have so much to do that I shall spend the first three hours in prayer." That quote has discouraged far more of us than it has inspired! The real issue is the cumulative impact of consistent reading and input, not the false dichotomy of quality time versus quantity time.

Spiritual reading is not ordinary reading. Instead, we read for spiritual impact and connection. When a word, phase, sentence, or concept "hits home" with us, capturing our attention or firing up our imagination, we stop and consider it. Von Hugel continued:

> Of course, such "reading" is hardly reading in the ordinary
> sense of the word at all. As well could you call the letting a very
> slowly dissolving lozenge melt imperceptibly in your mouth
> "eating." Such reading is, of course, meant as directly as possible
> to feed the heart, to fortify the will—to put these into contact
> with God—thus, by the book, to get away from the book to the
> realities it suggests…"[81]

In other words, savor, don't consume.

I read a great deal to accumulate knowledge and understanding, but
not when I'm practicing spiritual reading. Then, I read for engagement,
for encounter, for experience. We read the page to get beyond the page.

Baron von Hugel makes one more crucial point: set aside your
critical, analytic judgment for the time being, to engage with the
thoughts offered by the author.

> And above all, perhaps it excludes, by its very object, all
> criticism, all going off on one's own thoughts as, in any way,
> antagonistic to the book's thoughts; and this, not by any unreal
> (and most dangerous) forcing of oneself to swallow, or to "like,"
> what does not attract one's simply humble self, but (on the
> contrary) by a gentle passing by, by an instinctive ignoring of
> what does not suit one's soul.[82]

I consider Baron von Hugel's advice both wise and helpful, especially
considering the wide theological spectrum covered by many classics
of spiritual devotion. When we follow his counsel, we may discover
valuable insights that we had never considered.

Savor, don't consume.

You may need to read some books the way you eat fish: Enjoy the
meal but watch for bones. Despite the bones, many writers have
valuable insights for the spiritual journey we all travel. They will say
things you have thought but never put into words. Their honesty will
cause you to search your own heart.

When we read spiritually, we do so not to consume so many books
in a year or to gain intellectual mastery over some content. I liken
spiritual reading to taking a vitamin tablet. The tablet is much

smaller than a normal meal, but it supplies nutrients our bodies need. Small portions of material written by gifted spiritual pilgrims can nourish the soul for a day.

Read a little, then stop when you reach one thought that stirs your spirit—a morsel of grace for you to savor. Highlight it. Meditate on it. Journal about it. Write the thought at the top of a fresh page of paper and write your heart response and prayer. Then, return to it at the end of the day, reflecting on what it means.

Guidelines for Spiritual Input

Practice these guidelines to help you shift from ordinary reading to spiritual reading.

CHOOSE A RESOURCE THAT SEEMS BEST FOR YOU AT THIS POINT IN YOUR JOURNEY

Not every Christian will feel drawn to the weighty works of John Calvin or Martin Luther. Many believers appreciate devotional classics such as Oswald Chamber's *My Utmost for His Highest*.

Books of poetry, collections of quotations, and even fiction with biblical themes can nourish us. Storytelling inspires us in a way that's different from the benefits we receive from lectures or didactic writing. Some people get spiritually fed by reading journals or biographies and autobiographies of Christians whose stories they admire. Whatever author's work you choose, consider it in such a way that it leads you to reflection and prayer.

CONSIDER USING A DEVOTIONAL APP OR PODCAST

An abundance of inspirational/devotional apps and podcasts, in addition to reading, span the spectrum from very light to quite intense. My wife and I often begin our day by connecting our phone to a wireless speaker and playing a daily devotional from one of our favorite apps.

CONSIDER MEDITATING ON IMAGES FROM ART, INSTRUMENTAL MUSIC, OR MUSIC WITH LYRICS

Music of many styles, some instrumental and some with lyrics, has ministered to God's people for centuries. Paintings and sculptures can give us much to reflect upon. We feel especially blessed by the existence of many works of art inspired by Scripture, by stories and characters from the Bible.[83]

ENGAGE AND REFLECT

Our interaction with good content brings insight and inspiration. So, start asking yourself some questions. Why does this sentence, song, melody, sculpture, painting speak to me? What does it say? How does it instruct me? What does it reveal about my understanding of the Lord? Of myself? Of others?

JOURNAL YOUR REFLECTIONS

God uses all of these means to communicate to us his wisdom, love, and wonder, offered to us through the eyes, ears, and skills of people the Lord has gifted for just this purpose.

Spiritual reading will nourish your soul, help you commune with the saints, and open your vision to see much more of God than you ever could see with your eyes only.

Gain Spiritual Refreshment and Inspiration

Daily devotionals have been a standard resource in spiritual formation because they help us focus on the Lord, especially at the start of a day.

We can also find great inspiration in music. Song lyrics often compress great truth in a way that conveys hope and inspires vision. I realize selecting one or two sets of lyrics will date me and omit many other songs, but here goes!

I will never forget the first time our worship team introduced "Blessed Be Your Name" by Matt Redman. I came under the same conviction I felt when I read Habakkuk 3:17-19:

> Though the fig tree does not blossom,
>   and no fruit is on the vines;
>
> though the produce of the olive fails,
>   and the fields yield no food;
>
> though the flock is cut off from the fold,
>   and there is no herd in the stalls,

> yet I will rejoice in the Lord;
>> I will exult in the God of my salvation.
>
> God, the Lord, is my strength;
>> he makes my feet like the feet of a deer,
>> and makes me tread upon the heights.

Here's how Matt Redman expressed the same commitment to no-matter-what praise.

> Blessed be your name
> In the land that is plentiful
> Where Your streams of abundance flow
> Blessed be your name
>
> Blessed be your name
> When I'm found in the desert place
> Though I walk through the wilderness
> Blessed be your name
>
> Blessed be your name
> When the sun's shining down on me
> When the world's 'all as it should be'
> Blessed be Your name
>
> Blessed be your name
> On the road marked with suffering
> Though there's pain in the offering
> Blessed be your name[84]

Here's another song lyric I've appreciated more recently that reminds us that nothing can stand against Jesus' power and love.

> I stand on the chain-breaking,
> Miracle-making, powerful name of Jesus
> On the body-raising
> Prodigal-saving, powerful name of Jesus
>
> —Phil Wickham, "Where I'm Standing Now"[85]

And then there are the classic hymns of faith (many of which continue to be recorded by contemporary musicians):

> "Great Is Thy Faithfulness"… morning by morning new mercies I see.

"Amazing Grace"

"O for a Thousand Tongues to Sing" my great Redeemer's praise.

"Be Thou My Vision"

"How Great Thou Art"

Understand the Dynamics of Spiritual Life

Spiritual input helps us understand how the soul functions. Spiritual growth is not automatic. Many obstacles distract and deceive us.

One of the great preachers of the fourth-century Christian church, Gregory of Nazianzus, shares a message as contemporary now as it was when he first wrote it. Though he addresses pastors, the message speaks to all of us.

> Guiding humanity, the most variable of creatures, is the art of arts. Pastors have been called the "physicians of souls," and compared with physicians who treat the body. But as difficult as treatment of the body is, it pales in significance when compared with soul work.

> Physicians work with bodies and perishable, failing matter. Ministers work with souls that come from God and partake of heavenly nobility.

> Physical diseases remain basically the same under the watchfulness of the physician. Spiritual disease, on the other hand, puts up crafty opposition hostile to the work of the minister. Human selfishness is a great obstacle to the advance of virtue and acts like armed resistance to ministers eager to help. Indeed, patients actively eschew treatment and struggle against what is in their own spiritual self-interest.[86]

As I said at the outset of this book, Jesus did not die so we would stay the same. Countless books, podcasts, sermons, and other studies can illuminate our understanding of our heart, souls, and minds.

Develop a Biblical Worldview

Spiritual input also helps us interpret life in this world. No one says it more clearly than the apostle Paul:

> Don't let the world around you squeeze you into its own mold,
> but let God re-mold your minds from within, so that you may
> prove in practice that the plan of God for you is good, meets
> all his demands and moves towards the goal of true maturity
> (Romans 12:2, J B Phillips paraphrase).

Jesus' followers learn to look at the world from God's point of view.
Some call this the great reversal of values. The least becomes great.
The first become last and the last become first. Those who deny
themselves find themselves. In their provocative book on worldview,
Charles Colson and Nancy Pearcey write:

> Our major task in life is to discover what is true and to live in
> step with that truth.... Every worldview can be analyzed by the
> way it answers three basic questions: Where did we come from,
> and who are we (creation)? What has gone wrong with the
> world (fall)? And what can we do to fix it (redemption)? These
> three questions form a grid that we can use to break down the
> inner logic of every belief system or philosophy.[87]

Too often, Jesus' followers have neglected the life of the mind. Then
they feel puzzled about why the culture is so messed up.

Become Better Equipped for Living and Service

Spiritual input also equips us to live and serve like Jesus, who created
all of life and therefore redeems every aspect of life. Nothing is
beyond God's reach or outside of God's interest.

Followers of Jesus are called to develop competencies for life and
service. These include subjects ranging from prayer to financial
discipleship, from learning interpersonal skills, to setting boundaries
for healthy relationships. We also develop ministry skills to continue
in partnership with Jesus's ministry in the world where we live, work,
and play.

Interactive Reading that Changes Us

Another benefit of this discipline is the cultivation of what I call
interactive reading. Often, I allow my own responses and insights
during reading to pop like fireworks and fade away, but interactive
reading helps me take the spark of an author and allow it to light
a fire that gives sustained light for my own journey. It's a satisfying

experience to develop a thought more completely in terms of my
personal perspective.

Interactive reading helps me take the spark of an
author and allow it to light a fire that gives sustained
light for my own journey.

As with the discipline of meditation, I think it may help to show you
what spiritual reading is like by illustrating from my own experience.

The first book I intentionally read interactively was Augustine's
Confessions.[88] Let me reproduce here two journal entries I recorded
after reading brief sections from Augustine.

First, I copied in my journal Augustine's reaction to sin:

> My God and my mercy, how good you were to me in sprinkling
> so much bitterness over that sweetness [of physical desires and
> lust] … I was fettered happily in bonds of misery so that I might
> be beaten with rods of red-hot iron— the rods of jealousy and
> suspicion, and fears and anger and quarrels (Book III, Chapter 1).

In response, I wrote:

> Augustine continually penetrates the paradoxes of sin and of
> God's judgment and mercy. Sin is bittersweet bitterness and
> grace begins as bittersweet sweetness. The miseries attendant to
> sin are gracious spurs meant to turn us from sin; like thorns at
> the edge of a briar patch, to keep us from entering further into
> that dangerous wood.

At another point, Augustine wrote, "I was both confounded and
converted" (Book VI, Chapter 4). The combination of those simple
words arrested my attention. I have always endeavored to "assist the
process" of spiritual conversion by trying to answer every question.
Here Augustine speaks of conversion coming in the chaos of
uncertainties.

I wrote:

> I get a sense of assurance from Augustine: that I do not have
> to possess all the answers in order to experience the reality
> that God answers all. In other words, our minds and spirits

do not necessarily require detailed answers; they need to be assured that there is an answer in keeping with love, human worth, and rationality. It's a mistake to wait until all questions are answered. Life with God is not cut and dried. We may encounter God in such a way that all doubts vanish. We then apprehend reality in a way the mind cannot comprehend.

Spiritual reading gives us a fascinating way to be instructed and feel encouraged by profound spiritual leaders from the past. These writers are a product of their times, as we are of ours, so some writings may sound a bit stilted, and their expressions may at first sound foreign, but a little effort soon reveals that they have journeyed the same roads we travel. God has revealed insights to them that can illumine our own way. They will become trusted friends who challenge and comfort us and who encourage us by their own honesty. Whether or not we choose to walk as they walked, their accounts will greatly enrich us.

Guidelines: Spiritual Input

1   **CHOOSE A RESOURCE APPROPRIATE FOR YOU AT THIS POINT IN YOUR JOURNEY**

Consider an author's work in such a way that it leads you to reflection and prayer. I have provided a list of what I call "Soul-Stirring Books" in Appendix A. You can also check my Notes for additional ideas

2   **CONSIDER USING A DEVOTIONAL APP OR PODCAST**

Multitudes of inspirational/devotional apps and podcasts, in addition to reading, are widely available. They span the spectrum from very light in content to quite intense.

3   **CONSIDER MEDITATING ON IMAGES FROM ART, INSTRUMENTAL MUSIC, OR MUSIC WITH LYRICS**

Music of many styles, as well as the visual arts (including paintings and sculptures), can give you much to reflect upon.

4   **ENGAGE AND REFLECT**

Your interaction with the material brings insight and inspiration. Ask yourself, "Why does this sentence, song, melody, sculpture, painting speak to me? What does it say? How does it instruct me? What does it reveal about my understanding of the Lord? Of myself? Of others?"

5   **JOURNAL YOUR REFLECTIONS**

Capture the experience, insights, lessons, and life applications that arise from your reflections.

Pathways to God's Power

Chapter 15
Fasting

Some have theorized that if the mass of a single human body could be converted to nuclear energy, it would generate enough power to level a city the size of Los Angeles.

"If that is true," asked Presbyterian preacher Bruce Thielemann, "why is it most Christians go through life like 25 watt light bulbs?"[89]

Sam Moffett, of the missionary family who pioneered God's work in Korea, served as keynote speaker at a national conference I helped organize, attended by nearly 8,000 Presbyterians. His words sent a shock wave of conviction through the crowd.

"I've had my fill of decency and order," Sam began his message, taking a direct shot at a principle that church leaders hold dear. "Where is the power?"[90]

Don't miss the point. Although we have amazing potential in Christ, we see too little evidence of the Lord's power in our everyday lives.

Why?

Where's the Power?

We lead lives far below the level Jesus died and rose again to make possible. Let these verses of Scripture wash over you:

> Now all glory to God, who is able, through his mighty power at work within us, to accomplish infinitely more than we might ask or think (Ephesians 3:20 NLT).

> For God is working in you, giving you the desire and the power to do what pleases him (Philippians 2:12-13 NLT).

> …you belong to God, my dear children. You have already won a victory over those people because the Spirit who lives in you is greater than the spirit who lives in the world (1 John 4:4 NLT).

> For I can do everything through Christ, who gives me strength (Philippians 4:13 NLT).

> The eyes of the LORD search the whole earth in order to strengthen those whose hearts are fully committed to him (2 Chronicles 16:9 NLT).

Spiritual power flows from spiritual vitality. The disciplines of silence, solitude, and fasting help to break evil's power and tap God's power.

When he had completed his forty days in the wilderness near the beginning of his earthly ministry, Jesus returned from that season of fasting, silence, and solitude "in the power of the Holy Spirit" (see Luke 4:14 NRSV).

The disciplines of silence, solitude, and fasting help to break evil's power and tap God's power.

Most spiritual directors approach these disciplines in terms of "mortification" of the flesh, with the emphasis on detaching from the world, but that's only one aspect of their purpose. We detach *so we can attach to the Lord and experience the Lord's power*.

Food represents the power of our worldly needs and appetites that dominate, drive, and motivate us. Fasting breaks the control of food and other appetites so we connect with the power of God's Spirit that energizes the life of faith.

Words represent the power to understand, to impress, to manipulate, and even to deceive. Silence breaks the power of words and sounds and noise, so we connect with the power of God's instruction to renew our minds and lives.

People and crowds represent the power to get affirmation, recognition, and value from other human beings. We are often controlled by the power of others' influence and expectations. Solitude breaks the power of people-pleasing and peer pressure so that we connect with God's affirmation. Food, words, and people also represent the distractions of the world that keep us too busy for God.

We will study the disciplines of silence and solitude in separate chapters. This chapter will focus on fasting.

The Spiritual Messages in Physical Hunger

Physical hunger, one of the most basic and powerful drives of life, also represents one of the world's strongest attractions. Food has spiritual connotations beyond mere nutrition.

Food comforts us. (Especially when I come home from a long church meeting and head straight to the consolation of the refrigerator!) Food rewards us for a job well done—or at least, done. Food distracts us. I saw this when our children opened the refrigerator for the second or third time in half an hour, as if something new were going to appear. Food spoils us. We may indulge ourselves with an extra piece (or two or three) of chocolate cake, an extra scoop of ice cream, or "just one more…"

Paying attention to what our physical appetites reveal about us can give us insight into the many inner forces that strive to control us.

Work Your Appetites to Your Holy Advantage

Losing control debilitates the soul. When we lose control over our use of time or money, or over purity of thought, speech, or actions, we lose our sense of well-being and confidence.

The discipline of fasting is about control or, more properly, about what controls us. In my experience of discipling people in spiritual formation, fasting has an immediate impact on people, revealing what controls them. Nicole, whose experience with meditation I described earlier, wrote to me in response to her first fasting experience, about the fact that her daughter kept coming to mind.

> I *did* get hungry and immediately turned my thoughts to God, and my thoughts immediately turned to my daughter . . . weird? By the fourth time this had happened, I just was about ready to give up turning my thoughts towards God as obviously Erin was getting in the way (Oh, this is rich!). I was with my sister. We decided we would open the Bible at random and see where it led us.
>
> I first prayed; then the Bible fell open at Psalm 78. I read the first section about passing on the word of God to the next generation, etc. I looked at my sister and said, "God was turning my thoughts to Erin for a specific reason . . . wow!" The point of my fast seemed to be praying for God to watch over and protect my daughter. I did not expect that- but it's one of the greatest priorities of my life! [91]

Why Fast?

In *Spiritual Disciplines for the Christian Life*, Donald S. Whitney gives a helpful survey of fasting in Scripture. He summarizes the purposes for fasting in ten major categories:[92]

- to strengthen prayer

- to seek God's guidance
- to express grief
- to seek deliverance and protection
- to express repentance and a return to God
- to humble ourselves before the Lord
- to express concern for the work of God
- to minister to the needs of others
- to overcome temptation and dedicate ourselves to God
- to express love and worship to God

We could call fasting *the italics of the spiritual life*. Fasting adds emphasis to other activities we may already be pursuing, such as prayer or repentance or discerning God's purpose for us. Fasting enhances these with a sense of urgency and earnestness.

Fasting's impact on us is its key importance. As Whitney notes, "The Bible does not teach that fasting is a kind of spiritual hunger strike that compels God to do our bidding... Fasting does not change God's hearing so much as it changes our praying."[93] In addition to the biblical lessons on fasting, each of us will draw our own insights from our practice of it.

Guidelines for Fasting

We fast more effectively when we plan for it and know ahead of time its contours. Consider the following seven guidelines for a useful and satisfying fast.[94]

DETERMINE THE PURPOSE OF YOUR FAST

Fasting is not dieting. Fasting means abstaining from food for a particular purpose for a particular period of time. Simply going without food will not bring spiritual energy or restoration. Review Whitney's ten categories to see if any apply to your particular need or desire at this time.

Complete this sentence in your journal: "Lord, I am fasting now because . . ." Someone has said that fasting is praying with the body.

Then, for what are you praying? This purpose will guide and sustain you through your fast.

DETERMINE HOW LONG YOU WILL FAST

In a typical fast, you abstain from food for a set period of time, but permit yourself to drink water. The most common fast is 24 hours, from dinner one evening until dinner the next evening. In other words, fast from breakfast and lunch. Check with your physician to determine if you have any underlying medical conditions and/or medications that must be taken with food. Once you get accustomed to a 24 hour fast, you might try 48 or 72 hours.[95]

DETERMINE THE EXTENT OF YOUR FAST

What foods and liquids will you allow yourself? Some people, especially in the beginning, undertake a partial fast, while others commit to a complete fast except for water. Begin slowly and your body will adjust with experience.

A partial fast limits food and liquid intake, but does not completely exclude either. Daniel practiced a partial fast when he arrived in Babylon. He refused to eat the rich, non-kosher foods of the king and instead requested a simple diet of vegetables and water (see Daniel 1:12). Daniel also restricted his food to maintain his spiritual focus. At one point he fasted from rich food, meat, wine, and the use of fragrant oils over a three-week period of mourning following a vision of coming war and hardship (see Daniel 10:3).

To develop your fasting discipline, begin with a partial fast from lunch one day to lunch the next (skipping dinner and breakfast). Allow yourself only fruit juices and water for the twenty-four hours. After several weeks, try a normal fast, drinking healthy quantities of water. For variety, you may want to flavor your water with a slice of lemon or lime or drops of lemon or lime juice.

OBSERVE THE PHYSICAL AND SPIRITUAL DYNAMICS OF YOUR FAST

Initially, you likely will feel preoccupied with the discomfort and strangeness of the experience. Don't be hard on yourself. A few warm-up fasts will soon remove the distraction of the discipline. Then you can undertake some specific disciplines, such as prayer and Bible reading, to support and direct your fast.

SET ASIDE YOUR REGULAR MEALTIMES, AND OTHER TIMES, FOR FOCUSED PRAYER AND MEDITATION CONCERNING THE PURPOSE OF YOUR FAST

Fasting frees up time normally devoted to food preparation and eating. Use this time for specific disciplines of prayer, Bible reading, spiritual reading, or journaling. These also provide profitable times for silence and solitude, since being with people having meals can make your fast more difficult.

When I fast, I often use my lunch hour for personal worship and prayer. I may remain in my study, go for a walk, or visit the church sanctuary. I also keep a journal handy throughout the day since food-thoughts trigger God-thoughts and those God-thoughts often bring helpful insights.

CONSIDER HOW YOUR FASTING MAY AFFECT OTHERS

Jesus makes it clear that we should not parade our fasting in front of others (see Matthew 6:16-18). It may not be practical to keep it a total secret, however, especially from family, roommates, friends, or colleagues with whom you normally share meals. Tell them in advance of your fasting, so that meals and plans can be adjusted accordingly. You can choose whether to sit with others while they eat or ask to be excused. Simply explain that you want to show your love for God or are seeking the Lord's help in a special way. Be sensitive to others in your explanation so they won't feel pressure to participate with you or feel guilty if they don't.

BREAK YOUR FAST INTENTIONALLY AND NUTRITIOUSLY

How we conclude a fast can either carry its impact forward in our lives or disrupt and dilute the fasting experience. Break your fast with a light meal—with small amounts of fruits, vegetables, and juice. The length of the fast will influence how you should eat.

Remember that your body adjusts to less food. Some people feel tempted to indulge themselves in a large meal as a reward, or they simply start snacking on whatever they find available. This robs us of the power of the moment of gratefully receiving the nourishment our bodies need, as we celebrate the spiritual nourishment of the fast. Take a moment, also, to thank God for sustaining you through the fast.

What I've Learned from Fasting

My experience in fasting has made me aware of several forces besides food that influence and even control my daily life.

The clock

When I began fasting, I noticed that I tended to base my activities on the time of day, and especially the amount of time before a coffee break or a meal. I became aware of how much I would look forward to a break, lunch, and dinner. I saw how often I thought about food throughout the day. Quite a revelation!

The drive for instant gratification

Fasting exposed how much I allow impulse to control my time and the use of my other resources. I realized I often stopped what I was doing to get a cup of coffee or a snack, whenever I wanted it.

Impulse can easily control our days, fueled by the desire to have what we want when we want it. How unnerving to realize that we may be on the brink of a special touch of the Lord, but we break so we can eat!

In *The Screwtape Letters*, C. S. Lewis illustrated this concept in describing the demonic tempter Screwtape's "close call" at losing an atheist he had cultivated for twenty years. Screwtape warned Wormwood (his demonic apprentice) to guard against encouraging his human victim (called a "patient") in "the fatal habit of attending to universal issues and withdrawing his attention from the stream of immediate sense experience."

When Screwtape's atheist-patient began reading and thinking about things that might lead him back to God (whom Screwtape calls "the Enemy"), he struck the area of his patient's greatest vulnerability.

> If I had lost my head and begun to attempt a defense by argument, I should have been undone. But I was not such a fool. I struck instantly at the part of the man which I had best under my control and suggested that it was just about time he had some lunch... Once he was in the street, the battle was won.[96]

The power of choice

Fasting has made me aware of the abundant choices I enjoy in life. When we deny ourselves, even temporarily during our limited fast, we align ourselves with the poor and see how much of our abundance (and God's provision) we take for granted.

Break the Pull of Forces Inside and Outside Us

Spiritual fasting offers multiple advantages. First and foremost, it disrupts the magnetic pull of our appetites so that we may align our lives with God's purposes and values. Food-thoughts trigger God-thoughts.

Fasting brings God into the midst of our routine. Feeling physically hungry reminds us how hungry we are for God. "One does not live by bread alone, but by every word that comes from the mouth of the Lord," says Deuteronomy 8:3 (NRSV).

Feeling physically hungry reminds us how hungry we are for God.

Hunger pangs teach us. When we fast and pray for our loved ones, the hunger reminds us of our need for God's word to nourish us together. When we fast and pray for direction, our discomfort reminds us of the discomfort of trying to go our own way. When we fast and pray for a person's healing, we remember their pain, so much greater and more significant than our own.

Fasting reminds us how frail we are apart from God's gracious provision. Paul once put our freedom to do things in the context of our freedom *from* having to do them: "'All things are lawful for me,' but not all things are helpful. 'All things are lawful for me,' but I will not be enslaved by anything" (1 Corinthians 6:12-13, RSV).

Memorizing verses like this can remind us we do not merely give up food when we fast. We take back control over our lives. Fasting challenges the powerful drives of our physical bodies that control so much of our motivation and dictate so much of our activity. Fasting liberates us.

Fasting from Other Aspects of Life

Believers have applied the discipline of fasting to many other aspects of life. The same principle applies: We temporarily give up something for the sake of something better. People often fast from watching shows, videos, and movies, or from using social media. They also abstain from shopping and spending for spiritual reasons. The apostle Paul speaks of fasting from intimate relations for the sake of prayer. He wrote to married couples, "Do not deprive each other except perhaps by mutual consent and for a time, so that you may devote yourselves to prayer" (1 Corinthians 7:5).

A fast becomes a spiritual discipline when the individual fasting makes an intentional effort to fill that space with spiritual activity. Throughout the ages, God's people have celebrated events and seasons through harvests and feasts. They also have placed themselves before the Lord in an intense and vulnerable way through fasts—a spiritual resource as effective today as ever.

Guidelines: Fasting

1   **DETERMINE THE PURPOSE OF YOUR FAST**

Fasting means abstaining from food (or some activity) for a particular purpose for a particular time. Complete this sentence in your journal: "Lord, I am fasting at this time because..."

2   **DETERMINE HOW LONG YOU WILL FAST**

The most common fast is twenty-four hours, from dinner one evening until dinner the next evening. Remember to drink water and monitor your activity because of your reduced energy level.

3   **DETERMINE THE EXTENT OF YOUR FAST**

What foods and liquids will you allow yourself? In a partial fast you abstain from certain foods, in a complete fast you abstain from all food (but not from water). Begin slowly and your body will adjust with experience.

4   **OBSERVE THE PHYSICAL AND SPIRITUAL DYNAMICS OF YOUR FAST**

You may want to keep a journal handy since food-thoughts trigger God-thoughts and those God thoughts often bring helpful insights.

5   **SET ASIDE YOUR REGULAR MEALTIMES, AND OTHER TIMES, FOR FOCUSED PRAYER AND MEDITATION**

Fasting frees up time normally devoted to food preparation and eating. Use this time for specific disciplines of prayer, Bible reading, spiritual reading, or journaling.

6   **CONSIDER HOW YOUR FASTING MAY AFFECT OTHERS**

Tell others in advance of your intent to fast so they can adjust meals and other plans.

7

BREAK YOUR FAST INTENTIONALLY AND NUTRITIOUSLY

Break your fast with a light meal—with small amounts of fruits, vegetables, and juice. Do not indulge in a large meal as a reward, or snack on whatever you find available. Gratefully receive the nourishment your body needs as you celebrate the spiritual nourishment of the fast.

Chapter 16
Silence

A group retreat in which I frequently participate begins with a brief time of worship, introductions, and orientation. Then we move into a period of silence through the evening and the start of the next morning. I recall how I responded to my first experience of this silent retreat, and I have seen many others respond in a very similar way.

The first reaction is awkward embarrassment. You feel as if someone glued your lips together. You look at others, smile, and shrug your shoulders, as if to say, "This is weird—but I'll give it a try."

Soon, you begin to think about all the words that fill a day with constant chatter. How many of those words are necessary? You begin to think about how spoken words have served as your primary method of communication, even though we have so many other ways to communicate: touch, writing, facial expressions, kind gestures.

You may experience a sense of relief that you can be in someone's presence without feeling obligated to speak. You appreciate the intentional effort to communicate through courtesy instead of conversation.

When you awaken the next morning, the silence humbles you. You cannot use words to communicate or to distract. You move into the day with a sense of alertness, watching for cues, enjoying the countless other sounds you often miss in the relentless barrage of words.

When finally given permission to break the silence, many do so reluctantly.

"I wish we could have remained silent the whole weekend," a man told me after a morning chapel. "I was just beginning to get my mind to stop chattering when we were invited to pray aloud the Lord's Prayer. I'll be honest; I didn't pray aloud—but I can't remember when that prayer ever felt more meaningful."

After an extended period of silence—for example, a 24 hour silent retreat—the world can seem like a particularly noisy place.

What We Say Matters

"When words are many," says Proverbs 10:19 (ESV), "transgression is not lacking, but whoever restrains his lips is prudent." It continually amazes and sobers me to recognize the power of words for good and evil. As a preacher, I must take special care here—which I have learned the hard way.

Once, when speaking about the danger of impulsive decisions, I described a time when I was a teenager. I had attended a large youth conference and met a girl for the first time around the campfire. She seemed really great, so we agreed to meet for breakfast. When I saw her in the daylight, she didn't look as pretty as she had the night before.

"In fact," I said in my sermon, "she was a real dog." I told how I did my best to avoid her the rest of the week. The congregation laughed with me at my youthful impulsiveness and immaturity. But one woman didn't laugh. I had never met her, but she wrote me the following note:

> We have never met, but I have worshiped with you for nearly six months. I have been greatly helped by your sermons—until this Sunday. Your comment about the girl who was "a dog" cut me like a knife. I am not attractive—a fact my father made sure I understood. I have struggled for years with loneliness, because "beautiful people" get most of the friends. But I am learning that God loves me and is real in my life. I know you are a sensitive person. I can't imagine you would want to hurt anyone on purpose, but your words hurt deeply. Please think more carefully before you make a joke at another's expense.

I put down the letter. In my deep shame and regret I sensed the Lord's chastisement in her words. She had graciously signed the letter and gave her address, so I immediately wrote a letter of apology, expressing my appreciation for her bringing the issue to light.

Words Keep Sounding

"And I tell you this," Jesus once said, "you must give an account on judgment day for every idle word you speak" (Matthew. 12:36 NLT).

Jesus warns us that our words don't just die away. They continue to "sound," to have an impact, beyond the vibrations that strike our ears. As I struggled to comprehend this, I imagined an invention called the Sound Extraction Machine (SEM). This wonder of technology enables us to extract the sound vibrations absorbed by inanimate objects. In theory, the vibrations an object has "heard" leave a record within the object. (Yes, I'm making this up, but it wouldn't surprise me if some brilliant person figured out how to make it!)

What would happen if we put your steering wheel in the SEM? What would we hear? What about your phone? The walls of your home? What difference would it make if you paid attention to the fact that the Lord is always listening?

You may think, "Aren't you going a little too far with this idea? Can't we have any fun? What about joking and teasing? What are we supposed to do? Say as little as possible so that we don't offend anybody?"

That's not the point, of course. But appreciating the impact of words makes us think twice about our speech.

Appreciating the impact of words makes us think twice about our speech.

Silence: Listening to Your Soul

Far from being an impractical escape from the world, silence (and its twin discipline of solitude) enables us to function much more effectively in the world.

Dag Hammarskjold, General Secretary of the United Nations from 1953 until his death in 1961, became a great advocate of silence. Throughout his life he remained active in government service, both nationally and internationally. We learn from his writings that he sustained his intensive public life in politics by an intentional cultivation of silence, listening to his inner world:

> The more faithfully you listen to the voice within you, the better you will hear what is sounding outside. And only he who listens can speak. Is this the starting of the road towards the union of your two dreams—to be allowed in clarity of mind to mirror life and in purity of heart to mold it?[97]

Hammerskjold captures two dynamics at work in silence. First, we gain a clearer perception of the world outside us, "in clarity of mind to mirror life." Second, that clarity empowers us to discern places for positive influence and change—"to mold life." Silence enables us to mirror and mold life.

Silence also gives us time to consider our intuitions and test our perceptions. In the quiet, we deliberately process our experiences in light of an eternal perspective. We also can take a long, uncluttered look at the present world systems, as well as God's activity in the world.

A time of silence—possible once we quiet all the clatter within—provides a powerful antidote against jumping to conclusions based on our reflexes, which often gets us into awkward situations. We have the power to operate with the energy of integrity and clear thinking, as "in purity of heart" we seek to mold the world according to God's values.

Silence enables us to mirror and mold life.

Silence and reflection can break the cycle of assuming that fatalism and determinism will control the course of lives and events. When we stop talking and withdraw, we hear again the voice of faith, "For nothing is impossible with God" (Luke 1:37).

Guidelines for Practicing Silence

The following six guidelines for practicing silence should help make your experience more profitable.

FIND A SILENT PLACE

In addition to your home, a park or other natural setting, a quiet room, a corner in a public library, or a church sanctuary can greatly aid your experience. If no quiet place is available, some have found it helpful to put on headphones or use earbuds to listen to environmental sounds such as ocean waves or a rainstorm.

You might also consider going on a walk or running. Silence does not require us to remain motionless.

QUIET YOUR HEART AND MIND WITH A PASSAGE OF SCRIPTURE

God's word calms you, giving you the promise of his presence in the silence:

> The Lord leads me beside quiet waters, he restores my soul (Psalm 23:2-3, NKJV).

Be still and know that I am God (Psalm 46:10, NLT).

In quietness and trust is your strength (Isaiah 30:15, NIV).

BE STILL. REST. RELAX. TRUST GOD TO KEEP YOU.

In silence we release control. If you've ever had laryngitis, you know
that it leaves you with a sense of losing power and control. Treat your
silence as holy laryngitis. Let go of the need to speak so that your
inner voice can heal and be restored.

> You will keep in perfect peace
>   all who trust in you,
>   all whose thoughts are fixed on you! (Isaiah 26:3, NLT)

DO NOT STRAIN FOR THOUGHTS

In this spiritual discipline, consider the stillness itself the gift. Once
you renew your mind and fill your thoughts with God's truth, silence
enables these thoughts to percolate and permeate your heart and soul.
They put down deep roots in ways beyond understanding.

BE CONTENT AT EACH PHASE OF YOUR JOURNEY

At first, a sense of restfulness may last for a minute or two. With consistent practice, you will train yourself to be comfortable in the silence
for longer periods. You will find the silence a comforting experience.

LEARN TO BRING THE STILLNESS INTO THE MIDST OF DAILY LIVING

With practice, you will learn to bring the calm strength of silence
into the midst of your busy, word-filled, noise-filled day. Turning off
a podcast, news program, or whatever audio you use as background
noise opens up space for you to connect with God. Simply pausing
for a moment before responding to a difficult question or criticism
may allow you to draw from the reservoir of "quiet waters" instead of
tapping the broken cisterns of human weakness or defensiveness.

Take Time to Hear from Your Heart

As with many of the disciplines, our initial attempts at silence seem to
fill up with distractions. We often feel anxious to "do it right," with
expectations that dramatic things should happen.

"What am I supposed to think about?" one woman asked me anxiously during a seminar on the spiritual disciplines.

"Just be still and don't worry about what you're thinking," I replied.

"Well, can I read a Bible verse or something?" she asked.

"No, just be quiet."

"How about some music?" she persisted.

"Silence is silence," I said.

She returned from the hour of silence with a puzzled look. *Uh-oh*, I thought, *I pushed too hard*.

"That was . . . interesting," she said flatly. "As I sat still, my mind was ... on fast-forward. But after a while—I don't know how long because I put my watch away—it began to slow down. I felt relaxed and calm. That was all. How did I do?"

"How do you think you did?" I asked.

"If I was supposed to hear something from God, I didn't do all that great. But if I was supposed to trust God a little more . . . that's what happened!" she said, with a sudden start in her voice. "I didn't feel I had to *do* anything. I just felt peaceful and so calm. I can't remember *ever* feeling that way!"

The meaning of her silence came to her as she spoke with me. I've rarely seen such a delightful "dawning." Silence had shown her she could just *be*, and that just being with the Lord was all right.

We can practice silence throughout the day. When you drive your car, for example, turn off the media and your phone. Or perhaps you can leave your workplace to have lunch alone. Take half an hour or more for a walk. Be still. Silence is silence. You will find your own treasures in the stillness.

Be Aware of the Power of Words

Silence makes us more aware of the power of the words we use to excuse, rationalize, lie, deceive, persuade, hurt, minimize, exaggerate, and manipulate.

Silence makes us more aware of the power of the words we speak quickly in anger, slowly in apology, quickly in accusation, and slowly in admission of our guilt.

Silence makes us more aware of the words that fill our world with so much noise and confusion that we cannot hear the still, small voice of the Lord.

Silence makes us more aware of the limitations of human words, so we can appreciate the infinitely valuable Word of God.

Silence gives us space to process life.

We will either be disciplined by events, or we will discipline ourselves to redeem events. Therefore, God calls us to discipline our lives so that we may contribute to great events.

Silence makes us more aware of the limitations of human words so we can appreciate the infinitely valuable Word of God.

Silence can provide the emotional strength, mental clarity, and spiritual faith we need to bend to shocks and not allow panic to uproot us.

Our response to challenging events matters most. When forced to respond immediately to the demands of human relationships and the volatility of people's moods, we will likely find ourselves reactive, defensive, and emotionally exposed, quick to take fire. Silence can bring poise. Silence can lift us above the flood to a place of strength, serenity, and healing.

Guidelines: Practicing Silence

1   **FIND A SILENT PLACE**

If you have no quiet place available, listen to environmental sounds, such as ocean waves or a rainstorm. You may also want to go for a walk or a run to create a silent space.

2   **QUIET YOUR HEART AND MIND WITH A PASSAGE OF SCRIPTURE**

"Be still and know that I am God (Psalm 46:10, NKJV).

"In quietness and trust is your strength" (Isaiah 30:15, NIV).

3   **BE STILL. REST. RELAX. TRUST GOD TO KEEP YOU.**

Silence releases control. Treat your silence as holy laryngitis. Let go of the need to speak so that your inner voice can heal and be restored.

4   **DO NOT STRAIN FOR THOUGHTS**

Stillness is the gift.

5   **BE CONTENT AT EACH PHASE OF YOUR JOURNEY**

At first, restfulness may come for a minute or two. Consistent practice will allow you to experience silence's comfort and restoration.

6   **LEARN TO BRING THE STILLNESS INTO YOUR DAILY LIFE**

Bring the calm strength of silence into the middle of your day. Pause before responding to a difficult question or criticism. Take advantage of moments between meetings and be still.

Chapter 17
Solitude

Who tells you who you are? The discipline of solitude helps us find and remain connected with the source of our true identity.

Many years ago, I heard then-Secretary of State James A. Baker III speak at the National Prayer Breakfast in Washington, D.C. Someone asked him to name the most important thing he had learned since coming to Washington.

"It was the discovery that temporal power is fleeting," Baker replied.

He then told of an experience he had early one morning when serving as the White House Chief of Staff. As his limousine turned into the White House driveway, he looked down Pennsylvania Avenue and noticed a man walking alone. Many of us, perhaps, would have recognized him, a chief of staff in a previous administration. Yet, there he walked alone—no reporters, no security, no public attention, no trappings of power—just a man alone with his thoughts.

That mental picture burned a lesson in Baker's consciousness, continually reminding him of the impermanence of power and position. Not long before, that walking man had it all . . . but only for a short time. In a reflective mood, Baker continued to address leaders from all walks of life in the United States and from around the world who had gathered for the Prayer Breakfast.

"When I leave Washington," he asked, "what will remain? One thing I know for sure—the people who wouldn't return my telephone calls before I went to Washington won't return them after I leave!"

"Most importantly," he concluded, "having a position of power does not bring inner security and fulfillment. That comes only by developing a personal relationship with God, which for me is personified by Jesus Christ. Inner security and real fulfillment come by faith."[98]

Secretary of State Baker looked into a mirror that morning, but not the mirror of the world, which told him he was powerful. He looked into a mirror of faith, which reflected both the deceptions of life and the basis of his true significance. If this was true of a person of Baker's stature, how much more is it true for us?

What Mirrors Are You Using?

When we want to know how we look, we turn to a mirror. When we want to estimate our worth, we most often peer into the mirrors of the world.

The world's mirrors, however, cannot give a true reflection of our worth. They reflect only qualities and achievements the world deems important. The standards of worldly significance include power, position, prestige, and possessions. Using these is like looking at a funhouse mirror that distorts our true image. If we make the world's mirrors the basis for our self-evaluation, we will suffer a serious identity crisis.

Solitude shatters your old mirrors.

The mirror we use makes a *huge* difference.

Significance in the world's eyes carries tremendous liabilities. Those who thrive on the sound of clapping hands may one day have to flee when those same hands pick up rocks to stone them. Mansions and fame and personal bodyguards provide no security from the corrosive inner forces of selfishness, hypersensuality, and deception, nor from the destructive outer forces of gossip and false allegations.

Solitude shatters your old mirrors.[99]

Finding God and Ourselves Through Times Alone

Alzheimer's disease makes intense demands on the family of the patient. Robertson McQuilkin stepped down as president of Columbia Bible College and Seminary (now Columbia International University) to care for his wife, Muriel, who was rapidly succumbing to this dreaded condition. McQuilkin describes how solitude sustained him as he cared for Muriel. Referring to the stress he felt during this time, he wrote:

> Then I remembered the secret I had learned in younger days— going to a mountain hideaway to be alone with God. There, though it was slow in coming, I was able to break free from preoccupation with my troubles and concentrate on Jesus. When it happened, I learned what God had taught me more than once before: The heavy heart lifts on the wings of praise.[100]

In solitude, a journey of discovery we undertake by ourselves, we discover a deeper fellowship with God. We learn what really lives inside us, both the good and the bad. Once we truly search our soul, we find understanding, grace, and strength.

Solitude nurtures calmer confidence, stronger convictions, wiser discernment, and deeper compassion. Being alone is a disarming experience on the one hand, but as we discover that we are not alone—that God is with us in ways we never perceived—solitude becomes a place where we find spiritual treasure.

Solitude nurtures calmer confidence, stronger convictions, wiser discernment, and deeper compassion.

Jesus Practiced Solitude

Jesus modeled a rhythm of involvement with the outer world and withdrawal into solitude. As we study Jesus' life, we see that he sought the solitude of the wilderness before he entered the active ministries of preaching, teaching, and healing.

Solitude allowed Jesus to develop not only the message he presented but also his very character. Solitude also provided for the ongoing refreshment and reorientation required after extensive, demanding ministry (Mark 1:19-39; John 6:14-15).

The "kingdom within us" provides a vivid image for describing the inner life of the soul. We perceive this inner life most clearly in silence and solitude. Even those who profess no faith in Christ have caught a glimpse of the importance of this inner world. Solitude is the antidote to superficial living.

Henry David Thoreau's experiment with solitude confirmed for him this very understanding:

> When our life ceases to be inward and private, conversation degenerates into mere gossip. We rarely meet a man who can tell us any news which he has not read in a newspaper, or been told by his neighbor... In proportion as our inward life fails, we go more constantly and desperately to the post office. You may depend on it, that the poor fellow who walks away with the greatest number of letters proud of his extensive correspondence has not heard from himself this long while.[101]

In solitude we finally hear "news" from ourselves. We cease to rely on outward symbols of success, such as Thoreau's "mail from the post office." In my experience, credentials have a shelf life of two minutes—or less. We all know the experience of meeting people with impressive credentials who disappoint us once we interact with them. We expected more from a person with such a resumé.

Solitude is the antidote to superficial living.

The resumé that matters most is written on the heart by the Spirit of God in our times of communion with the Lord. Rather than drawing from the "broken cisterns" of the world, solitude brings us to the reservoir of Living Water supplied by the Holy Spirit. This water sparkles with purity and refreshes us with the cool, uncompromising taste of things beyond our present, physical world.

Guidelines for Practicing Solitude

You can practice solitude in two primary ways: in the press of life as well as in special times away from your normal schedule and location. The following guidelines are for a brief time of 15 to 60 minutes.

WITHDRAW TO A PLACE WHERE YOU CAN BE ALONE

Ideally, this is a physical place where no one will interrupt you. When you can't get away from people, you can withdraw by using headphones or earbuds to listen to environmental sounds while closing your eyes. Let those close to you know your intent. Strangers will usually respect the cues sent by your headphones and closed eyes.

LOOK INTO YOUR CUSTOMARY MIRRORS

Begin with confession and repentance. Use your imagination to see and then break the worldly mirrors you use to define your worth. Maybe you use mirrors for security, or mirrors that distract you from the Lord, or mirrors of relationships, work, school, performance, money, things, and so on. These aspects of life are not sinful in themselves, but cannot reflect your true nature and value.

LOOK INTO GOD'S MIRROR

Remind yourself that you live for the Lord, and the Lord is pleased with you. Imagine the person you are becoming in Christ.

REPLENISH YOUR SOUL

Solitude provides a flexible time and space to practice all the spiritual disciplines outlined in this book, as well as to express yourself freely and without self-consciousness. You can dance, sing, recite poetry, read, listen to music, paint, and draw. You get the idea!

PREPARE FOR AN EXTENDED TIME OF SOLITUDE

I once heard a counselor say that we all need a full day away for personal spiritual renewal, at least once every three months. On these days we can give ourselves to prayer, journaling, reading, and reflecting.[102] Starting with even an hour of solitude gives you a chance to become comfortable with the discipline and work your way up to a full day.

Just Another Form of "Navel Gazing"?

Some fear we can get too caught up in introspection, wasting our time and energy on self-concerns when we need to be about the Lord's business in the world. Is solitude really just another excuse to block out the world and obsess over our own problems?

As with any spiritual discipline, we can misuse solitude. But the spiritual discipline of spending time alone not only has historical precedent in the church, but the teachings and example of Jesus himself encouraged it: "The kingdom of God does not come with your careful observation, nor will people say, 'Here it is,' or 'There it is,' because the kingdom of God is within you" (Luke 17:20-21 NRSV).

Solitude does not mean permanent withdrawal. We do not make tabernacles on the mountain, as Jesus' disciples longed to do on their retreat at Jesus' transfiguration. Like them, we go back down to the valley, where we often find people caught in the throes of spiritual crisis. Solitude prepares us for involvement and service.

The Gifts of Solitude

The discipline of solitude offers many benefits. Let me suggest three of the most fruitful ways to experience these:

Explore the Landscape Of Your Soul

In solitude, you walk through the valleys of fear, the arid places of doubt, the lush pastures of conviction, the peaks of insight and communion, and the streams of creativity. The journey changes you from living as someone driven by the world and your unchecked desires, to being an individual called by God and filled with God's Spirit. We have more to offer others when we take time away from them.

We have more to offer others when we take time away from them.

Break the Hold of Worldly Expectations and Ambitions

Solitude releases the pressure of worldly expectations. Getting away enables us to recover the pace and perspective of spiritual vitality.

It's tough to learn "the unforced rhythms of grace"[103] when we feel tossed to and fro by the currents of daily activity. Until we get away, we often don't realize the cost of our continual involvement. Constant engagement makes us vulnerable.

Solitude can make us resilient. Dallas Willard illustrates this fascinating characteristic with a study in which scientists found that it takes 20 times more the amount of amphetamine to kill individual mice than it takes to kill them in groups. Experimenters also found that a mouse given no amphetamine at all will die within ten minutes of being placed in a group taking the drug.[104]

Harsh illustrations, I know, but so is the threat of continual engagement. The pressure of the crowd can distort our vision and pressure us to compromise our highest ideals and values. Solitude breaks the power of peer pressure by which we define ourselves and which influences so many of our choices. Solitude reminds us we live ultimately for an audience of One.

Make Space in Your Heart for Love

Solitude replenishes your inner reservoirs. Pastor William Lohe said,

> "Whoever must always give, must always have; and since he
> cannot draw out of himself what he must give, he must ever
> keep near the living fountain in order to draw… Solitude is the
> fountain of all living streams, and nothing glorious is born in
> public."[105]

Henri Nouwen makes a stark observation of the cost of ignoring
solitude:

> Without the solitude of heart, the intimacy of friendship,
> marriage, and community life cannot be creative. Without
> the solitude of heart, our relationships with others easily
> become needy and greedy, sticky and clinging, dependent
> and sentimental, exploitive and parasitic, because without the
> solitude of heart we cannot experience the others as different
> from ourselves but only as people who can be used for the
> fulfillment of our own, often hidden, needs.[106]

This is the spiritual basis for "Absence makes the heart grow fonder."
Absence does not create a deprivation that must be satisfied. Instead,
it generates a love rooted in God.

Being away from people for a time can enable us to engage more fully
when we rejoin them. We give others that which God has given us.
We cannot receive from God if we always have people around. But
when we receive from the Lord, we become eager to share his bounty
with others.

Solitude breaks the power of loneliness, enabling us to find our
affirmation in God. It reminds us that we secure our value in Christ
and then share it with others.

Guidelines: Practicing Solitude

1 **PREPARE FOR A BRIEF TIME OF SOLITUDE**

You can practice solitude in two primary ways: in the press of life and in special times away from your normal schedule and location. These guidelines refer to a brief time of 15 to 60 minutes.

2 **WITHDRAW TO A PLACE WHERE YOU CAN BE ALONE**

Ideally, make this a physical place where no one will interrupt you. When you can't get away from people, withdraw by using headphones or earbuds to listen to environmental sounds while closing your eyes. Let your associates know your intent. Strangers will usually respect the cues sent by your headphones and closed eyes.

3 **LOOK INTO YOUR CUSTOMARY MIRRORS**

Begin with confession and repentance. Use your imagination to see and then break the mirrors you use to define your worth. Mirrors of relationships, work, school, performance, money, things, and so on are not sinful in themselves, but cannot reflect your true nature and value.

4 **LOOK INTO GOD'S MIRROR**

Remind yourself that you live for the Lord and the Lord is pleased with you. Imagine the person you are becoming in Christ.

5 **REPLENISH YOUR SOUL**

Solitude provides a flexible time and space for you to practice spiritual disciplines. You can also express yourself freely without self-consciousness. Dance, sing, recite poetry, read, listen to music, paint, or draw. You get the idea!

Pathways to God's Purpose for Our Lives

Pathways to God's Pace for Living

Redeem Your Time | Enjoy Sabbath Rest | Celebrate Sacred Milestones

Pathways to God's Presence with Us

Preview | Review | Prayer

Pathways to God's Perspective

Bible Study | Meditation | Spiritual Input

Pathways to God's Power

Fasting | Silence | Solitude

Pathways to God's Purpose for Our Lives

Character | Community | Calling: Daily Call and Vocational Call

Chapter 18
Character

We have few joys greater than resisting temptation.

Late one evening, Steve lingered after a church committee meeting. He was usually one of the first out the door, but this time he hung around until everyone else was gone. He asked if I had time to talk to him privately. I could see he was deeply troubled. He was normally even-tempered, but that night, he was obviously rattled.

"There's a woman at my office..." and he began to tremble so much that he almost couldn't talk. His eyes filled with tears, "There's a beautiful woman at my office who is becoming more and more attractive to me—and I'm getting clear messages she's feeling something, too."

If you knew Steve, you'd know that this was probably not the product of an overactive imagination or ego. He was a young, trim, fit, handsome Ivy League graduate with a vibrant personality who was extremely successful in the financial world. Just a year earlier, Steve and his wife, Jenny, had prayed with me in their living room to commit their lives to Christ. They had committed to put their faith at the center of their marriage and home. I had baptized their first child, and another was one the way. Steve was not making dramatic progress in his faith, but I felt he was moving forward. Suddenly, he had been ambushed by desires and seemed shaken to the core as he described the situation:

"We've done some business deals together. We've had lunch together a few times. Nothing romantic ever happened ... But I'm struggling to resist this— I know it's wrong. But" and here he choked, unable to speak for a few moments. "Before coming here tonight, I drove past her house! I would never want to do anything to hurt my wife or our children... How do I stop this??"

Steve and I spent several hours together, late into the evening talking, reading Scripture, and praying. When he left, though he was completely wrung out, I could sense some relief.

We had our usual committee meeting the next month. Again, Steve lingered, but there was a difference this time. We walked out to the parking lot together, chatting about family and church.

When everyone else had gone, he said, "Doug, I think you saved my life. The morning after we talked, I told her exactly where I stood. I told her I was totally committed to my marriage and I didn't want there to be any confusion about our relationship. I asked her forgiveness for my words and behaviors that kept it going. If I hadn't been safe telling you, and turning to the Lord, I honestly don't know if I could have lasted."

Faith Incarnate

Steve faced an issue much larger than that of sexual temptation. It was a battle for his character that would have lifelong implications for many people, not just himself and his wife. He was not fully prepared for the ambush of feelings and desires. He began to pay much more attention to his spiritual life after this incident.

Spiritual disciplines equip us to live, work, serve, and play to the fullest. They are means, not ends. They enable us to draw life from the Lord so we can serve God's purposes in this world. Spirituality is not just about feeling good. Spirituality is about living well. As followers of Jesus, we may not do different things than everyone else, but we are meant to do everything differently.

Spirituality is not just about feeling good. Spirituality is about living well.

God's pace, presence, perspective, and power can show up through how we do whatever we do. Even as Jesus, the Word made flesh, lived among us, Jesus-living-in-us can become a reality to bless others.

Godly character is both an ingredient and a result of spiritual vitality. As we envision the person God wants us to become, energy and joy rise within us. Character gives us the confidence of honesty, the power of self-control, and the freedom of never having to hide, dodge, or deny.

You Can Count on Me

My personal definition of character expresses itself in the affirmation, "You can count on me."

You can count on me to be honest and direct.

You can count on me to keep my promises.

You can count on me to admit my mistakes and ask forgiveness.

> You can count on me to act with integrity, whether I am with
> you or away from you.

Such simple affirmations carry a tremendous amount of power. Read them aloud and see what I mean.

Godly character shares the fruit of spiritual vitality with those around us. They have the privilege and, we hope, the inspiration, of harvesting from the seeds of life that God has sown in us. In relationships, others reap the blessing of patience and kindness. In business, employers, employees, and customers reap the benefits of a trusted, conscientious worker or the security of integrity in leadership.

The Character Gap

Over coffee one day, my friend Gary and I spoke about a colleague who had left the ministry because of misconduct. As in so many cases, the news had surprised and saddened us. It also raised the troubling paradox of an obviously gifted pastor who had been caught leading a secret life over many years. He had inspired many individuals to commit their lives to Christ. As an effective communicator, he had discipled many others in the ways of Christ. Yet he himself had fallen prey to dark desires, hurting countless others in the process.

Why? How did this happen?

Gary took a napkin (one of his favorite writing surfaces!) and a felt-tip pen and drew two lines, as on a graph. The lower line gradually sloped upward. The second line, just above it, started to slope upward slowly, then shot up dramatically, leaving a huge gap between the two.

"The lower line with the gradual slope," Gary said, "is the 'character line.' The upper line is the 'gift-success line.' Our friend's gifts in ministry promoted him to a place that couldn't be supported by his character. His opportunities outgrew his character. That's what makes many people so vulnerable."

A character gap develops when we allow activity in the outer world to distract us from the daily business of bringing our attitudes, desires, words, and behavior under the sanctifying power of the Holy Spirit. Developing character is like developing physical strength and skill. As in physical exercise or any form of learning, you cannot cram, hoping to do in a day or week what can be accomplished only by months and years of consistent practice.

The weakness of a character gap will become apparent when the circumstances or stresses of life converge and reach a breaking point. We may be able to coast for a while and yet feel quite secure. But raw talent, personality, and fortunate circumstances cannot substitute for the forging of inner holiness, resilience, and the convictions that constitute integrity of character.

Raw talent, personality, and fortunate circumstances cannot substitute for the forging of inner holiness, resilience, and the convictions that constitute integrity of character.

Character does not develop in a vacuum. I can tell myself, in the sanctuary of silence and solitude, that I will control my temper, but not until someone insults me and I have returned a blessing instead have I taken a step forward in character development.

> "But solid food is for the mature, *who by constant use have trained themselves to distinguish good from evil*," says the writer to the Hebrews (Hebrews 5:14, NIV, italics added).

We make our faith incarnate by developing an awareness of the character issues we face, especially in our daily choices and temptations. Then we make a plan for developing the character traits we believe the Lord most desires to nurture in us at this time. It's best to focus on one trait at a time (though life has a way of frustrating such neat divisions).

Guidelines for Building Character

We all could use some help in building our character. Use the following six guidelines to kickstart your own character-building program.

STUDY YOUR OWN LIFE

What in your lifestyle and circumstances most needs transformation? How would "the new you-in-Christ" respond differently to character struggles? Respond to prompts such as, "The area that causes me most regret now is…" or "When I think of a recent difficult interaction, I had with someone, I wish I had…" or "Lord, I would like people to describe me as…"

STUDY AND MEDITATE ON SCRIPTURES THAT APPLY TO YOUR PARTICULAR DESIRE

A concordance or Bible dictionary can lead you to passages on most any character trait you may want to consider.[107] Consider biblical characters and explore how they model these qualities. Choose one or two passages that speak most clearly to your heart and journal on what difference these would make in your life.

CULTIVATE GOD'S VISION FOR YOUR NEW ATTITUDE AND/OR BEHAVIOR

Vision rather than willpower can best help to unlock the energy of change. Prayerfully reflect and journal to formulate the specific qualities you want to cultivate. You might frame this as moving from the undesirable quality to the desirable one. For example, "Lord, I want to move from the irritability that focuses on my needs to the patience that focuses on others."

Rescript a situation where you responded inappropriately, picturing as vividly as possible a positive, godly interaction. Redefine your identity in Christ. "In Christ, I am patient and kind. In Christ, I bear the fruit of love, joy, and peace in my attitudes and interactions."

CONFESS AND REPENT OF THE NEGATIVE TRAIT

I have listed repentance after visioning because our new vision helps us understand the way in which the negative trait has cheated God, others, and ourselves. It makes us more eager to be free from that which compromises our integrity and weakens our discipleship.

Write a specific prayer in your journal in which you release your guilt to God and receive his forgiveness in Christ. Consider it an ongoing source of encouragement and incentive.

DEVELOP A PLAN FOR IMPLEMENTATION AND ACCOUNTABILITY

If you have a problem with anger, for example, plan how to cultivate patience, gentleness, and kindness. Make a list of your trigger points and all-too-typical responses. Then make a list of new ways to break the habitual response cycle.[108] Consider asking a spiritually mature friend to keep you accountable. "Accountability is not spiritual policing but spiritual partnership," according to Dave Rhodes.[109]

BE GRACIOUS TO YOURSELF AND PERSISTENT IN YOUR COMMITMENT

Scripture calls us to have realistic expectations based on a clear understanding of the natural resistance of our hearts. As Jeremiah 17:9 (NIV) says, "The heart is deceitful above all things and beyond cure. Who can understand it?" Jeremiah does not mean we should abandon our efforts. But we undertake the task in full reliance upon the Lord and his resources. As Jeremiah proceeds to say, "I the Lord search the heart and examine the mind" (Jeremiah 17:10). As the Lord leads us, step-by-step, his Spirit transforms us into the likeness of Christ.

The choices we make today shape us for eternity. Our salvation remains secure through faith in Christ, but our choices now *will* affect us. God has provided the foundation in Christ and supplied all the materials we need. How will we respond?

> For no one can lay any foundation other than the one that has been laid; that foundation is Jesus Christ. Now if anyone builds on the foundation with gold, silver, precious stones, wood, hay, straw—the work of each builder will become visible, for the day will disclose it, because it will be revealed with fire, and the fire will test what sort of work each has done. If what has been built on the foundation survives, the builder will receive a reward. If the work is burned up, the builder will suffer loss; the builder will be saved, but only as through fire (1 Corinthians 3:11-15, NRSV).

Lord, have mercy! I do not want to arrive in heaven smelling of smoke!

With Character Comes Authority

As God shapes your character, you will discover a new sense of authority in Christ. Authority is the force of presence, not the presence of force. Authority is not a matter of position but of person. Your authority grows out of your integrity.

By authority, I mean the freedom to take the initiative and influence others for godly purposes. I mean the confidence to stand up to

intimidating circumstances, the strength to stand against sin and
wickedness, and the power to stand firm against evil.

Authority is the force of presence, not the presence of force.

I have experienced the authority of character in completely unexpected
places. John worked in automobile repair for most of his life. Anyone
who shook hands with him couldn't help but notice the grease
embedded in every wrinkle and crack of those hard-working hands.
His dirty hands, however, were good. *Very* good.

John didn't talk much, and he didn't feel at all comfortable on church
committees. But you could count on John. If your car had a problem,
he told you exactly what it needed—never more, never less. Many
times, he spent a few hours on a car and would not charge a penny,
especially to elderly customers on fixed incomes. "I have all I need,"
he would say.

But more than these things, John developed a ministry that you'd
never expect: a ministry of letter writing. I got my first letter from
John on a day I really struggled, one of those days when you'd like to
roll the clock back and just start over. The late afternoon mail came,
bearing John's letter:

> Dear Doug,
>
> Jesus is pleased with you. I know you already know that, but the
> Lord told me to tell you again. You may not feel you do enough
> for God, or that you don't do all the right things, but that's not
> what God is looking for. He just wants your love—that's all.
>
> I try to remember this when I'm fixing cars. I do the best I can,
> but I know that what people want most is an honest man they
> can trust. So, if I don't do it right the first time, I just apologize
> and do it again for free. They like that. I tell them that's what
> love is all about.
>
> We love you. If there is anything my wife and I can do for you,
> just call us. I'm not the type to get up in front of groups, but I
> love being backstage. I pray for you every day when I unlock
> my shop. As I open that door, I thank God I opened the door

of my heart to him, and I pray that he will use you as a key for others to unlock their hearts.

John wrote with *authority*. That letter renewed me for days and weeks. His simple exhortation, "Jesus is pleased with you," felt like a warm, healing hand reaching right into my heart, relieving much of my burden. The impact lay in John's clear grasp of Christ and his unwavering commitment to honoring Jesus in his life and work. *How* he did what he did made the difference.

Character Is Formed Through Faithfulness in the Little Things

While we may feel tempted to think of character as the ability to pass the big tests, it truly is evident in the little quizzes we're given each day. Charles Spurgeon's advice to young preachers is apt for us all:

> Let us so act that we shall never need to care if all heaven, and earth, and hell, swelled the list of spectators… Take care of your life, even in the minutiae of your character… We cannot afford to run great risks through little things. Our care must be to act on the rule, "giving no offence in anything, that the ministry be not blamed."[110]

While we may feel tempted to think of character as the ability to pass the big tests, it truly is evident in the little quizzes we're given each day.

C. S. Lewis used the image of a "central core" of personality within each of us that is formed and molded by daily decisions. At the end of life, we will see the results of our efforts.

> People often think of Christian morality as a kind of bargain in which God says, "If you keep a lot of rules I'll reward you, and if you don't, I'll do the other thing." I do not think that is the best way of looking at it. I would much rather say that every time you make a choice you are turning the central part of you, the part of you that chooses, into something a little different from what it was before.

And taking your life as a whole, with all your innumerable
choices, all your life long you are slowly turning this central
thing either into a heavenly creature or into a hellish creature:
either into a creature that is in harmony with God and with other
creatures, and with itself, or else into one that is in a state of war
and hatred with God, and with its fellow creatures, and with
itself. To be the one kind of creature is heaven: that is, it is joy and
peace and knowledge and power. To be the other means madness,
horror, idiocy, rage, impotence, and eternal loneliness. Each of us
at each moment is progressing to the one state or the other.[111]

Whenever some choice confronts us, our character is on the line. Each
choice shapes us. Every action bends us in a certain direction, toward
or away from the light, toward or away from qualities you may
consciously reject or embrace. Let's seek the Lord's power to bring
our faith to life.

Guidelines: Building Character

1   STUDY YOUR OWN LIFE

What part of your lifestyle and circumstances most needs transformation? How would "the new you-in-Christ" respond differently?

2   STUDY AND MEDITATE ON SCRIPTURES THAT APPLY TO YOUR SPECIFIC DESIRE

Use a concordance or Bible dictionary to find passages on the character trait you are considering. Choose one or two passages that speak most clearly to your heart, and journal on what difference these would make in your life.

3   CULTIVATE GOD'S VISION FOR YOUR NEW ATTITUDE AND/OR BEHAVIOR

Vision rather than willpower best helps unlock the energy of change. Prayerfully reflect and journal to formulate the specific qualities you want to cultivate. You might frame this as moving from an undesirable quality to the desirable one. Rescript a situation, picturing as vividly as possible a positive, godly interaction. Redefine your identity in Christ. "In Christ, I am patient and kind..."

4   CONFESS AND REPENT OF THE NEGATIVE TRAIT

In your journal, write a prayer in which you release your guilt to God and receive his forgiveness in Christ. Consider this an ongoing source of encouragement and incentive.

5   DEVELOP A PLAN FOR IMPLEMENTATION AND ACCOUNTABILITY

Plan how to cultivate the quality the Lord wants to form in you. Make a list of new responses to break your habitual response cycle. Consider asking a spiritually mature friend to keep you accountable.

6 **BE GRACIOUS TO YOURSELF AND PERSISTENT IN YOUR COMMITMENT**

Scripture calls us to have realistic expectations based on a clear understanding of the natural resistance of our hearts. Undertake this task in full reliance upon the Lord and his resources.

Remember, the choices you make today shape you for eternity.

Chapter 19
Community

In the early years of my ministry, I had the privilege of meeting with
Bishop Festo Kivengere and his associate, John Wilson, both of whom
ministered in Uganda at the height of Idi Amin's brutal dictatorship
(1971-1979). Ironically, in that time of intense persecution, the church
in Uganda experienced revival.

When I asked Bishop Festo if he could name any factors critical to the
success of the revival, he replied, "We guard our relationships. If an
issue is causing division or anger, we face it immediately so that our
fellowship is unbroken. A community of Christian love draws others
to it. We cannot afford to tolerate alienation."

Bishop Festo told countless stories of conflicts that the community of
faith dealt with immediately and effectively. Such a response requires
discipline. As we practice this discipline, we learn that love is the soil
of vitality and revival.

Fellowship with Others Can Make God More Real in Our Experience

In a culture that values self-reliance and individualism, Jesus calls his
followers to the radical alternative of active interdependence. Like the
parts of a body, each person plays an essential role for the well-being
of all. The spiritual life is not a solo quest but is intimately tied to our
relationships with others.

> The spiritual life is not a solo quest but is intimately
> tied to our relationships with others.

> The community is the first place where you will make God's
> kingdom incarnate... The quality of your community does not
> depend on age or numbers. The only thing that counts and will
> bring you a blessing is that you should be always seeking each
> other in the Spirit of Jesus. From Him alone comes salvation.[112]

An African proverb says, "If you want to go fast, go alone. If you
want to go far, go together." We mature in Christ as we move "from
me to we" and confidently rely on one another.

Jesus did life with others. He called twelve to be with him. Following
Jesus' ascension, his followers stayed together in the upper room.
They formed a waiting, praying community, filled by the Holy Spirit.

First and foremost, the early church was a caring *fellowship*.

One of the greatest manifestations of Jesus' resurrection was the quality of life and community demonstrated by his followers. The book of Acts illustrates the new community Jesus lived, died, and rose again to create. Our faith comes alive when we connect in authentic fellowship centered in Christ, not just our natural affinities and preferences.

The book of Acts makes a direct correlation between unity, the apostles' testimony, and the experience of great grace:

> All the believers were one in heart and mind. No one claimed that any of his possessions was his own, but they shared everything they had. With great power the apostles continued to testify to the resurrection of the Lord Jesus, and much grace was upon them all (Acts 4:32- 33, NIV).

Jesus' prayer in John 17 reveals that Jesus most earnestly desired unity among his followers. Their unity would loudly testify to the world and would release grace among and through them.

We can call the practices that facilitate our involvement with others "spiritual disciplines" in that they become "policy decisions" we make by virtue of our faith in Jesus Christ and our commitment to love others as he has loved us. A policy decision is a choice made in advance concerning how we will respond to a particular matter. When we weave these disciplines into our lives, our relationships generate spiritual energy.

Guidelines for Building Relationships in the Body of Christ

Community does not just happen. Community arises from intentional engagement with each other. These guidelines present some of the most basic principles for healthy fellowship.

BE AVAILABLE

To be unavailable is to be out of fellowship. Be available both physically and emotionally. In addition to your time, your willingness to connect with others communicates their value and importance.

TIME, NOT MONEY, IS THE MOST SIGNIFICANT CURRENCY IN RELATIONSHIPS

It takes discipline to pace our schedules to include time for others. Consider what it will take for you to be available to others.

No system of spiritual disciplines can substitute for love.

In our fast-paced lifestyles, we so often hear, "I hate to bother you, but…" or "I know you are busy, but…" Relationships should not feel like intrusions or interruptions. Instead, we enjoy fellowship as a gift. In the process, we celebrate one another. If we are too busy for people, especially the special people in our lives, we are too busy! No system of spiritual disciplines can substitute for love.

BE INTERRUPTIBLE

Some of Jesus' most powerful ministry happened in the unplanned moments. You can hold a valid and wise schedule too tightly. Trust the Lord to redeem the time you sacrifice to another. I greatly appreciate the wisdom of Dietrich Bonhoeffer:

> We must be ready to allow ourselves to be interrupted by God. God will be constantly crossing our paths and canceling our plans by sending us people with claims and petitions. We may pass them by, preoccupied with our more important tasks, as the priest passed by the man who had fallen among thieves, perhaps reading the Bible. When we do that, we pass by the visible sign of the Cross raised athwart our path to show us that, not our way, but God's way must be done.[113]

SHOW OTHERS THEIR VALUE

Community grows through tangible affirmations and demonstrations of valuing each other. We will experience deeper community when we intentionally affirm and encourage others. Consider three ways you can show your appreciation for the people God brings into your life.

Value Others by Paying Attention

Pay attention to the ways in which others perceive their sense of worth. Do they value verbal affirmation or acts of kindness?[114] Learn how to provide opportunities to release their gifts. You need to ask some people to do a specific task, while others will offer themselves if given the chance. Some need lots of reassurance, while others need just a few well-chosen words. Some like to work alone, others in groups. Our joy comes from observing people in action and then matching gifts with needs. In the process, a joyful community grows.

Value Others by Involving Them

You may feel tempted to do a project yourself, but by including others in the process you will deepen your relationships. Ask opinions. Invite people to make their own contributions. Seek ways to utilize their gifts.

I vividly remember my parents building a new home when I was in elementary school. They showed me the blueprint for my room and asked if I would like to figure out how to arrange its furniture. Dad explained the scale drawing and helped me make scale cutouts of my furniture. I placed them in the room in various ways until we found the best fit.

It might be quicker to do it yourself—but speed isn't the issue in matters of community.

I enjoyed the task so much that my parents asked me if I would make scale furniture patterns for *all* the rooms in the house. When the movers brought in our furniture, I told them where each piece went (I'm sure they appreciated my supervision!). My parents' request for my participation made me feel like I played a significant role in our move into a new home.

The process of connecting with others is as important as the project itself. We miss so much if we value only the result of accomplishing tasks. We can become impatient and frustrated at how long it takes to do things when we involve others. It might be quicker to do it yourself—but speed isn't the issue in matters of community. What happens in our relationship as we grow together will last far longer than any event or object—after all, it will shape us for eternity!

Value Others by Sharing Freely

When we connect in community, things that we considered our

personal possessions become community property. Generosity with possessions marked the early church and characterized God's people across the centuries. Generosity generates connection. Whether you give or receive, an act of kindness creates a special bond. I've found that the more I share, the more I enjoy what I'm sharing.

KEEP SHORT ACCOUNTS

Conflict and disappointment are inevitable in a fallen world. We feel tempted either to nurse grudges or keep up our defenses to protect ourselves against disappointments. In either case, community suffers.

In addition to developing realistic expectations for yourself and others, develop the discipline of keeping short accounts. Address an offense or problem as soon as possible. Don't let a debt accumulate bitterness interest by waiting to see if the other person will do something. You address it.

Festo Kivengere and the Ugandan fellowship made this their primary discipline. They brought differences to light so that those disputes wouldn't have the chance to divide the fellowship. This takes courage and tact, but it is worth the effort.

The simple fact of viewing this commitment as a spiritual discipline moves it from being a nice option to becoming an important discipline in love.

I have a friend deeply committed to this principle. If he feels things aren't quite right, he will reach out and ask, "Are we doing OK?" Or, he'll say, "I really value our relationship, and I feel there's something I need to talk over with you." He then proceeds in a thoughtful way to explain his concern. Time and again, his prompt calls (usually on the same day as the problem) and his nondefensive approach bring understanding and reconciliation.

FORGIVE, FORGIVE, AND FORGIVE AGAIN

Perhaps no more important a discipline exists than releasing the power of forgiveness into our relationships. Forgiveness is so essential to spiritual health that the Lord's Prayer singles it out for special comment (see Matthew 6:14-15).

When people ask me if a lack of forgiveness puts their eternal destiny in danger, I refocus them on their earthly destiny. This much is clear:

Our *experience* of forgiveness is directly related to our *expression* of forgiveness toward others.

Our experience of forgiveness is directly related to our expression of forgiveness toward others.

Forgiveness releases us from the chains that would hold us in bitterness and bondage. It may help to remember the difference between forgiveness and reconciliation. As David Stoop clarifies:

> Forgiveness is unilateral: It is something I can do all by myself. Reconciliation is bilateral: It is something both parties must do together. If you have hurt me, and we are estranged as a result, I can forgive you on my own, without your permission, without your even knowing about it. But we are not reconciled until we sit down and take mutual action together.[115]

Practically speaking, this means that we take care of our own "stuff" concerning what others have done to harm us. We do not allow it to block the flow of living water to and from our own hearts. "If it is possible, *as far as it depends on you*, live at peace with everyone" (Romans 12:18, NIV, italics added). This takes discipline as we deliberately choose to obey God, often despite our feelings. As we put forgiveness in this light, we find hope for freedom from the paralysis of anger and the resentment of bitterness, both of which drain our spiritual energy.

CONFESS AND MAKE THINGS RIGHT

Confession drains sin of its power and strengthens our fellowship with others. Confession doesn't earn God's forgiveness, but it makes God's forgiveness real to us. Confession opens the door that our sin shut and locked.

Generally speaking, the circle of the confession should extend only as far as the circle of the offense. But restitution may also be necessary. If we have done something that can be repaired or replaced, the honorable choice is to do whatever we can to set the situation right.

When Zacchaeus received Christ, he not only repented but also made a promise of restitution: "Look, half of my possessions, Lord, I will give to the poor; and if I have defrauded anyone of anything, I will pay back four times as much" (Luke 19:8, NRSV). Such restitution went beyond the expected. It conveyed his immense gratitude for the riches of salvation in Christ. It may also indicate Zacchaeus's personal integrity. Even though most Israelites viewed tax collectors with disgust as *yes-men* of the occupying Romans, Zacchaeus may well have maintained his integrity in a vocation riddled with corruption. Otherwise, how could he possibly have had the resources to reimburse people four-fold?

Confession doesn't earn God's forgiveness, but it makes God's forgiveness real to us.

Connecting with Others Deepens Our Connection with the Lord

Thomas Kelly well presents the goal of discipline in our relationships:

> Can we make all our relations [to others] relations which pass through Him? Our relations to the conductor on the trolley? Our relations to the clerk who serves us in a store? . . . For until the life of men in time is, in every relation, shot through with Eternity, the Blessed Community is not complete.[116]

Viewing each relationship through Christ moves us to a different level of interaction. At the least, it interrupts our frequently careless attitudes towards others so that we value each person not only for themselves but for the Lord. "And the King will say, 'I tell you the truth, when you did it to one of the least of these my brothers and sisters, you were doing it to me!'" (Matthew 25:40, NLT).

Guidelines: Building Relationships In The Body Of Christ

1   BE AVAILABLE

To be unavailable is to be out of fellowship.

2   TIME, NOT MONEY, IS THE MOST SIGNIFICANT CURRENCY IN RELATIONSHIPS

Pace your schedule to include time for others. Consider what it will take for you to be available, physically and emotionally, to others.

3   BE INTERRUPTIBLE

Jesus' most powerful ministries happened in the unplanned moments. Valid and wise schedules can be held too tightly. Trust the Lord to redeem the time you sacrifice to another.

4   SHOW OTHERS THEIR VALUE

Community grows through tangible affirmations and demonstrations of valuing each other. You can do this in at least three ways:

Value others by paying attention
Value others by involving them
Value others by sharing freely

5   KEEP SHORT ACCOUNTS

In a fallen world, conflict and disappointment happen. Instead of nursing grudges or withdrawing from others, develop the discipline of keeping short accounts. Address an offense or problem as soon as possible.

6   FORGIVE, FORGIVE, AND FORGIVE AGAIN

Forgiveness is so central to spiritual health that the Lord's Prayer singles it out for special comment. Forgiveness releases us from the chains that would hold us in bitterness and bondage. Our *experience* of forgiveness is directly related to our *expression* of forgiveness toward others.

7   ## CONFESS AND MAKE THINGS RIGHT

Confession drains sin of its power and strengthens our fellowship with others. Confession opens the door that our sin shut and locked. Generally speaking, the circle of the confession should only go as far as the circle of the offense. If we have done something that can be repaired or replaced, the honorable choice is to do whatever we can to set the situation right.

Chapter 20
Calling

The Lord wants more for you than you could ever imagine.

Since creation, the Lord has called us, as his image-bearers, to reflect God's nature in a holy partnership in life and work. Language strains to communicate both our privilege and our responsibility. Theologians describe our call to be "vice-regents" who exercise authority in the responsible care for creation.

In his essay, *"On Tree and Leaf: On Fairy-Stories,"* author J. R. R. Tolkien described humanity as "sub-creators." The term fits well with the theological implications of being created in the image of God. Tolkien wrote, "Fantasy remains a human right: we make in our measure and in our derivative mode, because we are made, and not only made, but in the image and likeness of God."[117]

What Tolkien applies to fantasy applies very much to real life. God has called us to utilize our creativity and personal resources to make God's redemptive presence real in this fallen world.

A Living Reminder

While on vacation with our family in Florida, I turned on the news at the end of one of our delightful, sun-drenched days and heard of the collapse of L'Ambiance Plaza, a thirteen-story building under construction in Bridgeport, Connecticut. That building lay about four miles from our home at the time. Of the seventy men working at the site, 28 were reported missing under tons of concrete and steel.

When we returned from Florida, I immediately joined the pastoral care team at the L'Ambiance disaster site. The pastoral team made itself available to the affected families, construction workers, police, firefighters and medical personnel. When I arrived, they had recovered 16 bodies and continued their search for the remaining 12.

I took the 9 PM to 2 AM shift. I felt troubled not only by the catastrophe but also by my own helplessness and unimportance as I stood at the edge of the pit. They soon located four more bodies but could not get to them for hours. What could I do? I remember feeling intimidated by the workers who operated the heavy equipment and provided practical help.

I spoke with a union boss (a rough, burly guy) who'd been there from the very beginning. Had we met outside of these circumstances, I doubt we would have conversed much.

As we talked, I expressed my appreciation for all he and his men had done. Many were doing the physically grueling, emotionally stressful work of recovery, all on minimal sleep.

"I only wish I could do more," I said.

"You're doing enough," he said. "I am so glad you pastors come here. This place is like hell—and you keep reminding us God's still around."[118]

Spiritual Vitality Calls Us to Intentional Living

On countless occasions I have recalled the comment by that union boss: "You keep reminding us that God's still around." While I could not dig through concrete, operate an acetylene torch, or provide medical care, I could be present as a visible representative of Jesus Christ—his presence in the middle of tragedy.

As followers of Jesus, we are living reminders that God exists and cares.[119]

Being a "living reminder" is not as abstract as it sounds. We reveal Jesus' presence by how we care for hurting people. We can serve as a quiet conscience in times of decision. We exercise ethical influence in leadership, model hope in discouragement, and witness to recovery in brokenness.

The spiritual director Francois Fenelon (1651-1715) exhorted us to move from knowledge to action: "A persuaded mind and even a well-intentioned heart is a long way from exact and faithful practice." Fenelon went on to say:

As followers of Jesus, we are living reminders that God exists and cares.

> Nothing has been more common in every age, and still more so today, than meeting souls who are perfect and saintly in speculation. The spiritual life is not an escape from life but the preparation for encountering life in this world. True spirituality is not a leisure time activity, a diversion from life. It is essentially subversive, and the test of its genuineness is practical.[120]

Spiritual disciplines can seem self-centered if we focus only on our experience of God. Spiritual disciplines channel the life of Christ through us as we play our part in Christ's continuing work in the world.

Spiritual disciplines can seem self-centered if we focus only on our experience of God. Spiritual disciplines channel the life of Christ through us as we play our part in Christ's continuing work in the world.

Spiritual health and vitality bear fruit in our lives on a personal level and contribute to bringing God's kingdom here on earth. We have the privilege of standing at life's disaster sites, reminding the world that God does exist and that the Lord can make a difference.

Two Expressions of Our Call in Christ

We have one call in life—to live for Jesus Christ—that expresses itself in two ways. The first is the discipline of our Daily Call as Disciples; the second is the discipline of our Vocational Call. Let's take them one at a time.

Our Daily Call as Disciples

All of us face what I term the "Fit or Form" challenge. Jesus' encounter with Mary and Martha illustrates this challenge, a choice between two distinct approaches to life (Luke 10:38-42 NLT).

Martha felt distracted, anxious, and troubled about many things, while Mary sat at Jesus' feet as he taught. When Martha complained about Mary's lack of help, Jesus responded, "Martha, Martha, you are worried and upset about many things, but few things are needed—or indeed only one. Mary has chosen what is better, and it will not be taken away from her."

Martha tried to *fit* Christ into her already-full life, while Mary *formed* her life around Christ, choosing the "one necessary thing."

Which choice best describes your approach to faith: fit (Martha) or form (Mary)? Your choice will radically affect your daily call.

Guidelines for the Discipline of Daily Call

The following six steps are designed to help you better follow your daily call as a disciple of Jesus.

BEGIN EACH DAY AFFIRMING YOUR COMMITMENT TO FOLLOW JESUS

"Lord, I live for you today."

Three Scriptures bring our call into sharp focus. Memorize these verses and repeat them to yourself throughout the day to empower your daily commitment.

- "… for me, to live is Christ" (Philippians 1:21).

- "Then Jesus said to them all: 'Whoever wants to be my disciple must deny themselves and take up their cross daily and follow me'" (Luke 9:23).

- "For it is by grace you have been saved, through faith—and this is not from yourselves, it is the gift of God—not by works, so that no one can boast. For we are God's handiwork, created in Christ Jesus to do good works, which God prepared in advance for us to do" (Ephesians 2:8-10).

PRACTICE THE DISCIPLINE OF PREVIEW WITH SPECIAL ATTENTION TO BEING A "LIVING REMINDER" TO THOSE AROUND YOU

Look at your schedule and prepare your soul for your day. Visualize the Lord with you in every moment, every encounter, every project. See the Guidelines for Preview on page 104.

PRAY

"Lord, make this day your day."

We rely on God's power and direction to fulfill God's call for our daily lives. Prayer centers us, reminding us whose we are.

SEE YOURSELF AS A HOST

The world includes two types of people, guests and hosts. *Guests* expect to be taken care of, while *hosts* make others feel welcome and valued. How are you most likely to see yourself, as a guest or a host? Which role do you most naturally take?

Practicing my role as host has changed the way I interact with others. While I am by no means a strong extrovert (though I have that tendency), when I view myself as a host, it becomes more natural to put others first. I take the initiative in reaching out, looking out for their welfare, and making them feel welcome.

PAY ATTENTION

"Lord, where are you working?"

What a difference when we approach our day with "resurrection eyes." Paul prayed for disciples to exercise faith by seeing life from God's perspective:

> I keep asking that the God of our Lord Jesus Christ, the glorious Father, may give you the Spirit of wisdom and revelation, so that you may know him better. I pray that the eyes of your heart may be enlightened in order that you may know the hope to which he has called you, the riches of his glorious inheritance in his holy people, and his incomparably great power for us who believe. That power is the same as the mighty strength he exerted when he raised Christ from the dead and seated him at his right hand in the heavenly realms (Ephesians 1:17-20 NIV).

PRACTICE THE DISCIPLINE OF REVIEW AT THE END OF YOUR DAY

Where did you see the Lord working today? What "coincidences" occurred that revealed God's hand? Thank the Lord for these provisions. What failures and sins do you want to confess? Receive God's forgiveness and cleansing. See the Guidelines for Review on page 115.

Our Vocational Call as Disciples

God has given you life so that you might make a unique contribution to his continuing work in this world. Your primary call is to fulfill the design God has woven into your heart. You are to do what you love to show others God's love.

By "vocation," I do not mean simply how you earn a living or how you make money. Your vocation is your primary contribution to life. You might not earn any money from your vocation, but you know you're meant to contribute here, even if it costs you.

Do what you love to show others God's love.

The subject of Vocational Call is vast. While I provide some basic guidelines for it, I highly recommend that you investigate the resource developed by Will Mancini with Dave Rhodes and Cory Hartman called *Younique: Designing the Life God Dreamed for You*.[121]

Guidelines for the Discipline of Vocational Call

None of us will automatically frame our daily life and work as callings unless we intentionally choose to engage in our daily responsibilities in light of our faith in Jesus Christ.

BEGIN EACH DAY AFFIRMING YOUR COMMITMENT TO SERVE JESUS

"Lord, may I bring your presence wherever I am, whatever I say, and whatever I do."

We experience freedom when we view Jesus as the ultimate boss of our work and other responsibilities. I vividly remember pouring out my heart in prayer when I struggled as a pastor early in my ministry. I felt frustrated because I was doing everything I knew how to do, but saw little progress in the congregation. Sarah and our children were paying the price, and I just didn't understand why God seemed to have little interest in honoring my work.

"Lord," I cried out in prayer, "Why is it so hard? Why aren't things changing? I have tried to be a faithful servant of this congregation..."

At that point it was as if God broke into my thoughts. I didn't hear an audible voice, but it seemed as though God said to me, "What did you just say?"

"Umm, I said, 'I have tried to be a faithful servant of this congregation...'"

"That's part of the problem. You are *my* servant, *not theirs*. You are my servant, temporarily assigned to this congregation. Serve me— and you will be serving them, whether or not they respond."

That became a turning point in my understanding of my role in ministry and it gave me a new freedom in Christ. "And whatever you do, whether in word or deed," Paul wrote, "do it all in the name of the Lord Jesus, giving thanks to God the Father through him" (Colossians 3:17, NKJV).

FOCUS ON YOUR BEST OFFERING

While you have many responsibilities, the important thing to remember is that *how* you do what you do matters as much as *what* you actually do.

Discover the unique contribution you can offer in life. In the Gospel-based life design course called *Younique,* people use the "Passion Funnel" to discern their most important contribution.[122] The Passion Funnel asks four key questions:

> What am I interested in? (What do I enjoy?)
> What am I excited about? (What gives me energy?)
> What drives me? (What gets me up in the morning?)
> What burdens me? (What keeps me up at night?)

Seminary professor Howard Hendricks warns, "There are lots of things you could do. But there is only one you must do. Most opportunities are distractions in disguise."[123] Remind yourself daily to focus as much as possible on the one thing you believe God has called you to do.

PAY ATTENTION TO LIFE-GIVING EXPERIENCES IN YOUR WORK/SERVICE SETTING

Life-giving experiences provide clues to our calling. My wife, Sarah, felt called to the nursing profession. She excelled at providing medical care. Connecting with patients, however, interested her most. She discovered she has a pastor's heart for helping people find comfort, strength, and hope in times of illness and suffering.

Review your work responsibilities to identify the aspects that attract your positive interest and that generate energy as you do them.

PAY ATTENTION TO LIFE-DRAINING EXPERIENCES IN YOUR WORK/SERVICE SETTING

Life-draining experiences also provide clues to our calling—but you still may have to do such tasks. "You may not feel called to do it," I heard someone say, "but everybody has to take out the trash."

What responsibilities, tasks, and relationships sap your energy? Why? What steps can you take to manage them more effectively?

Follow Jesus' Rhythm of Life

Jesus showed us the rhythm of a healthy, active spiritual life. In him, we see a life marked by involvement and solitude, by action and reflection, by engagement and withdrawal.

Jesus' time apart with his Father energized his ministry. Jesus' time in ministry became the fuel for his intercession (see Matthew 11:25-27).

Jesus kept a balance between gathering strength and wisdom from solitude and then applying that strength and wisdom to the situations around him.

We all develop spiritually in this arena called "the world." While we may have countless questions about the suffering and trials of this life, some aspects of our spiritual growth can happen only in the context of difficult days. In vivid images, Forbes Robinson says that, far from being a hindrance, life on this fallen planet shapes us in ways impossible in any other way:

> If angels could envy, how they would envy us our splendid chance, to be able, in a world where everything unseen must be taken on sheer faith, in a world where the contest between the flesh and the spirit is being decided for the universe, not only to win the battle ourselves but also to win it for others! To help a sister or brother up the mountain while you yourself are only just able to keep your foothold, to struggle through the mist together—that surely is better than to stand at the summit and beckon.[124]

We all are embroiled in "the contest for the universe," no matter what our specific vocation happens to be. In such a world, spiritual disciplines not only address the weaknesses of our own inner lives but also release God's truth, grace, and power to work through us.

We remind ourselves of the practical nature of the spiritual life by our being "in the world but not of it" (John 17:14). How are we to conduct ourselves in the daily pressures and expectations of life?

We operate in the world through who we are (as we develop Christlike character), through the quality of our interaction with others (community), and through our continuing role in Christ's work as disciples in our daily and vocational lives (call).

Again, spiritual disciplines are not ends in themselves. While we may think of them as retreats from life's battles, in fact they equip us for service. God has much for us to do in bringing the world to a redeeming knowledge of himself. But to fulfill that high calling, we must connect to God, be filled with the mind of Christ, and empowered by the Holy Spirit. Only then can we accomplish what God intends.

Guidelines: The Discipline Of Daily Call

1   **BEGIN EACH DAY AFFIRMING YOUR COMMITMENT TO FOLLOW JESUS**

"Lord, I live for you today." Three Scriptures bring our call into sharp focus. Memorize these (on page 230) and repeat them to yourself throughout the day to empower your daily commitment.

2   **PRACTICE THE DISCIPLINE OF PREVIEW WITH SPECIAL ATTENTION TO BEING A "LIVING REMINDER" TO THOSE AROUND YOU**

Look at your schedule and plan for your day. Visualize the Lord with you in every moment, every encounter, every project. See the Guidelines for Preview on page 104.

3   **PRAY**

"Lord, make this day your day." Rely on God's power and direction to fulfill God's call for your daily life.

4   **SEE YOURSELF AS A HOST**

Being a host changes how you interact with others. Even if you are not an extrovert, take the initiative in reaching out, looking out for the welfare of others, and making them feel welcome.

5   **PAY ATTENTION**

"Lord, where are you working?" Approach your day with "resurrection eyes." Exercise faith by seeing life from God's perspective.

6   **PRACTICE THE DISCIPLINE OF REVIEW AT THE CONCLUSION OF YOUR DAY**

Where did you see the Lord working today? What "coincidences" occurred that revealed God's hand? Thank the

Lord for these provisions. What failures and sins do you want to confess? Receive God's forgiveness and cleansing. See the Guidelines for Review on page 115.

Guidelines: The Discipline Of Vocational Call

1 **BEGIN EACH DAY AFFIRMING YOUR COMMITMENT TO SERVE JESUS**

"Lord, may I bring your presence wherever I am, to whatever I say, and in whatever I do." You will experience a sense of freedom when you view Jesus as the ultimate "boss" of your work and other responsibilities.

2 **FOCUS ON YOUR BEST OFFERING**

Remember that *how* you do what you do matters as much as what you actually do. Complete your *Younique* Passion Funnel exercise to discern your most significant offering. Remind yourself daily to focus as much as possible on what you sense God has called you to do.

3 **PAY ATTENTION TO LIFE-GIVING EXPERIENCES IN YOUR WORK/SERVICE SETTING**

Life-giving experiences provide clues to your calling. Review your work responsibilities to identify the aspects that attract your positive interest and that generate energy as you do them.

4 **PAY ATTENTION TO LIFE-DRAINING EXPERIENCES IN YOUR WORK/SERVICE SETTING**

Life-draining experiences also provide clues to your calling (even though you may have to continue doing some of them.) What responsibilities, tasks, relationships sap your energy? Why? What steps can you take to better manage them?

Part Three
Walking Toward Spiritual Vitality

Chapter 21
Seasons of
the Soul

Spiritual life is a living reality. It is not mechanical, but rather organic, dynamic, and nonlinear.

We so easily forget this while living in a technology-driven world. We are so accustomed to controlling our external environment that we become impatient when our inner environment goes off course and doesn't get back on track quickly. You cannot manipulate your soul like a thermostat. You cannot turn it on and off like a switch.

The annual seasons that characterize most of the globe remind us of the cycle of life. We plant, grow, harvest, and recover. These seasons can serve as helpful metaphors for our spiritual journey. If we are to cultivate true spiritual growth, we must respect the natural movement of the soul. Rather than thinking of your present spiritual state as a static condition, you can view your spiritual life in terms of seasons.

If we are to cultivate true spiritual growth, we must respect the natural movement of the soul.

Even as seasons come and go in a predictable cycle, so our souls move through patterns of stirring, growth, fruitfulness, and recovery. We respond differently to different seasons. A down parka doesn't fit a hot summer day any more than a swimsuit works in a frigid winter. A person in spiritual spring will invest a great deal more energy in their new beginning than a person enjoying a summer of steady growth.

As we consider the metaphor of seasons to assess our soul condition, don't feel surprised if you find yourself in spring in one area of life but in winter in another. Each season has distinctive qualities, with wide variance within that season.

Spring: A Time of New Beginnings

The messy season of spring, filled with sudden warmth and dreary days, gradually comes on as winter takes its final breaths. Days of clouds and rain alternate with dry, sunny ones. The overall feel of the season sparks refreshment, expectancy, and renewed vigor.

Spiritually, in spring our love for God stirs anew. We feel excited about new opportunities and consider undertaking new commitments to ourselves and to others. We've had enough of the status quo; we long for a richer, more meaningful life. The time has come to risk sowing new seeds.

Spring is the season of resurrection. Easter is the ultimate expression of new life. Both the reality and the metaphor of resurrection awaken our faith that nothing is impossible for God.

Our spiritual growth and personal development do not proceed at an even pace. We move in stages of rapid progress and then consolidate our gains. We see this principle in botany. The annual growth rings of a tree show how much growth the tree added each year. The tree adds that growth in the first six weeks of spring. The rest of the year, the fiber hardens.

The spiritual life often follows a similar pattern. Personal maturity and mastery come from continuing through the periods of growth and hardening, both the climaxes and plateaus. Most people do not gain mastery because they allow the plateaus to discourage them rather than seeing them as places to prepare for the next stage.

ASSESSMENT FOR SPRING

- In what areas of your spiritual life do you sense the stirring of new interest and energy?

- Review your journals (or your memory) and note those times you've had a spiritual growth spurt.

- What was happening in your life and circumstances at that time?

- What stimulated your growth?

- What continuing change resulted from that season?

- What does spiritual springtime mean to you?

Summer: A Season of Cultivating Growth

In summer, we begin to see the fruit of our labor, as well as those things that didn't take root.

Early summer can bring a time of thinning out overplanted crops. We may have tackled too many new projects in the spring and now need to step back and reevaluate what stays and what we need to release.

We also think of summer as a time of easing up a bit from the rigorous schedule of the rest of the year. Vacations vary our pace and bring brief adventures.

In spiritual summer we may want to experiment with a new discipline or spiritual activity. We can commit to a specific, limited period for the project. Summer is a growing season. We've planted a spiritual crop, chosen a spiritual direction, and continue doing whatever nurtures that choice.

ASSESSMENT FOR SUMMER

- Where do you feel like you are growing spiritually?

- What will help you maintain steady growth?

- Review your journals (or your memory) and note those times you've had a summer season of steady growth.

- What was happening in your life and circumstances at that time?

- What sustained your growth?

- What continuing change resulted from that season?

- What does spiritual summer mean to you?

Fall: A Season of Harvesting Fruit

The energy of spring and the discipline of summer move into a fall season when we see tangible changes in our lives. We see the truth of the principle that "life adds up." If we sow generously, we reap generously.[125] We hope it will bring a season of thanksgiving as we savor God's faithfulness and the satisfaction of our work done well in God's strength.

Without doubt, however, fall can discourage us if we look for fruit and find only a poor crop. We may find ourselves in situations that demand resources we haven't taken the time and effort to cultivate.

The threat of a spiritual famine can devastate us. We may have to take some extraordinary measures to secure the resources we need. We will find that God's mercy is ever present. This may not come, however, without a bittersweet sense that the recovery of our spiritual health requires some immediate, significant action.

ASSESSMENT FOR FALL

- Where are you experiencing a "harvest" in your spiritual life? What factors have brought this about?

- Review your journals (or your memory) and note those times you've had a fall season of spiritual harvest.

- What was happening in your life and circumstances at that time?

- Where and how did you see the fruit of your spiritual vitality?

- What continuing change resulted from that season?

- Is there a situation where you're experiencing a shortfall or, perhaps, a spiritual famine? If so, what actions would be most helpful?

- What does spiritual fall mean to you?

Winter: A Season of Reflection and Anticipation

As with the other seasons, winter has its positive and negative nuances.

Winter can delight us as we rest and recover from the rigors of fall. Telling stories with friends around crackling fires, enjoying the falling snow that blankets the earth in beauty and brings a hush over all activity—winter can bring us all these gifts.

In winter, we may take stock of our lives, gather with our friends, and tell the stories of God's faithfulness. We may take time to muse, with no urgency for action. Action will come with spring. The ground rests, and so do we.

Of all seasons, winter requires a grace-spark of memory to ignite a spiritual fire that can sustain us through the season.

Yet winter can feel harsh: cold, barren landscapes, darker days, longer nights. When we find ourselves in a bleak winter, God may seem far away indeed. We may hear talk of God's presence as a callous mockery of our emptiness.

Of all seasons, winter requires a grace-spark of memory to ignite a spiritual fire that can sustain us through the season. It may help us to remember that the first day of winter has the fewest hours of daylight. From that day on, the days get longer and brighter. We may want to stay put, conserve our energy, and realize that we walk by faith, not by sight.

A friend of mine, a horticultural specialist in fruit trees, once mentioned the necessity of cold or "chill hours" to set the blossom and ensure fruit for the coming year. I see a spiritual principle here that correlates with the concepts of pace, rest, and what we could call holy dormancy. Times of inactivity can refresh and replenish our depleted reserves.

ASSESSMENT FOR WINTER

- Are you in a time of recovery and rest from extensive soul work?

- Review your journals (or your memory) and note those times you've had a winter season of spiritual rest and recovery.

- What was happening in your life and circumstances at that time?

- What gave you that sense of rest and recovery?

- What continuing change resulted from that season?

- Have you experienced a harsh spiritual winter? How did you survive it? How can you guard against that happening again?

- What does a spiritual winter mean to you? Do you see it as more positive or negative? Why?

The Seasons Cycle

These seasons do not occur one time only. We experience each of them many times over. And as we consider our vision for spiritual growth, we need to consider our current season. Not every discipline is for every season.

A spiritual winter may call for reflection and reading to prepare for a busy spring ahead. A spiritual spring may call for great activity when you must draw on your reserves to keep up with the changes and pace of projects. A spiritual summer may require you to dial back a bit, maintaining your core disciplines, but not pressing too hard. A spiritual fall can be a time to celebrate and record in your journal the stories of fruitful experiences.

Chapter 22
Soul-Specific Disciplines

We should avoid thinking of spiritual disciplines as a hodgepodge of optional activities for our spiritual amusement. God has provided these tools to help us mature as beloved sons and daughters and valued servants as we live in God's

Pace

Presence

Perspective

Power

Purpose

A great way to profit from these disciplines is to relate each one to the result, or the fruit, that it produces in your life.

When I studied piano, my teacher continually made the link between the music I wanted to play and the scales and other technical exercises I needed to practice. Seeing the link between exercise and result helped inspire my commitment to practice.

As in a physical fitness program, certain exercises move us toward certain goals. We work the cardiovascular system through running or swimming, and we work various muscle groups through targeted weight training. Some exercises address multiple needs. Running, for example, gives excellent cardiovascular exercise while also building strength and endurance. Different exercises produce different results.

Likewise, some spiritual disciplines address many spiritual needs. We might consider Bible study and prayer the cardio workout of spiritual fitness, building both stamina and strength. The essential disciplines of study and prayer support and supply all the other disciplines.

Some disciplines focus primarily on personal intimacy with God, others shape our relationship to the world, while still others build us up in the ways we function in the body of Christ.

Different exercises produce different results.

What spiritual needs do you feel? What responsibilities do you carry? What do you sense the Lord calling you to do in the near future and beyond? Responding to these questions and other considerations will help you develop a soul plan that will generate spiritual vitality.

Tailor Your Disciplines to Fit Your Temperament

In this book I cannot fully develop the complex relationship between spirituality and personality preferences and or/temperament.[126] Still, it is worth mentioning. To give you a sense of what I mean, consider these questions:

- What spiritual disciplines best suit a task-oriented person?

- What spiritual disciplines best suit a relationship-oriented person?

- What spiritual disciplines best suit an idea-oriented person?

- What spiritual disciplines best suit a more artistic person?

You likely know of several personality inventories that help individuals identify and measure their personality and behavioral preferences. Probably the most widely known are the Myers-Briggs Type Indicator (MBTI) and The DiSC Personality Profile.[127]

Since at least the time of Hippocrates (450 BC) observers began recognizing distinct differences in human personality and temperament. Hippocrates based his classic paradigm on the differences or imbalances in the four humors or secretions of the body. These secretions came from the heart (blood, sanguine), liver (yellow bile, choleric), lungs (phlegm, phlegmatic) and kidneys (black bile, melancholic).[128]

It's intriguing to consider the dynamic possibilities of the interaction between personality and spirituality. Here are four broad generalizations to illustrate what I mean.

Some personality types are highly talkative, enthusiastic, active, and social. They find it easy to be social, outgoing, and charismatic. Individuals with this personality prefer to stay active. In terms of spiritual disciplines, they can benefit from disciplines of God's pace, providing a check to over-extension.

Other personalities are independent, decisive, goal-oriented, and ambitious. These traits, combined with their dominant, result-oriented outlook, make them natural leaders. These task-oriented temperaments can benefit from the disciplines that emphasize God's presence and God's purpose because these disciplines help to balance and direct the activist lifestyle.

Still others tend to be analytical and detail-oriented, thinking and feeling deeply. They are introverted and try to avoid getting singled out in a crowd. They may be self-reliant individuals who often strive for perfection within themselves and their surroundings. This can express itself in detail-oriented behavior. These temperaments can find comfort and freedom in the disciplines cultivating God's presence and God's perspective with the emphasis on grace and acceptance.

Other individuals tend to be relaxed, peaceful, quiet, and easy-going. They are sympathetic and care about others yet may hide their emotions. These individuals are also good at generalizing ideas or problems to the world and making compromises. They may find direction and engagement through the disciplines of God's purpose.

If you have taken any of the well-known personality inventories, you may find it helpful to reflect on which spiritual disciplines fit best with your temperament. An idea-focused person, for instance, could find new depth of understanding and appreciation for the Lord by moving beyond cognitive analysis to contemplative meditation.

Conversely, you might consider which spiritual disciplines will help balance your natural tendencies. An extrovert, for instance, can benefit greatly from silence and solitude to tap the power of relying on the Lord for a sense of identity, security, and independence.

Keep in mind that *all* the disciplines promote spiritual growth. Try each one for a time so you can access it as a resource whenever your circumstances require it.

Tailor Your Disciplines to Respond to Your Symptoms of Soul Neglect

Understanding the soul-specific nature of the disciplines will help you avoid counterproductive practices. The Reference Chart: Remedies for the Symptoms of Soul Neglect gives you a starting point.

A person who feels depressed, for example, would be unwise to fast. The loss of food will aggravate the sense of loss that fuels the depression. This person needs a recovery of energy, both spiritually and physically.

Likewise, the intensive confession of examen connected to the discipline of Review (God's presence) may not help a person with an overactive conscience and much misplaced guilt. This person will find it more beneficial to read testimonies that convey the "no-matter-what you've-done-I-love-you" nature of God's acceptance. The thief on the cross provides a great example (see Luke 22:32-43). He needed only a simple admission of guilt.

Ironically, in times of special need we may feel drawn to those disciplines that may help us least. Hot packs may feel good and provide initial relief from muscle ache, but a hot pack applied immediately after a muscle injury will complicate the problem, because it brings more blood and swelling to the tissues. A cold pack may not feel comfortable, but it reduces blood and fluid accumulation, reducing the stress on the strained or torn tissue.

If God seems far away, extensive Bible reading may seem like the best course of action, but it may not touch the heart. Reading spiritual biographies or inspirational literature, combined with times of prayer and conversation with a spiritual mentor (or spiritual director), will likely produce better results.

For the person who feels overwhelmed by perfectionism, I recommend a fast from spiritual activities and a good, long dose of recreation and diversion from the heavy issues of life. Those on the edge of burnout, who find themselves out of cope and emotionally drained, should step away from disciplines of service and take some time to renew themselves in non-demanding ways.

When used wisely, spiritual disciplines enhance our lives in ways we could never imagine. The time has come for Jesus' worn-out, burned-out believers to rediscover the energy, joy, and productivity so thrillingly pictured in his statement, "I came that they may have life, and have it abundantly" (John 10:10, RSV).

Spiritual growth means weaving faith into *every* aspect of life. Not only are we saved by faith, but we also learn to live by faith in our character development, our relationships, our careers, our recreation, and in every other way.

Reference Chart: Remedies for the Symptoms of Soul Neglect

Symptoms of Soul Neglect	Indicators	Pathways and Spiritual Disciplines
Having a Low-Grade "Depression Fever"	A sense of loss, whether real or perceived loss	**Presence:** *Review* to inventory your soul for sense of loss and to discover God's daily presence. *Prayer* to engage with the Lord, as the psalmists did in their struggles. **Perspective:** *Spiritual Input* for awakening faith and hope. **Purpose:** *Community* for encouragement and support.
Being Busy but Bored	A loss of connection between activity and its meaning and purpose	**Presence:** *Prayer* to rediscover identity and re-engage with God. **Power:** *Silence* to listen to your heart and to the Lord. **Purpose:** *Daily Call* to discern God's invitation to good works.
Losing Control over Life's Routine	Overwhelmed by the press of demands, unable to keep all the fires burning	**Pace:** *Redeem Your Time* and *Enjoy Sabbath Rest* to be more intentional about your spiritual health. **Presence:** *Preview* and *Review* to bring God into every moment. **Perspective:** *Bible Study* to encounter the living Word through God's written word.

Symptoms of Soul Neglect	Indicators	Pathways and Spiritual Disciplines
Losing Responsiveness to Others	Irritable, impatient, weary with others. Key Scripture — Numbers 20	**Pace:** *Redeem Your Time* and *Enjoy Sabbath Rest* to provide personal soul time and rest from responsibilities. **Power:** *Solitude* to provide respite from others' expectations and demands. **Purpose:** *Community* to find refreshment with a few who encourage and support you.
Withdrawing from Responsibility and Leadership	Unwilling or unable to give of ourselves; emotional burnout.	**Pace:** *Redeem Your Time* and *Enjoy Sabbath Rest* to regain a sense of your life in Christ. **Purpose:** *Daily Call* and *Vocational Call* to clarify your priorities and identify the context for serving God and others.
Paying More Attention to Less Important Things	Doing fewer demanding activities and choosing busywork instead of meaningful work.	**Pace:** *Redeem Your Time* and *Enjoy Sabbath Rest* to refresh from burnout. **Perspective:** *Meditation* to generate creative encounter with the Lord. **Presence:** *Preview* and *Review* to be aware of each moment's value. **Call:** *Daily Call* and *Vocational Call* to recapture self-worth and renew your partnership with God.
Experiencing Restlessness and Dissatisfaction	Lack of contentment. Fear of missing out.	**Presence:** *Preview* and *Review* to focus on God's continual presence. **Purpose:** *Daily Call* and *Vocational Call* to discern your vital contribution to God's kingdom work.

Symptoms of Soul Neglect	Indicators	Pathways and Spiritual Disciplines
Falling into Unhealthy Habits and Temptation	Resurgence of unhealthy habits; impulsivity; diminished ability to resist temptation.	**Perspective:** *Spiritual Input* to inspire desire for God's ways. **Purpose:** *Community* for support and accountability. **Purpose:** *Character* to develop a vision and plan for becoming the person Jesus died to redeem.
Being Preoccupied with Guilt and Shame	An objective state of having violated a law or personal value (guilt). A sense of lowered self-esteem (shame). "Guilt says, 'I did wrong,' while shame says, 'I am wrong.'"	**Presence:** *Review* for naming sin and meeting God in grace. *Prayer* for confession and accepting forgiveness. **Pace:** *Redeem Your Time* and *Enjoy Sabbath Rest* to create space to experience grace. **Perspective:** *Bible Study* to renew your mind and revise your self-talk.
Becoming Spiritually Apathetic and Indifferent	Knowingly refusing to do what is right or being unwilling to stop doing what is wrong.	**Perspective:** *Spiritual Input* to inspire faith. **Presence:** *Review* to be reminded of the reality of God's redemptive activity in the world. *Prayer* to repent and seek a softening of heart. **Purpose:** *Community* for support, encouragement, and loving accountability.

Tailor Your Disciplines to Respond to Your Life Situation

You can tailor spiritual disciplines to fit your life circumstances and role. While a high-level executive can practice the spiritual discipline of simplicity (covered in other books on spiritual disciplines), for example, it could actually impede her ability to share her faith with friends who might view her "scaled down" life as religious fanaticism. On the other hand, that same executive could practice weekly fasting or lead an office Bible study.

One person may feel most drawn to spiritual reading, while another comes alive through a discipline of quiet service. God has provided a spectrum for the full range of human personalities and preferences. When properly understood, this is the joy of the disciplines.

To determine which disciplines suit you best for your current soul condition, you can ask questions such as:

- What spiritual season am I in?

- Which disciplines best suit the need I feel now?

- What disciplines will help me when I look for…

  o   spiritual stamina?
  o   victory over temptation?
  o   a new challenge?
  o   a deeper sense of God's presence?
  o   something to cling to when God seems far away?
  o   recovery after getting hurt?
  o   recovery from guilt?

The final chapter of *SoulShaping* takes you through the process of developing your personalized soul plan. By now, you see the rich opportunity that God provides with a variety of resources. The disciplines provide you a full buffet for the joyful nourishment of spiritual health in your daily life.

Our satisfaction depends on our self-awareness. You can choose the disciplines to fit you, appropriate for the season you're in, tailored to fit your unique temperament, and chosen to address the most important need(s) you feel at the time.

Our satisfaction depends on our self-awareness.

Chapter 23
Developing Your Soul Plan

Commitments shape our lives. In a wedding ceremony, a couple makes a commitment to stand by each other "in plenty and in want, in joy and in sorrow, in sickness and in health." In school, sports, careers, and relationships, we make commitments that determine both the narrow boundaries and the broad expanse of our lives.

Commitments have power to make or break our lives. Winston Churchill is credited with saying, "First we shape our buildings, then our buildings shape us." The same can be said of our commitments. Once chosen, many other choices follow as a matter of course.

We first make our commitments and then our commitments make us.

As we come to the commencement of our journey toward heightened spiritual vitality (I prefer not to think of it as a conclusion), view it as your launch to a new level of living. Like high school and college commencements, your work in spiritual vitality equips you to live and work fruitfully.

We first make our commitments and then our commitments make us.

What kind of commitments shape *your* life? Is life just happening to you, or are you shaping an abundant life? If you want to become all that God created you to be, you must discover how to tap the power of a committed life.

If you feel dissatisfied with your life, an inventory of your experience will most likely reveal two things: First, you are investing too much in unworthy pursuits. Second, you are not investing enough in worthy commitments. Commitment unlocks the energy of life.

The decision to invest yourself in a valued course of action satisfies your mind, energizes your will, and engages your emotions. Any commitment must be worthy of the name. It's important to invest your energy and personal resources in proportion to the value of your objectives.

God has designed you so that the resources develop and circumstances adapt to support the commitments you make. You probably have experienced this but may not have appreciated the principle.

A friend decided to return to college to finish his degree. He had a full-time job and a young family, but committed to his education because he saw it as the best way to provide for his family's security. He succeeded wonderfully. Today, as he looks back after more than a decade, he marvels that he did it. How did he succeed? Commitment.

Commitment unlocks the energy of life.

The resources developed and circumstances adapted to support a choice he truly embraced. I could offer other examples, but the best ones come from looking back over your own life.

You now have the tools to experience the abundant life Jesus died and rose to make possible. Will you commit to a plan that moves you into that life? Discipline supports a goal you value. Discipline brings your commitments to life.

Keep in mind that you don't have to master all of the spiritual disciplines at once. Spiritual vitality is a process. Think of it like good nutrition. It may feel overwhelming to imagine all the meals you eat in a week, in a month, in a year. If someone took you into a warehouse filled with all the meals you had to eat in a lifetime and said, "OK—start eating!" you'd collapse. No one can eat, in a single sitting, all the food they will ever consume.

Eating is a daily matter. You focus on consuming your daily bread, not on building a bakery. *Daily* bread, *daily* discipline.

God has designed you so that the resources develop and circumstances adapt to support the commitments you make.

What will nourish you *now*? In spiritual formation, the process *is* the product. You will get results simply by paying attention to your spiritual condition and committing to one discipline to promote your spiritual health.

You have the information you need to make an intentional commitment to *SoulShaping*. Now you need a plan, developed through honest reflection and the guidance of the Holy Spirit. A common name for this plan is a rule of life. Adele Ahlberg Calhoun defines a rule of life as a plan "to live a sane and holy rhythm that reflects a deep love for God and respect for how he has made me."[129]

Guidelines for Developing Your Soul Plan

The following nine brief guidelines are designed to help you think through the major issues and to help you take practical steps toward the restoration and holy shaping of your soul.

BEGIN SOUL-SEARCHING

You can begin just about anywhere, but I find it most effective to pay attention to what you feel stirring in your heart already. Where do *you* want to start? What has stirred your heart as you've read this book? Why? What seems most intriguing or meaningful to you?

REVIEW YOUR SYMPTOMS OF SOUL NEGLECT

Review the list of ten symptoms on pages 14–23, along with any you've added. What area most needs your attention? Look at the chart on pages 251–253 in chapter 22 to see disciplines I've suggested to address that symptom.

DETERMINE THE SEASON OF YOUR SOUL

Discern your current spiritual season with respect to the area you've selected. What characteristics of that season should you consider as you make your plan? If you're in a winter of recovery, for instance, how will you honor your need for rest as you develop your plan?

SELECT A FOCUS FROM YOUR SOUL LIFE VISION

What one step toward glory do you believe God would like you to make? Picture yourself with this change. How would it affect your attitude, behavior, knowledge, or skills? How could your schedule adapt to allow this? What would change in your life by next week? What could change in the next eight weeks?

REVIEW THE SOUL-SPECIFIC DISCIPLINES AND SELECT THE ONE(S) THAT SEEM MOST APPROPRIATE AT THIS TIME

While all disciplines have great value, some are more appropriate based on your personal preferences and circumstances. What disciplines "fit" you best? Why? How would you like to weave these into your life? What discipline(s) would best help you move forward toward your vision? Look over the following list and prioritize the ones you want to practice.

Pathways to God's Pace for Living

> Redeem Your Time
> Enjoy Sabbath Rest
> Celebrate Sacred Milestones

Pathways to God's Presence with Us

> Preview
> Review
> Prayer

Pathways to God's Perspective

> Bible study
> Meditation
> Spiritual Input

Pathways to God's Power

> Fasting
> Silence
> Solitude

Pathways to God's Purpose for Our Lives

> Character
> Community
> Calling: Daily Call and Vocational Call

SUMMARIZE AND ASSESS YOUR PLAN

Why have you chosen these disciplines? What specific soul needs do they address? How? What specific symptom of soul neglect do you hope to remedy? Considering questions like these moves you to a different level of awareness, commitment, and motivation. If you neglect this diligent work at the outset, you may find yourself starting with a burst of energy that soon fizzles.

What additional information or resources do you need to begin this discipline? Why not buy your spiritual journal today and write in it your vision and initial plan? Select the book you will use for spiritual reading or call a friend to arrange a time to discuss a spiritual friendship. Start a personal prayer guide.[130] Immediate action will help cement your intention.

MAKE SPECIFIC COMMITMENTS

Someone has said, "Performance has more to do with commitment than with competence." When you make commitments, your heart, mind, soul, and body join to bring those commitments to fulfillment. When you add to this the gracious power of God, you will make great progress.

Make a simple plan of commitments to yourself. Set specific goals or commitments for each time frame:

Each day I will _____

Each week I will _____

Each month I will _____

Each year I will _____

The night before, prepare for the day ahead. You give yourself a significant incentive when you know everything will be ready for you when the alarm sounds in the morning.

Clearing your desk or other quiet space and having your journal and Bible ready remove some of the most common obstacles to a disciplined soul time. Eliminate as many distractions as possible so you can more easily center your attention on the Lord and his word.

BE ACCOUNTABLE

How will you handle accountability? You may need only to log your goals and plans in your personal calendar or daily planner. A simple chart to track your activity may be enough. On the other hand, you might benefit from the support and encouragement of another person.

While most athletes have natural talent, it takes a coach to get them to invest the effort required to move from talent to skill. Ask someone to hold you accountable. A fellow traveler can be a partner to encourage you to keep the commitments you value.

Remember, your spiritual life will *always* be in process. While such knowledge discourages some and makes others impatient, imagine your soul condition if you do nothing at all!

By now, you know too much to allow the world to shape your soul. See the vision of what you can become in Christ and determine to move ahead, relying on God's grace and the indwelling power of God's Holy Spirit.

Understand How Progress Works

You don't immediately notice the results of spiritual discipline, any more than you instantly recognize the results of physical exercise.

In physical exercise, the body experiences what Kenneth Cooper called "the training effect." After about six weeks of regular exercise, a series of changes seem to happen "all at once" in the body. [131] This is the product of vascularization, the development of additional capillaries to supply blood to the muscles.

Athletes report "plateaus of progress," improving not only day by day, but in quantum jumps. Vascularization is the most essential factor in building endurance and reducing fatigue in the skeletal muscles, saturating the tissue with oxygen and carrying away more waste.

Spiritual experience shows a similar trajectory to physical conditioning. After sustained discipline, our spiritual lives respond and deepen with increased vitality and sensitivity to God's presence and direction.

Spirituality is an adventure of love.

At the same time, we cannot reduce spiritual vitality to systems and methods. It is an adventure of love. Even as you grow in your knowledge of the spiritual disciplines, you can never substitute them for the natural interaction of your relationship with the Lord.

Lasting vitality resembles lasting love: you carefully nurture it day by day with little courtesies, frequent affirmations, and a delight in your beloved. You look more carefully and closely at the qualities of your beloved and remember more clearly the gracious acceptance that your beloved has shown you over the years.

God is at work in you, shaping you for all eternity. You are his beloved son or daughter, and he longs for you to love him and to be transformed by his love for you. Have your way, almighty potter, empower us to join you in shaping our souls! Have your way.

Jesus did not die so we could stay the same. Enter into Jesus' joy by pursuing the abundant life he offers. You will be blessed and will bring blessing to everyone around you.

Guidelines: Developing Your Soul Plan

The following guidelines for developing your personal soul-care plan are designed to help you think through the major issues and help you to take practical steps toward the holy shaping of your soul.

1 **BEGIN SOUL-SEARCHING**

You can begin just about anywhere, but I find it most effective to pay attention to what you feel stirring in your heart already.

2 **REVIEW YOUR SYMPTOMS OF SOUL NEGLECT**

Review the list of ten symptoms on pages 14–23, along with any you've added. What area most needs your attention? Look at the chart on pages 251-253 in chapter 22 to see disciplines I've suggested to address that symptom.

3 **DETERMINE THE SEASON OF YOUR SOUL**

Discern your current spiritual season with respect to the area you've selected. What characteristics of that season should you consider as you make your plan?

4 **SELECT A FOCUS FROM YOUR SOUL LIFE VISION**

What one step toward glory do you believe God would like you to make? Picture yourself with this change. How would it affect your attitude, behavior, knowledge, or skills?

5 **REVIEW THE SOUL-SPECIFIC DISCIPLINES AND SELECT THE ONE(S) THAT SEEM MOST APPROPRIATE AT THIS TIME**

While all disciplines have great value, some are more appropriate based on your personal preferences and circumstances. What disciplines fit you best? Why?

6 ## SUMMARIZE AND ASSESS YOUR PLAN

Why have you chosen these disciplines? What specific soul needs do they address? How? What specific symptom of soul neglect do you hope to remedy? What additional information or resources do you need to begin this discipline?

7 ## MAKE SPECIFIC COMMITMENTS

When you make commitments, your heart, mind, soul, and body join to bring those commitments to fulfillment. When you add to this the gracious power of God, you will make great progress.

Make a simple plan of commitments to yourself. Set specific goals or commitments for time:

Each day I will _____

Each week I will _____

Each month I will _____

Each year I will _____

8 ## BE ACCOUNTABLE

How will you handle accountability? You may need only to log your goals and plans in your personal calendar, daily planner, or a simple chart to track your activity. On the other hand, you might benefit from the support and encouragement of another person.

Acknowledgments

In the years since its first publication in 1996, I have desired to rewrite *SoulShaping*. I've learned and experienced much that not only confirmed my original concept, but also refined and expanded it. The daily requirements of pastoral ministry and a lack of clarity on the overall strategy for the revision delayed my rewrite. Then my dear brother in Christ, John McAlpine, took me to lunch in spring 2021, and encouraged me with not only words, but also by providing the financial resources to pursue this dream. That's when God rekindled the creative fires.

Special thanks to The McAlpine Family Foundation for the vision and funding to bring this dream to reality.

I also want to express my abundant gratitude to:

My editor, Steve Halliday, who helped me "crack the code" for this revision. Steve brought not only his skills as an editor for some of the finest authors writing today, but also the mind and heart of a pastor. We connected as friends and as partners in the ministry of communication. I am honored to have him as part of my team—hopefully for many more projects.

The pastors, staff team, elders, and covenant partner members of Trinity United Presbyterian Church, Santa Ana, CA, who prayerfully supported this project and persuaded me to "go for it" with a churchwide "*SoulShaping* Experience." It's been an honor and privilege to serve the Lord with you all.

Alix Riley and Gail Herrmann, who both served as excellent copy editors.

Our daughter-in-love, Katie King Rumford, who designed both the cover and the book, and *The SoulShaping Journal*.

Efraim Meulenberg, my producer at Crazy Creative.

The board of Lorica Ministries, my newly established not-for-profit ministry. To John McAlpine, Jeff Herrmann, Bill Hoyt, and Steve Komanapalli. I'm humbled by your support and excited about the vision the Lord has given us to empower individuals, leaders, and congregations to experience spiritual vitality and intentional living through practical resources and dynamic support in curriculum, coaching, and consulting.

And to my amazing partner in life and ministry, my wife Sarah, and our family. Words fail to express my love and gratitude for you all. You have been part of God's shaping an abundant life.

Appendix A

A List of
Soul-Stirring
Books

The following is a selective list of books from the many fine resources that are available. I have chosen these because they have stood the test of time and have had a significant impact on my own spiritual vitality. I have not included specific bibliographical information because many of these are published in various editions. All can be found easily with the author and title. Many other books are listed in my Notes.

- E. M. Bounds, *Power through Prayer*
- John Bunyan, *The Pilgrim's Progress*
- Franois Fenelon, *Christian Perfection*
- Thomas R. Kelly, *A Testament of Devotion*
- William Law, *A Serious Call to a Devout and Holy Life*
- Brother Lawrence, *The Practice of the Presence of God*
- Andrew Murray, *With Christ in the School of Prayer*
- Henri J. M. Nouwen, *Making All Things New*
- J. I. Packer, *Knowing God*
- J. B. Phillips, *Your God Is Too Small*
- Arthur T. Pierson, *George Muller of Bristol*
- Don Postema, *Space for God*
- Dr. & Mrs. Howard Taylor, *Hudson Taylor's Spiritual Secret*
- A. W. Tozer, *The Knowledge of the Holy*
- A. W. Tozer, *The Pursuit of God*
- *The Confessions of Saint Augustine*

Two compilations that provide wonderful introductions to spiritual classics are:

Richard J. Foster and James Bryan Smith, ed., *Devotional Classics: Selected Readings for Individuals and Groups* (San Francisco: HarperSanFrancisco, 2005).

Julia L. Roller, ed., *25 Books Every Christian Should Read: A Guide to the Essential Spiritual Classics* (New York: HarperOne, 2011).

Appendix B
Remedies for the Symptoms of Soul Neglect

Symptoms of Soul Neglect	Indicators	Pathways and Spiritual Disciplines
Having a Low-Grade "Depression Fever"	A sense of loss, whether real or perceived loss	**Presence:** *Review* to inventory your soul for sense of loss and to discover God's daily presence. *Prayer* to engage with the Lord, as the psalmists did in their struggles. **Perspective:** *Spiritual Input* for awakening faith and hope. **Purpose:** *Community* for encouragement and support.
Being Busy but Bored	A loss of connection between activity and its meaning and purpose	**Presence:** *Prayer* to rediscover identity and re-engage with God. **Power:** *Silence* to listen to your heart and to the Lord. **Purpose:** *Daily Call* to discern God's invitation to good works.
Losing Control over Life's Routine	Overwhelmed by the press of demands, unable to keep all the fires burning	**Pace:** *Redeem Your Time* and *Enjoy Sabbath Rest* to be more intentional about your spiritual health. **Presence:** *Preview* and *Review* to bring God into every moment. **Perspective:** *Bible Study* to encounter the living Word through God's written word.

Symptoms of Soul Neglect	Indicators	Pathways and Spiritual Disciplines
Losing Responsiveness to Others	Irritable, impatient, weary with others. Key Scripture — Numbers 20	**Pace:** *Redeem Your Time* and *Enjoy Sabbath Rest* to provide personal soul time and rest from responsibilities. **Power:** *Solitude* to provide respite from others' expectations and -demands. **Purpose:** *Community* to find refreshment with a few who encourage and support you.
Withdrawing from Responsibility and Leadership	Unwilling or unable to give of ourselves; emotional burnout.	**Pace:** *Redeem Your Time* and *Enjoy Sabbath Rest* to regain a sense of your life in Christ. **Purpose:** *Daily Call* and *Vocational Call* to clarify your priorities and identify the context for serving God and others.
Paying More Attention to Less Important Things	Doing fewer demanding activities and choosing busywork instead of meaningful work.	**Pace:** *Redeem Your Time* and *Enjoy Sabbath Rest* to refresh from burnout. **Perspective:** *Meditation* to generate creative encounter with the Lord. **Presence:** *Preview* and *Review* to be aware of each moment's value. **Call:** *Daily Call* and *Vocational Call* to recapture self-worth and renew your partnership with God.
Experiencing Restlessness and Dissatisfaction	Lack of contentment. Fear of missing out.	**Presence:** *Preview* and *Review* to focus on God's continual presence. **Purpose:** *Daily Call* and *Vocational Call* to discern your vital contribution to God's kingdom work.

Symptoms of Soul Neglect	Indicators	Pathways and Spiritual Disciplines
Falling into Unhealthy Habits and Temptation	Resurgence of unhealthy habits; impulsivity; diminished ability to resist temptation.	**Perspective:** *Spiritual Input* to inspire desire for God's ways. **Purpose:** *Community* for support and accountability. **Purpose:** *Character* to develop a vision and plan for becoming the person Jesus died to redeem.
Being Preoccupied with Guilt and Shame	An objective state of having violated a law or personal value (guilt). A sense of lowered self-esteem (shame). "Guilt says, 'I did wrong,' while shame says, 'I am wrong.'"	**Presence:** *Review* for naming sin and meeting God in grace. *Prayer* for confession and accepting forgiveness. **Pace:** *Redeem Your Time* and *Enjoy Sabbath Rest* to create space to experience grace. **Perspective:** *Bible Study* to renew your mind and revise your self-talk.
Becoming Spiritually Apathetic and Indifferent	Knowingly refusing to do what is right or being unwilling to stop doing what is wrong.	**Perspective:** *Spiritual Input* to inspire faith. **Presence:** *Review* to be reminded of the reality of God's redemptive activity in the world. *Prayer* to repent and seek a softening of heart. **Purpose:** *Community* for support, encouragement, and loving accountability.

Notes

Chapter 1: From Soul Neglect to Spiritual Vitality

1   I'll give you tools to help you develop your personal "picture" in Chapter 5.

Chapter 2: Recognize the Symptoms of Soul Neglect

2   Parker J. Palmer, *Let Your Life Speak: Listening to the Voice of Vocation* (San Francisco: Jossey-Bass, 2000), 30-31.

3   I sometimes use the words "disciplines," "practices," and "exercises" interchangeably throughout this book. Each word conveys different nuances, but they have similar meanings. Discipline expresses intentional effort with an emphasis on order and structure. Practice communicates a pattern of behavior chosen to prepare for executing a larger task. Exercise makes us think about conditioning and getting in shape. All of them help us to understand the scope of spiritual formation.

4   Charles H. Spurgeon, *Lectures to My Students* (Grand Rapids, MI: Baker Book House, 1977), 167.

5   For more information on this view of depression, see Archibald D. Hart, *Feeling Free: Making Your Emotions Work for You* (Old Tappan, NJ: Fleming H. Revell, 1979).

6   Henri J. M. Nouwen, *Making All Things New: An Invitation to the Spiritual Life* (San Francisco: Harper & Row, 1981), 29-31.

7   King Pyrrhus' experience is the basis for the phrase, "Pyrrhic victory," referring to a military success that is gained at such a high price that, ultimately, it wasn't worthwhile.

8   Thomas Traherne, *Centuries* (Wilton, CT: Morehouse-Barlow, 1960), 11-12.

9   John Calvin, *Institutes of the Christian Religion*, Edited by John T. McNeill, Translated by Ford Lewis Battles (Philadelphia: The Westminster Press, 1950), Book 1, Chapter 1, 35.

Chapter 3: Vital Signs of a Healthy Soul

10   https://en.wikipedia.org/wiki/Palais_Garnier

11   Playbill and website for Phantom of the Opera https://us.thephantomoftheopera.com/

12   From the website https://ia600702.us.archive.org/11/items/St.BernardOnTheSongOfSongs/StBernardOnTheSongOfSongsall.wps.pdf, page 93.

13   Henry Blamires, *The Christian Mind* (London: SPCK, 1966), 44.

14   I approach the disciplines of fasting, solitude, and silence in terms of power, different from most other paradigms on spiritual growth.

Chapter 4: Understand the Process of Spiritual Growth

15   Richard Foster, *Celebration of Discipline*, (San Francisco: Harper & Row Publishers, 1978).

16   Dallas Willard, *The Spirit of the Disciplines*, (San Francisco: HarperSanFrancisco, 1988), 158.

17   I just presented these in the preceding chapter, but this is the backstory for how I arrived at these.

Chapter 5: Develop Your Vision for Spiritual Growth

18   See John 1:35-42 (NIV).

19   George Barna, *The Power of Vision* (Ventura, CA: Regal Books, 1992), 28, 48.

20   This concept does not displace God's sovereignty with human responsibility. We are to think of human responsibility acting in concurrence with God's sovereign power, as taught in Philippians 2:12-13.

21   Ethel May Baldwin and David V. Benson, *Henrietta Means and how she did it!* (Glendale, CA: Gospel Light Regal Books, 1966), 17.

22   The ministry is now known as Cru.

23   I first learned this concept of moving from A to B from Will Mancini and his training on the vision process in his book *Church Unique* (San Francisco: Jossey-Bass, A Wiley Imprint, 2008), 126-127.

24   Jim Rohn, "How to Be a Bigger Winner," *Success Strategies* cassette tapes (Niles, IL.: Nightingale-Conant, n.d.).

25   Mark Landfried, *This Service of Love* (United Presbyterian Church in the United States of America: Synod of the Trinity, 1978), 52.

Chapter 6: Redeem Your Time

26   To quote the title of Charles Hummel's classic booklet, *Tyranny of the Urgent*, 1967, Inter-Varsity Christian Fellowship.

27   This material has been adapted from Stephen R. Covey, A. Roger Merrill, Rebecca R. Merrill, *First Things First* (New York: Simon and Schuster, 1994), 88-89.

28   Quadrant I in the Covey/ Merrill material is titled "Urgent and Important." It contains projects, relationships, and appointments that meet the criteria of both "urgent" and "important." These are the deadlines and crises, big and small, of life. Covey observes, "But we also need to realize that many important activities become urgent through procrastination, or because we don't do enough prevention and planning."

29   Quadrant II in the Covey/ Merrill material includes activities identified as "important but not urgent." Covey says these activities land in "The Quadrant of Quality." We use this time for long-range planning, to anticipate and prevent problems, empower others, broaden our minds, and increase our skills through reading and continuous professional development, and cultivate vision and strategies. "Ignoring this quadrant feeds and enlarges Quadrant I," Covey writes, "creating stress, burnout, and deeper crises for the person consumed by it. On the other hand, investing in this quadrant shrinks Quadrant I. Planning, preparation, and prevention keep many things from becoming urgent. Quadrant II does not act on us; we must act on it. This is the Quadrant of personal leadership."

30   In the Pathways to God's Presence section, you can read about the practice of Preview that teaches you how to pray over your schedule, listening for God's direction.

31   Alan Lakein, *How to Get Control of Your Time and Your Life* (New York: Signet, 1989), 23-24.

32   Lakein, *How to Get Control of Your Time and Your Life*, 24.

33   Leslie B. Flynn, "It's About Time" (Newtown, PA: Timothy Books, 1974), 39., cited in Tim Hansel, *When I Relax, I Feel Guilty* (Elgin, IL: David C. Cook Publishing Co. 1979), 67-68.

Chapter 7: Enjoy Sabbath Rest

34   I wrote the following "Grade Covenant" in my journal during my freshman year at college:

Covenant: Grades will never come between me and my heavenly father. My fellowship with you, Lord, will always be maintained, regardless of tests, papers, or piles of homework. This means daily devotions.

Responsibilities in Christian Work: I will decide what I can handle, considering my academic load. Once the decision is made, nothing must interfere. In other words, I will keep my commitment to do whatever I promised to do, even if I have tests. God will honor that commitment. He has before and will continue to do so.

Work Hard at Studies: Considering the above commitments, I will do my best in my studies. Remember, a "B" is good and will serve as well as an "A." God always is uppermost. Glorify him in all. Colossians 3:17.

I want to testify, not boast, that I graduated Magna Cum Laude from Miami University in Oxford, Ohio, and was inducted into Phi Beta Kappa. I also received the President's Award as the valedictorian of my graduating class at Gordon-Conwell Theological Seminary.

35   Parkinson's Law says the amount of work required adjusts to the time available for its completion. Cyril Northcote Parkinson first coined the term in a humorous essay written for *The Economist* in 1955. https://www.atlassian.com/blog/productivity/what-is-parkinsons-law

36   Ironically, our culture of leisure has deliberately torn down the structures meant to protect our time and pace in life. With the elimination of the "Blue Laws," Sunday became the nation's biggest shopping day. Now, no day differs much from any other.

37   Rueben P. Job and Norman Shawchuck, *A Guide to Prayer for Ministers and Other Servants* (Nashville: The Upper Room, 1983), 384.

38   The date shows the survey is pre-Covid, which is important because of how rapidly the work landscape is changing. Nevertheless, this is informative on people's continuing attitudes.

39   Chloe Della Costa, "Top 5 Reasons Americans Don't Use Their Vacation Days," February 23, 2018. https://www.cheatsheet.com/money-career/the-top-5-reasons-people-dont-use-their-vacation-days.html/

40   Jesus' resurrection on Sunday drove this shift to celebrate the first day of the week as the Sabbath.

41   Exodus 31:12-18.

42   Abraham Joshua Heschel, *The Sabbath: Its Meaning for Modern Man*, (New York: Farrar, Straus and Giroux, 1951 renewed 2005), 13.

43   Heschel, *The Sabbath*, 10.

44   Dave Rhodes in the seminar *Younique: Gospel-Based Life Design*, developed with Will Mancini.

45   My blog is titled, "Heart and Mind: A Spiritual Journal," at <u>www.</u>
      <u>dougrumford.com</u>. This specific blog, "Drink Before You're Thirsty", was
      posted on July 2, 2018.

Chapter 8: Celebrate Sacred Milestones

46   Heschel, *The Sabbath*, 15, 16.
47   Chester P. Michael and Marie C. Norrisey, *Prayer and Temperament: Different
      Prayer Forms for Different Personality Types* (Charlottesville, VA: The Open
      Door, Inc. 1984), 46.
48   You can find instructions for all these festivals in Leviticus 23.
49   The Western calendar and some practices vary from churches in the Eastern
      and Orthodox traditions.
50   Immediately following Advent are Christmas and Epiphany. Epiphany
      celebrates the coming of the Wise Men, recorded in Matthew 2:1-12. This
      day celebrates the initial fulfillment of God's promise to give "light to the
      Gentiles" (Isaiah 49:6). Epiphany celebrates evangelism, reaching out to those
      who have not yet heard. As with the Wise Men, we trust that God already
      has begun revealing himself to those who will seek him.
51   The name "Lent" is derived from "lengthening," a reference to the longer days
      that result when the season shifts from the darkness of winter to the spring.
52   Sundays are not counted as part of the forty days of Lent because, even
      during Lent, every Sunday is a "little Easter."
53   *Palm Sunday/Passion Sunday* remembers Jesus' entry into Jerusalem when
      the crowds shouted "Hosanna," an expression of messianic praise. The
      word "passion," when applied to Jesus and the events of this week, has the
      technical meaning of "undergoing suffering." Jesus "passively" surrendered
      to the crowds and the cross.
      Maundy Thursday recalls Jesus' experience with his disciples in the Upper
      Room. The name "Maundy" (not "Maunday") comes from the Latin word
      maundatum which means "commandment," referring to Jesus' words at the
      Last Supper: "I give you a new commandment; that you love one another…"
      This night also included Jesus' washing the disciples' feet, instituting the
      Last Supper (communion), and Jesus' prayer of agony in the Garden of
      Gethsemane.
      Good Friday refers to the horror of seeing the Lord crucified. The name Good
      Friday is a contraction of "God's Friday," similar to the linguistic contraction
      that shifted the phrase "God be with ye" to "Goodbye."
54   *Eastertide* culminates in Pentecost and Ascension Sundays. We reflect on
      Jesus' resurrection appearances during this season. It is the dawning of the
      new era that comes with the ascension of Christ to the right hand of God and
      the descending of the Spirit to indwell the believer.
55   *Kingdomtide* or *Ordinary Time* refers to the balance of the year, from
      approximately June through November. These weeks are devoted to the
      spreading Kingdom of God in our hearts and in the world. Our worship
      focuses on topics such as the growth of the church recorded in the Book of
      Acts, as well the full range of biblical themes.

Chapter 9: Preview

56 I believe this saying comes from Alcoholics Anonymous.
57 www.lindastone.net. https://www.csmedia1.com/paseodelrey.org/continuous-partial-attention.pdf
58 *Lectio 365* app.
59 Dallas Willard, *The Divine Conspiracy: Rediscovering Our Hidden Life in God* (New York: HarperCollins, 1998), 283.
60 I discuss interruptions more fully under the discipline of Community.

Chapter 10: Review

61 Karen Mains, *The God Hunt* (Downers Grove, IL: Intervarsity Press, 2003), 11.
62 Richard Foster, *Prayer: Finding the Heart's True Home* (San Francisco: HarperSanFrancisco, 1992), 27-28.
63 As you practice the examen consistently, over time you will notice patterns that can inform your spiritual life and your actions.
64 Parker J. Palmer, *Let Your Life Speak* (San Francisco: Jossey-Bass, 2000), 63.

Chapter 11: Prayer

65 Excerpted and rewritten from Richard H. Schneider, "Quake," *Guideposts* (Nov. 1983), 2-7.
66 Hart, *Feeling Free*, 85.
67 Dr. David Stoop, *Self Talk: Key to Personal Growth*, (Old Tappan, NJ: Fleming H. Revell Company, 1982), 32-33.
68 Jack Canfield with Janet Switzer, *The Success Principles* (New York: HarperCollins publishers, 2015), 271.
69 Canfield and Switzer, *The Success Principles*, 271.
70 Nouwen, *Making All Things New*, 72-73.

Chapter 12: Bible Study

71 *American Bible Society Record*, March 1990.
72 A good example is Chapter 3, "You Feel the Way You Think," in David D. Burns, M. D. *Feeling Good: The New Mood Therapy*, (New York: HarperCollins Publishers, 1980, 1999), 37-53.
73 Blamires, *The Christian Mind*, 3.
74 John R.W. Stott, *Your Mind Matters*, (Downers Grove: InterVarsity Press, 1972), 55.

Chapter 13: Meditation

75 Two interesting books on this are written by Tony Buzan. *Make the Most of Your Mind* (New York: Simon & Schuster, 1984) and *Use Both Sides of Your Brain* (New York: E. P. Dutton, 1983).
76 Marcus Aurelius, quoted by Douglas V. Steere, "A New Set of Devotional Exercises," in *An Anthology of Devotional Literature*, ed. Thomas S. Kepler (Grand Rapids, MI.: Baker Book House, 1947), 769.

77   I developed this model using a variety of resources, including Carolyn
Stahl, *Opening to God* (Nashville: The Upper Room, 1977), and Elizabeth
O'Connor, *Search for Silence* (Waco, TX: Word Books, 1972), 141-142.

78   How do we keep our meditations from heresy, from false and deceptive
guidance, from clever rationalizations that we may love more than the Lord,
from concepts that draw us into unfruitful lives? I follow three principles:

1. We affirm the authority of God's Word over all human experience.
Our techniques must never contradict the Word of God, nor must
our conclusions. Initially, we may have a fascination with imaginative
encounters with God's Word, but we must balance them with the careful
exegesis of the texts upon which we meditate.

2. We consult the witness of history.
How have God's people dealt with these issues in the past? A continuous
thread of spiritual formation affirms and develops this discipline of
meditation across the centuries. The community of faith has left us rich
resources, such as the Spiritual Exercises of Ignatius of Loyola. We also
have wise cautions, such as the counsel of Jonathan Edwards concerning
spiritual excesses. Referring to Loyola's Exercises, Puritan scholar J. I.
Packer writes, "They remain a potent aid to self-knowledge and devotion
to the Lord Jesus, even for those outside the Catholicism in which they
are so strongly rooted." (J. I. Packer, "Ignatius of Loyola," *Eerdmans'
Handbook to the History of Christianity*, (Grand Rapids, MI: Eerdmans,
1977, 411).

*3. We dwell in a faithful community that nurtures us and holds us accountable
in our pilgrimage of discipleship.*
A disconnected disciple is a contradiction in terms. Christ has called us not
only to himself but to his people. Even as we shouldn't scuba dive without
a buddy, so we don't venture into the deeper areas of spiritual life without
the support, guidance, accountability, and cautionary influence of peers
and mentors. We find the greatest security in honest friendships submitted
to Christ.

Spiritual experience can be disconcerting, even as it shook Moses at the
burning bush, Ezekiel in the desert with the vision of wheels within the
wheels, and Paul with his vision of the third heaven. But the greater risk
is to cut ourselves off from the Lord, who wants to reach us, transform us,
equip us, and mobilize us for God's kingdom.

Chapter 14: Spiritual Input

79   For example, Robert Fulghum's 1988 No. 1 bestseller fits: *Everything I Ever
Really Needed to Know I learned in Kindergarten*. It sold over seven million
copies.

80   Baron Friedreich von Hugel, *Selected Letters* (1927), p. 229. Quoted in John
Baillie, *A Diary of Readings* (New York: Scribner's, 1955), Day 1.

81   Von Hugel, *Selected Letters*.

82   Von Hugel, *Selected Letters*.

83   A good example is Henri Nouwen's book, *The Return of the Prodigal Son:*

A Story of Homecoming (1994) in which Nouwen reflects on Rembrandt's painting on *The Prodigal Son* in light of his own life experience.

84 © 2002 ThankYou Music

85 Composers Brian Johnson/Brandon Lake/Phil Wickham Essential Music Publishing SONG ID 25557 Copyright 2021.

86 *Leadership: A Practical Journal for Church Leaders*, A Publication of Christianity Today, Inc. Summer 1984, p. 22-23.

87 Charles Colson and Nancy Pearcey, *How Now Shall We Live* (Wheaton: Tyndale House Publishers, 1999), 14.

88 Don't let Augustine's title put you off. In our day, the title *Spiritual Reflections or My Spiritual Autobiography* might better describe the content of the book.

Chapter 15: Fasting

89 Sermon *Legions of the Unjazzed*. No other information available.

90 Keynote address given at the National Presbyterian Congress on Renewal, Dallas, TX, January 1985.

91 Letter from Nichole Wichert (reprinted by permission).

92 Donald S. Whitney, *Spiritual Disciplines for the Christian Life* (Colorado Springs: Navpress, 1991), 156-170.

93 Whitney, *Spiritual Disciplines*, 157-158.

94 Richard Foster also offers some helpful counsel on the mechanics of a productive fast in Richard Foster, *Celebration of Discipline* (San Francisco: Harper & Row, 1978), 49-53.

95 During special personal seasons, you may want to try extended fasts of two or more days. I would suggest reading Richard Foster's advice in *Celebration of Discipline* on the spiritual and physical dynamics of such a fast.

96 C. S. Lewis, *The Screwtape Letters* (New York: Macmillan, 1961), 8-9.

Chapter 16: Silence

97 Dag Hammarskjold, *Markings*, (New York: Alfed A Knopf, 1964), 13.

Chapter 17: Solitude

98 Secretary of State James A. Baker, III, National Prayer Breakfast, February 1, 1990. Unpublished manuscript of his message. I published this story in my book *Scared to Life: Awakening the Courage of Faith in an Age of Fear*, (Wheaton: Victor Books, 1994), 38-40.

99 I've adapted this material from my book, *Scared to Life*, 38-40.

100 Robertson McQuilkin, "Muriel's Blessing," *Christianity Today* (February 5 1996), 34.

101 Henry David Thoreau, *Walden and Other Writings* (New York: Modern Library, 1950), 723-724. Quoted in Henri J. M. Nouwen, *Reaching Out*, (New York: Doubleday, 1966), 18.

102 Many churches and Christian camps often make a simple room available for such a day. Some individuals make overnight plans so that they arrive in the evening after dinner and have the night to quiet themselves. Then, they

arise in the morning for the discipline they have set. Doing this at least once a year kindles renewal. My experience tells me that solitude is like a salt that makes us thirst for more such times.

103   Matthew 28:28-30, *The Message.*

104   Willard, *The Spirit of the Disciplines*, 160.

105   William Lohe, quoted in *Minister's Prayer Book*, ed. John W. Doberstein (Philadelphia: Fortress Press, 1986), 279-280.

106   Nouwen, *Reaching Out*, 30.

Chapter 18: Character

107   *The TouchPoint Bible* and other *TouchPoints* resources from Tyndale House Publishers provide thorough compilations of Scriptures and helpful commentary on hundreds of topics.

108   Many resource groups and 12-Step programs are available to support recovery from addiction. Deeper issues of character may require ministries such as counseling and inner healing prayer. A person can be discouraged by expending efforts to correct a problem that needs more specialized care. A spiritual friend, pastor, or spiritual director can offer guidance in this area.

109   From workshop teaching on *Younique: Gospel-Based Life Design.*

110   Spurgeon, *Lectures to My Students*, 17.

111   C. S. Lewis, *Mere Christianity* (New York: Macmillan, 1943), 86-87.

Chapter 19: Community

112   *Rule for a New Brother* (Springfield, IL: Templegate Publishers, 1976), 10.

113   Dietrich Bonhoeffer, *Life Together* (New York: Harper & Row, 1954), 99.

114   Gary Chapman, *The Five Love Languages: How to Express Heartfelt Commitment to Your Mate* (Chicago: Northfield Publishing, 1992) is a helpful resource here.

115   David Stoop, *Making Peace with Your Father* (Wheaton: Tyndale House, 1992), 234-235.

116   Thomas Kelly, *A Testament of Devotion* (New York: Harper & Row, 1941), 88.

Chapter 20: Calling

117   J. R. R. Tolkien, *The Tolkien Reader* (New York: Ballantine Books, 1966), 55. The Lord empowers us to fashion stories and frame messages that enrich our lives. Tolkien identifies four purposes of fairy-stories: Fantasy—the exercise of imagination. Recovery—regaining a clear view of life, "freed from the drab view of triteness or familiarity" (57). I call this refreshment. Escape—from the bounds and bonds imposed by modern life, secular existence. "Don't confuse the escape of a prisoner with the flight of a deserter" (60). Consolation—the happy ending; the eucatastrophe (or the good catastrophe) which denies the universal final defeat. I think this involves meaning, inspiration, and joy.

118   This dreadful collapse happened April 23, 1987.

119   I later learned that Henri Nouwen used this term in his book, *The Living Reminder: Service and Prayer in Memory of Jesus Christ* (Minneapolis: The

Seabury Press, 1977).

120   Francois Fenelon, *Christian Perfection* (Minneapolis: Bethany House Publishers, 1975), 3.

121   Will Mancini with Dave Rhodes and Cory Hartman, *Younique: Designing the Life God Dreamed for You* (Nashville, TN: B & H Publishing, 2020). https:// lifeyounique.com/. I have found this material so effective that I have become a certified coach and master trainer in *Younique*.

122   Mancini with Rhodes and Hartman, *Younique*, 54-56.

123   *Younique: Journey 1 Workbook*, 15.

124   George Christian Dieffenbad and Christian Muller, *Evangelishes Brevier* (Gotha: Gustav Schloessmann, 1869), 416f, quoted in *Minister's Prayer Book*, ed. John W. Doberstein (Philadelphia: Fortress Press, 1986), 203. Adapted.

Chapter 21: Seasons of the Soul

125   Galatians 6:7-8 presents this "law of the harvest": "Do not be deceived; God is not mocked, for you reap whatever you sow. If you sow to your own flesh, you will reap corruption from the flesh; but if you sow to the Spirit, you will reap eternal life from the Spirit." We find it as well in 2 Corinthians 9:6, which says, "The point is this: the one who sows sparingly will also reap sparingly, and the one who sows bountifully will also reap bountifully."

Chapter 22: Soul-Specific Disciplines

126   A useful resource here is Chester P. Michael and Marie C. Norrisey, *Prayer and Temperament: Different Prayer Forms for Different Personality Types* (Charlottesville, VA: The Open Door, Inc., 1984).

127   Many also use the Enneagram. It is also fascinating to use CliftonStrengths, formerly known as StrengthsFinder (https://www.gallup.com/ cliftonstrengths) and Alan Hirsch's APEST model of Apostle, Prophet, Evangelist, Shepherd, and Teacher, based on Ephesians 4:1-16

128   I draw this summary from https://en.wikipedia.org/wiki/Four_ temperaments.

129   Adele Ahlberg Calhoun, *Spiritual Disciplines Handbook*, (Downers Grove, IL, IVP Books, 2005) 13.

130   I prefer the word "guide" to "list," since it sounds more open and freer; "list" has the ring of fulfilling a mechanical obligation.

131   Kenneth H. Cooper, M.D., *Aerobics*, (New York City, Bantam Books, 1968), 93-94.

About the Author

Doug Rumford has served as an ordained pastor in Presbyterian churches for over 40 years. He is also founder and president of Lorica Ministries.

In addition to *SoulShaping* (first and second editions) Doug has authored several books:

> *Scared to Life: Awakening the Courage of Faith in an Age of Fear* (Wheaton, IL: Victor Books, 1994).
>
> *Questions God Asks, Questions Satan Asks* (Wheaton, IL: Tyndale House Publishers, 1998).
>
> *What About Unanswered Prayer?* (Wheaton, IL: Tyndale House Publishers, 2000). (Also translated and published in Korean by Word of Life Press, 2022)
>
> *What About Heaven and Hell?* (Wheaton, IL: Tyndale House Publishers, 2000).
>
> *What About Spiritual Warfare?* (Wheaton, IL: Tyndale House Publishers, 2000).

Doug developed and wrote the notes for *The Promise Bible*, *The Promise New Testament*, *TouchPoint Bible Promises,* and *TouchPoints for Leaders*, all from Tyndale House Publishers.

Doug received his Doctor of Ministry degree from Fuller Theological Seminary, Pasadena, CA. He earned his Master of Divinity degree from Gordon-Conwell Theological Seminary, South Hamilton, MA, graduating summa cum laude, as valedictorian. He earned a Bachelor of Arts in English from Miami University, Oxford, OH, graduating magna cum laude and Phi Beta Kappa.

Doug's blog, "Heart and Mind: A Spiritual Journal" can be found at www.dougrumford.com

For information and inquiries about Doug's resources and availability, visit the website www.loricaministries.org. Lorica Ministries is a not-for-profit ministry committed to empowering individuals, leaders, and congregations to experience spiritual vitality and intentional living through practical resources and dynamic support in curriculum, coaching, and consulting.

Doug and his wife, Sarah, live in Southern California and have four adult children and five grandchildren.

Doug's greatest joy is equipping people to experience Christ's abundant life through spiritual vitality and intentional living.

An Additional *SoulShaping* Resource

The **SoulShaping** Journal: Pathways to Spiritual Vitality

The SoulShaping Journal: Pathways to Spiritual Vitality is an additional resource to help readers translate information into genuine personal transformation. It highlights primary disciplines that form the foundation for spiritual vitality.

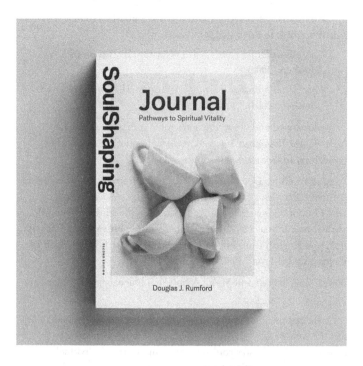

The SoulShaping Journal: Pathways to Spiritual Vitality provides input on how to keep a spiritual journal, along with exercises for daily reflection on Scriptures and the material in *SoulShaping*. Detailed steps guide readers through a ten-week process of developing their personal vision and soul plan.

SoulShaping is also available as an eBook and an audiobook.